SCHOOL OF THE PILGRIM

SCHOOL OF THE PILGRIM

*An Alternative Path
to Christian Growth*

Brett Webb-Mitchell

Westminster John Knox Press
LOUISVILLE • LONDON

Scripture quotations, unless otherwise indicated, are from the New Revised Standard Version of the Bible, copyright © 1989 by the Division of Christian Education of the National Council of the Churches of Christ in the U.S.A., and used by permission.

Book design by Sharon Adams
Cover design by Lisa Buckley
Cover art: Festival of Lights, © *2000 by John August Swanson, Serigraph 30 ¾" × 24",*
  www.JohnAugustSwanson.com

First edition
Published by Westminster John Knox Press
Louisville, Kentucky

This book is printed on acid-free paper that meets the American National Standards Institute Z39.48 standard. ∞

PRINTED IN THE UNITED STATES OF AMERICA

07 08 09 10 11 12 13 14 15 16 — 10 9 8 7 6 5 4 3 2 1

Library of Congress Cataloging-in-Publication Data is on file at the Library of Congress, Washington, D.C.

ISBN-13: 978-0-664-22744-9
ISBN-10: 0-664-22744-9

*With heartfelt thanks for
all the pilgrims who
have taught me about the life of
pilgrimage: Dean Blackburn,
Parker and Adrianne Webb-Mitchell,
Liz and Don Mitchell, Sister Stefanie Weisgram,
Father Aelred, Matt Norvell, Rita Bennett,
Wally Hannum, Richard Rodriguez,
and many others.*

Contents

Acknowledgments

*W*hile lecturing on pilgrimage material that would become this book, I was asked, "Which kind of pilgrim are you?" Baffled by the question, the student continued: Is there a difference between John Bunyan's lone pilgrim, "Christian," versus the merry band of raucous pilgrims who make their way with little to no hurry to Canterbury, as told by Geoffrey Chaucer? Almost without thinking I said, "I am a Chaucerian pilgrim," enjoying a good tale told, seeking out and finding solace in the unexpected events on life's journey by being a member of the body of Christ. The reason I knew the answer was because I was asked a similar question only weeks before by my friend Richard Rodriguez, who told me that I was one of Canterbury's pilgrims.

Having been named a pilgrim among pilgrims by Richard and other friends, I have come to see that this book, while in parts a personal account of my life as a pilgrim, was made possible by the many friends who have become and are my community on this journey. I have traveled life's road in the company of good people, who have been a blessing in my life. My thanks begin with Dean Blackburn, who has been with me on this pilgrimage of life together. He has walked with me in territory in which we were not welcomed because of who and whose we are.

My parents Liz and Don Mitchell taught me the art and love of travel, not knowing at the time that it would lead to a book on pilgrimage. My father enjoyed taking us to forts, while my mother stopped at quilt shows, all leading me to snoop at cathedrals, ancient chapels, and pilgrim roads.

My thanks go out to Sister Stefanie Weisgram, who has been a pilgrim guide, taking me to the Abbey of the Crucified Christ and the basilica in Esquipulas, Guatemala, that holds within its walls the beautiful statue of the Black Christ, *El Cristo Negro*. Richard Rodriguez thankfully reminded me that pilgrimage is a road leading to the unknown God. Thank you to Rita Bennett, who is one of the musicians on this pilgrimage. Wally Hannum has

x   Acknowledgments

been a faithful friend and pilgrim companion who has repeatedly told me to
write this book and start the actual School of the Pilgrim. Thanks to Paul
Ilecki who first told me of the pilgrimage to El Santuario de Chimayo in
northern New Mexico. My thanks also extend to the Rev. Dr. Phillip Leach
and Barbara Campbell Davis, who provided me much support for my pilgrimage interests.

My "laboratory" for learning that the way of pilgrimage is a better way of
educating Christians to understand growth took place in two courses at Duke
Divinity School: one on human development and the other on pilgrimage as
education. Thank you to all those fantastic students who were brave enough
to take courses with me as I was learning the road of pilgrimage. I thank other
pilgrims I have met along the way: Sister Agatha Zwilling, Jane Scott, John
Jerry Anthony Parente, David Malone, Jeffrey Hutson, Martin Connell,
Father Aelred of Mepkin Abbey, David Ferreiro, Robert Lewis, and Rachel
Downs-Lewis.

St. John's Presbyterian Church and Ernest Myatt Presbyterian Church
(U.S.A.) have been great communities to be part of as I have found myself
walking through the land of transition. Thanks for the masterful editing work
of David Maxwell, who saw the artist in me and the art in my writing.

I thank God for traveling on pilgrimage with the next generation of pilgrims, my children, Adrianne and Parker. Finally, I write this book for those
pilgrims today, and those generations of pilgrims who will follow us as we,
together, follow Christ.

Introduction: Being a Pilgrim

Happy are the people whose strength is in you!
Whose hearts are set on the pilgrims' way.
                    (Ps. 84:4, Book of Common Prayer, *1979)*

We are pilgrims through time.
                    (St. Augustine, City of God*)*

We all go on pilgrimage. It is part of our human yearning to associate
places with people we love, with experiences which are precious, with
events which are holy.
                    (Brother Ramon, SFF)

*W*hat made you think about taking a pilgrimage in the first place?" is a
question people often ask. After all, the majority of mainline Christians of
all stripes do not normally engage in this practice. Yet people are often surprised to know that many Christians throughout the ages have taken this very
seriously.

For over a decade I have been engaged in a hands-on study of Christian
pilgrimage. Besides reading and lecturing on the subject, I have also been a
participant, both as pilgrim and guide. I am convinced that the length and
breadth of the Christian life is a pilgrimage and that it is through the actual
practice of pilgrimage that we may best understand the experience of growth
and change in the Christian life.

I am also convinced that Christian leaders and those preparing for leadership in the church can benefit greatly by learning this ancient spiritual discipline. It is not only transformative for those who participate, but it also is a
wonderful teaching tool leaders can use in all kinds of settings.

Pilgrimage as Intellectual Curiosity

My intellectual interest in pilgrimage began as I was striving to better understand growth and change that occurred in the lives of children and adults in general, and people with disabilities in particular. In my undergraduate years I spent hours studying theories and conducting experiments around the topic of growth in the discipline of music therapy and special education, poring over the plethora of human development studies that tried to advance certain patterns of growth and change. I believed in the persuasive logic of these theories, even though they competed or clashed against each other at certain theoretical points. However, in teaching children and adults with disabilities, in which the aim was to bring those considered "disabled" to be more like "able-bodied" people, I began to look carefully at the language, philosophy, theology, and cultural assumptions that were implied in all theories of growth and change. More importantly, I began to understand that each theorist of human growth was formed by certain cultural constructs and storied communities.

My belief that the theories of human development were the sole way of understanding growth and change came crashing down when I applied James Fowler's interview questions in *Stages of Faith* to a young adolescent with a dual diagnosis of mental illness and mental retardation. To my surprise, this young man had reached the apex of Fowler's theory: The young man had "Stage Six" universal images and mature impressions of faith, though mentally this same young person (who was sixteen years old chronologically) tested at the cognitive level of a second-grader.[1] Either the child was a savant in the area of faith, or there was an error in the testing tool and thus a problem in the overall theory of "faith development."

To locate where the error was in this diagnosis, I read theorists from Sigmund Freud to Robert Kegan. I kept seeing in their theories generalized structures of steps, stages, or ladderlike movements of growth, with a similar internal mechanism for encouraging growth over a person's life. None of the theorists could explain how people with severe developmental or multiple sensory disabilities could know God in such mature yet simple expressions of faith.

My interest in pilgrimage came out of the way that the theorists themselves would speak of steps and stagelike sequences with a certain pathway orientation. Robert Kegan used "roadway of life" to talk about his theory of growth. With the theorists using such words, images, and metaphors, I began to pursue a scholarly interest in Christian pilgrimage, especially in my work with children and adolescents with disabilities. One of the first essays I wrote told how many of these young people were like pilgrims among us, who appear as strangers in a land that is alien to them.[2] Each of us is constantly growing in some form or fashion, but we may not all be on the very same road or pathway. We move alongside one another from some location toward some destination. This seemed a way of honoring the life of another person who is not like me but is still worthy of respect. This seemed a worthy project to pursue.[3]

Becoming a Pilgrim: Confession and Affirmation

The other reason that I began this investigation into the ancient practice of pilgrimage is that I went on an actual pilgrimage and my life has never been quite the same. I have a better understanding and appreciation for the serendipitous nature of Christian growth through the prism and practice of pilgrimage than from other practices, metaphors, or analogies used to describe growth. As the Christian life includes a myriad of gestures, rituals, relationships, virtues, and the cultural context in which we live, Christian pilgrimage amplifies their importance in profound ways.

Identifying myself as a pilgrim is an odd, quirky, surreal at times, and usually comical confession for someone who has been a youth leader, college professor, former seminary professor, and an ordained clergyperson in the Presbyterian Church (U.S.A.). In the Presbyterian *Book of Order,* there is no called position for "pilgrim." Yet John Calvin writes that Christ "teaches us to travel as pilgrims in this world that our celestial heritage may not perish or pass away."[4]

Unlike my medieval counterparts I wear the modern dress of pilgrims: T-shirt and shorts, white socks, sweat pants for the evening and walking into sanctuaries, suntan lotion, bug spray, baseball cap, a comfortable pair of running shoes, and a kit with foot powder, moleskin, bandages, needles, matches, and petroleum jelly. On my right hand I wear a ring with a small scallop shell carved on it, and I carry a small scallop shell in my pocket. Around my neck I wear a Benedictine medallion. In my backpack I carry clothes and a medicine kit, a water bottle and granola bars, a book of Benedictine prayers, a Bible and some other interesting books and magazines to read, and a journal to write. A rosary a friend gave me is in my pocket.[5] I carry a metal walking stick and a small silver flask two students gave me, on which is inscribed this quote: "No matter where you go, there you are." Another student carved "Pilgrim 2001" in a stained and polished wooden walking stick resting by my front door, reminding me of pilgrimage.

I discuss clothes because being and becoming a pilgrim is also being and becoming a Christian, which is like putting on a set of clothing items and growing into them. Consider the following Scriptures: "Do not lie to one another, seeing that you have stripped off the old self with its practices and have clothed yourselves with the new self, which is being renewed in knowledge according to the image of its creator" (Col. 3:9–10); "Clothe yourselves with love, which binds everything together in perfect harmony" (Col. 3:14); "Clothe yourselves with the new self, created according to the likeness of God in true righteousness and holiness" (Eph. 4:24); "Put on the Lord Jesus Christ" (Rom. 13:14). The very imagery of growing into Christ that the apostle Paul gives us, as if Christ were a loose garment that we grow into, is a way of understanding our growing in the Christian life as pilgrims of Christ. The clothing of a Christian is Christ, and thus the clothes of the pilgrim may be baggy and sacklike at first, maybe uncomfortable at times, hard to get around in, dragging behind perhaps, and hanging in all the wrong places. In these clothes of Christ there is no tailored, hand-in-glove fit. Instead, there is only room to grow.

We grow *into* the clothes of Christ. We learn how to wear these clothes, how to be Christians, while on the road of life. The body of Christ is not a stagnant, passive vessel on which we climb and do nothing. It is dynamic and fluid and constantly changing. As a parent, every few months I kneel down before my son Parker and measure his growing feet by doing the thumb test: placing my right thumb against the big toe area of the new shoe that he is trying on to see if there is room to grow. Likewise, the clothes we wear as Christian pilgrims are clothes that won't be fitting us anytime soon, probably not until our coming to the end of the journey. Pilgrims grow and change over time. With each new experience we grow.

Since going on my first pilgrimage to El Santuario de Chimayo outside of Santa Fe, I have learned and experienced growth in the faith both with companions and alone; with arduous physical training, over many miles and many days, and in meeting strangers along the way. In my first pilgrimage I experienced change as I ate different foods along with "comfort foods." I was busy collecting new stories and remembering old tales, practicing ancient gestures in timeless rituals in new places in the arid desert places, or learning new rituals and adapting different habits to foreign habitats.

But from this first pilgrimage I have a better understanding of how the entirety of the Christian life is a pilgrimage. After my divorce, I learned to grow when I got lost in this desert place of my life but suddenly found myself at peace with God. In raising teenagers in middle-class America, I appreciate spiritual discernment, wrapped in the warmth of solitude when feeling frantic. In facing discrimination at numerous institutions of higher education, rituals affirming that I was created in God's image bring hope. In working with congregations where there are deep wounds, I no longer try to quickly fix them up, but have learned to sit and listen to the stories before moving too fast.

As I have learned these lessons on the road of life, the obverse is true as well. It is constantly revealed to me by God's Spirit that there are no guarantees that learning happens in intentional moments in preplanned places, like Sunday schools or adult Bible studies. Rather, God educates the Christian in spontaneous, nonsystematic, serendipitous moments. When asked one day by a Christian educator, "What are the learning objectives of Christian pilgrimage?" I wanted to say sincerely, "I have no clue—ask God," but knew it would come out too flippantly, even though it was the most honest answer or response I could have given. Sometimes the instruction or "objective" of pilgrimage comes from a guide or teacher we walk with or meet along the way. The guide provides intentional instructions that may be a matter of life and death, lead us to a new life in Christ embraced after nothing else made sense or would work, or engage us in a deepening and meaningful dialogue. I would like to say that I have always been mindful of Christ's presence on pilgrimage. More honestly, I am searching for God constantly, exhaustingly, and am frustrated on the days that I find myself playing "hide-and-go-seek" with the Holy of Holies.

This is but a brief description of learning experiences that come to mind from pilgrimages, always with Jesus Christ as guide, as companion, as comforter along the entire way. The degree of freedom I gain from this realization is that I don't have to be the exemplary pilgrim for anyone else, because Christ is the exemplary pilgrim for us all.

A Story of a Modern-Day Pilgrim

Having named the idea of pilgrimage as a way of understanding the growth of Christians, I can admit that pilgrimage is the basis of how I comprehend growth and change in the Christian life in its totality. More days than not, in the middle of wondering what is going on in my life, living in situations that I never contemplated occurring, near the end of my tether of self-understanding, I have to consciously remind myself that I am writing a book on pilgrimage and that this book is borne out of my experience of life that is becoming more or less a pilgrimage. The various experiences of intentional pilgrimages I have been on—pilgrimages that had a beginning, middle, and end, and that occurred in a specific place with a particular group of people—and the many pilgrimage narratives I have read over the last few years convince me again and again that these moments of constant worrying, wonder, stress, and edgy agony are really to be understood as periods of grace. If I remain still and in one place long enough, amid the sacrifice of time and energy—and money—I may actually find some moments blessed and some arduous times a godsend. Upon reflection, I discover over and over again that these intentional or volitional periods of pilgrimage in my crowded life are not only a great metaphor for the Christian life but that Christian pilgrimage *is* the Christian life.[6] The pilgrimage narratives of others remind me that the Christian life can be understood as a pilgrimage, in which we are born and baptized as pilgrims among a people who are already on a pilgrimage. We are not at the beginning of the line of pilgrims, though the experience will seem forever new for us. But Christ is at the head of the line, and we are the followers, being led by the cross of Christ. Likewise, we are not at the end of the line, for there are many who will follow us, hearing and receiving stories of our time on the pilgrim's way.

The School of the Pilgrim is a different approach to educating individual Christians, congregations, and parishes about understanding our entire life as a pilgrimage, in which we follow the Pilgrim God, Jesus Christ. In following the Pilgrim, we learn what Christ taught, performing the movements, or the gestures, commissioned by Christ in our world today.

In this ongoing conversion or transformation, we gain a clearer understanding of what it means to be members in the body of Christ, and we accept that being a Christian requires performing Christly gestures of service, praise, and prayer in company with fellow pilgrims both from today and from ages past.

The School of the Pilgrim approach follows the gospel mode of simplicity filled with divine mystery. First, individuals become acquainted with the tradition of pilgrimage through familiarity with the literature and resources on pilgrimage.

Second, pilgrims flourish through the rich interchange and journey to authenticity with other companions. All this culminates in the experience of pilgrimage. Fellow pilgrims grow increasingly comfortable in the presence of the Holy Spirit as well as in their Christian connection to and with one another. The School of the Pilgrim experience touches a fuller revelation of the *imago Dei* among us.

The School of the Pilgrim advocates reappropriating the ancient practice of pilgrimage and instructing people as to how the Christian life is a lifelong pilgrimage in today's world. As I will explain in this book, the School of the Pilgrim will incorporate the various aspects or characteristics of a prototypical pilgrimage, using these characteristics as the basis for further developing pilgrimage practices that will help us see, hear, touch, and move along life's pilgrimage. These characteristics include focus on the gestures of pilgrimage; understanding that educating pilgrims involves our mind, body, and spirit; becoming part of a community of pilgrims, discovering the gift and art of friendship and companionship along the way; relying on the saints before us and among us to guide us by focusing on the importance of memory—remembering—along the pilgrim's way; learning the act of teaching and seeing Christ on pilgrimage; utilizing the rituals and sacraments that are essential for pilgrimage; focusing on the way that education of Christians on the pilgrim's way shapes and nurtures our very character in the virtues of Christian life; awakening to the importance of the land, the environment, our context, in life's pilgrimage; lifting up the profound need for prayer and contemplation on our pilgrimage; and underscoring the pivotal place that our beginning point and destination have on being God's pilgrim people.

In the end, in the School of the Pilgrim we realize we are on an ongoing, lifelong pilgrimage, moving collectively toward the realm of God that is already breaking into our world today. Like pilgrims of old, today's pilgrims are on a transforming trek, in which our knowledge of God and each other is deepened as we walk with Christ.

I am well aware that traditional Christian education models do not follow the lessons learned through pilgrimage. This book may seem strange and even heretical for some. Yet, in fact, the practice of Christian pilgrimage is older than Christian education programs. I am convinced that traditional teaching in our seminaries and places of learning is missing some time-proven lessons on how to respect and nourish the Christian faith of disciples. My hope is that new approaches will become clear through these pages.

Chapter 1

The Story of Christian Pilgrimage

The figure of the pilgrim was not a modern invention; it is as old as Christianity. . . . St. Augustine jotted down the following observation: "It is recorded of Cain that he built a city, while Abel, as though he was merely a pilgrim on earth, built none."

(Zygmunt Bauman, Life in Fragments*)*

Go from your country and your kindred and your father's house to the land that I will show you.

(Gen. 12:1)

While they were talking and discussing, Jesus himself came near and went with them.

(Luke 24:15)

I have often caught myself looking at the footsteps of others while on pilgrimage. I forget to look up and see what wonders are around me. Remembering to seek what my predecessors have sought seems key to understanding pilgrimage. Matsuo Basko wrote, "Don't seek to follow in the footsteps of the men [and women] of old—seek what they sought." Basko believed we are to embody the art of seeing, of noticing, rather than focusing on the step before us. Basko would also remind us that while we are traveling outwardly along the roads of this world, there is an internal experience in this spiritual quest, which allows a freer play of our imagination.[1]

What is a pilgrimage? Is it an outer journey, or an inner quest, or both? And what is a pilgrim? It seems there are as many definitions and descriptions of pilgrims and pilgrimage as there are people who have been on such a journey or who have studied such a historical yet current practice.

What Is Pilgrimage? Who Is a Pilgrim?

Diana Webb argues that "pilgrimage did not originate with Christianity, and that it has never been, nor is it now, an exclusively or peculiarly Christian phenomenon."[2] Yet others understand pilgrimage from primarily its Jewish and Christian roots, beginning with the nomadic travels of Abram and Sarai, who left their home in Ur of the Chaldeans. Other scholars of world religions show us that the impetus to travel with such a purposefulness and resoluteness to seek the sacred is a trait found around the world, throughout time. In Islam there is the *hajj*, or devotional trip to Mecca. Hindus make a trip to the river Benares for pilgrimage. Many Japanese practice a pilgrimage to a shrine on Mt. Fuji. Some Native Americans in Taos Pueblo in New Mexico make a journey to the top of the mountain region for the Blue Corn celebration. In certain Central American countries, there are the ancient ruins of indigenous people who built temples for their pilgrimages. Aboriginal people in Australia go on mysterious walks over land on "Dreaming tracks."[3]

By many accounts, there is a kind of universality to the idea and practice of pilgrimage, and such travel seems almost foundational in its core, as people have a desire to move from one place to another for whatever reason they so claim is central to their way of understanding themselves and the world. The journey itself is the crucial component of the enterprise, as the motion of the pilgrimage is an almost kinesthetic mapping of space, a charting of bodily movement of the contours of the religious landscapes as they rise "upwards from the peripheral homelands of the nation to a sacred center," as Michael Sallnow writes.[4] Huston Smith writes that since we are embodied souls, we have to act out our faith with our bodies as well as our minds and spirits. Pilgrimage is not only an act of body, mind, and spirit. Smith thought that pilgrimage is "belief in action."[5] There is the low bow to natural law as many pilgrims think that the practice of pilgrimage "is due to the natural desire of men to visit the places where their great heroes have lived and died and to the deep-seated conviction that certain localities are particularly favored by the Godhead."[6] For the purposes of this book, let me narrow this investigation by focusing on the question of what is a Christian pilgrimage and pilgrim.

An Anthropology and Sociology of Pilgrim and Pilgrimage

The word "pilgrim" comes from the Old French *pelegrin*, Middle English *pelegrim,* or French *pelegrinius*. The Latin *pelegrinus* refers to the wayfarer or foreigner, or the journey of a person who travels to a shrine or holy place.

The Latin, *pelegrinus*, can also mean "from abroad," and *per agrum*, "through the field."[7] To be a pilgrim on pilgrimage is to be a person who is on the move, making a journey, which may be difficult and often long, to some specific place, such as a religious or sacred shrine or important physical marker, with or without a group of people, over a span of time. Richard R. Niebuhr writes that a pilgrim is a person in motion—on unknown ground—moving toward completion or clarity, a goal to which only the Spirit's compass points the way.[8] Ambrose Bierce defines a pilgrim as "a traveler that is taken seriously."[9]

Pilgrimage is different from travel or vacation. Victor and Edith Turner argue that a tourist is half pilgrim, while a pilgrim is half tourist. It is impossible to totally separate the sacred from the secular.[10] There is the mix of the tourist and the pilgrim in the throng who goes to celebrate seasonal changes at Stonehenge in England, or in those who make their summer vacation a trip to Graceland in Tennessee to visit Elvis's shrine. In the South, I have participated in church reunions or "Homecoming" events at several Protestant churches, in which members of churches from some years ago will come back to visit a congregation where they once worshiped. On St. Patrick's Purgatory I was told by some women that this pilgrimage was as much a break from their husbands and an excuse to spend time with their "girlfriends" as it was a pilgrimage.

It can be argued that all pilgrims are travelers, since the root of the word for travel is "travail," from the Latin *tripalium*, which in the Middle Ages meant "torture rack." To travel is to travail or to be in travail.[11] To be on pilgrimage involves some kind of obstacle that will become travail along the pilgrim's way. To quote the Arabian proverb, "It's not the road ahead that wears you out—it's the grain of sand in your shoe."[12]

But there are some distinctive characteristics of pilgrimage that make it different from mere travel or a vacation. First, as Philip Cousineau writes, a pilgrimage is different from a journey or a vacation because it has the added component of being a "soulful journey," which makes it more rigorous than a vacation or a tourist odyssey. He suggests that when we no longer know where to turn, our real journey has begun: "At that moment, a voice calls to our pilgrim soul."[13] He writes, "Ancient wisdom suggests if you aren't trembling as you approach the sacred, it isn't the real thing. The sacred in its various guises as holy ground, art, or knowledge, evokes emotion and commotion."[14]

Second, pilgrimage is a kind of sacred travel. "Sacred" comes from the word "sacrifice." To have or be on a sacred journey, one has to give up something—one has to make a sacrifice.[15] I have been told on pilgrimages that we who are pilgrims are blessed because of the sacrifice of time, energy, and talent that we now share with other pilgrims, the church, and the saints along a pilgrimage route.

In sum, while tourists might escape reality or the world where they live, pilgrims go deeper into what is real, what is of God. To be on vacation is to literally "vacate," to leave, to depart, for rest and relaxation, perhaps some recreation—to get away from it all. Meanwhile, pilgrimage is "the kind of journeying that marks just this move from mindless to mindful, soulless to soulful travel."[16] Huston Smith writes that to be on pilgrimage is "to throw down a challenge to everyday life. Nothing matters now but this adventure."[17] Pilgrimage is the art of movement, "the poetry of motion, the music of personal experience of the sacred in those places where it has been known to shine forth. If we are not astounded by these possibilities, we can never plumb the depths of our own souls or the soul of the world," writes Cousineau.[18]

Third, pilgrimage comes from an act of the heart, as a means of exploring either the unconscious or the deeper questions of life in general, and life in God in particular.[19] Martin Robinson says that the *act* of pilgrimage "echoes questions that come to us from that deeper journey of the heart. What is the reason for my being? It is no coincidence that many who go on pilgrimage are at a critical stage of life—the transition from childhood to adulthood, and adulthood to the start of retirement."[20] Sometimes the question of pilgrimage focuses our attention on the seemingly simple act of turning our lives in the right direction of the pilgrimage, for in the frenzy of life it is easy to get turned around from where we should be heading. Thus, the pilgrim's very body is a conduit of knowledge, a medium of communication, a means of connecting with some agent of social change. A pilgrim's very act of walking or riding a bike, hiking or even crawling along a paved roadside is a protest against the modern age: We pray with our feet or on our bicycles.[21] Anthropologically, John Eade and Michael Sallnow write that pilgrimage is a break from the mundane and secular:

> Pilgrimage, being stereotypically focused on powerful but peripheral shrines commanding widespread recognition and devotion, is *anti*-structural: it always tends towards communitas, a state of unmediated and egalitarian association between individuals who are temporarily freed of the hierarchical secular roles and statuses which they bear in everyday life. The achievement of communitas is the pilgrim's fundamental motivation. . . . Pilgrimage, in other words, to the degree that it strips actors of their social personae and restores their essential individuality, is the ritual context *par excellence* in which a world religion strives to realize its defining transcultural universalism; for to reach the individual is to reach the universal.[22]

Furthermore, the Turners, under the influence of religious scholar Mircea Eliade, write that the pilgrimage's raison d'être is the notion of a holy place, a shrine, marked off by the secular space surrounding it, where "heaven and earth intersect and where time stands still, where there exists the possibility of breaking through to the realm of the transcendent."[23] But sometimes it is not a place per se but a relic, a person who is entombed or had visited a spot, that becomes the raison d'être of a pilgrimage, such as the bones of St. James in Compostela, or the bones of St. Peter in St. Peter's Basilica in Rome. Such shrines with their relics have a power that is almost sui generis: "Its power is internally generated and its meanings are largely predetermined."[24]

Lastly, it is often the case that the sacred geography is considered worthy of a pilgrimage as it illuminates the sacred and authoritative text upon which it is founded. Such is the case with places around Jerusalem and the Holy Land, the very cradle of Christianity, in which the attraction is Christ himself, who causes the power of the place to recede against the far greater power of the written word. Eade and Sallnow write that what matters most for Christian pilgrims is the triad of the person, place, and text. In the sacred places, led by holy texts, persons seek to experience a growing awareness of God as they grow more aware of who a person is *in* God. That is why pilgrimage is a journey of the religious imagination, or what the Turners calls an "exteriorized mysticism, the private mystical journey made public, a journey of the spirit which is physically enacted . . . [,] an allegory of the journey of the soul to God."[25] As such it cannot be readily comprehended by those who have not undertaken such a journey.

The walking, the movement, is a necessity of pilgrimage. Pilgrimage is a "kinesthetic mapping of space, a charting by bodily movement of the contours of the religious landscape as they rise upwards from the peripheral homelands" of one's hometown to a sacred center, a hallowed site, writes Michael Sallnow.[26]

That which is sacred is not given or something fixed, waiting for the pilgrim to come. Instead, it takes a conscious effort on the part of the pilgrim to use the appropriate symbols, myths, rituals, worship, and other practices in order to experience on pilgrimage the Holy of Holies made real in this time and space.[27]

Pilgrimage in the Bible

Pilgrimage is as old as the biblical tales we grew up with, beginning with the texts of the Old Testament. For example, God chose to be on a pilgrimage with God's people in their exodus out of Egypt: "The cloud covered the tent of meeting, and the glory of the LORD filled the tabernacle" (Exod. 40:34). In 1 Kings 8:10–13, we read that it was not until later in history when God, who would "dwell in thick darkness," received an exalted house or temple to dwell in forever.[28] Philip Cousineau cites Abraham as the earliest recorded pilgrim when he left Ur four thousand years ago.[29] In the Psalms (see, e.g., Ps. 84), the Wisdom literature, and the prophetic books, the theme of journey, of being moved by God, led by God in the wilderness, and traversing the land when taking to exile is a continuous theme.

In the New Testament, the stories of Jesus and his disciples are one of almost constant movement. In the infancy narrative of Luke 1–2 we read of the holy family's journey to Egypt. Jesus spent forty days and nights in the wilderness, which could be construed as a pilgrimage of sorts. Jesus' participation in Passover with his disciples, in which are born the eucharistic practices of the church, was a celebration of the Israelites' pilgrimage out of Egyptian slavery.

According to the late Brother John of the Taizé Community, Jesus is the pilgrim *par excellence*:

> A pilgrim with no fixed abode in this world, Jesus is far more than a "new Abraham" or a "new Moses." These typologies, though present in the gospel portrait of Jesus, do not yield the key to his identity. At a first level, Jesus is certainly the man who answers God's call and sets out to follow in his footsteps. But he fulfills this mission in a unique way, because he is primarily the one who comes into the world to call men: like the *Shekinah*, he comes to chart God's path in the heart of our history. In the context of the story of Abraham, we may liken him first to the pilgrim-God who speaks, and only then to the human being who hears the divine Word and conforms his existence to it.[30]

Brother John cites the Synoptic Gospels (Mark, Matthew, and Luke) as portraying a Jesus whose public life unfolds in two stages: first is the itinerant ministry of Jesus in the villages and rural areas of Galilee, and the second stage is his ministry in the holy city of Jerusalem. John portrays Jesus as a pilgrim who is sent from heaven by God in order to give life to the world (John 6:33; 8:42) and who then leaves this world: "But now I am going to him who sent me" (John 16:5) and "If I go and prepare a place for you, I will come again and will take you to myself, so that where I am, there you may be also" (John 14:3). In the story of Palm Sunday, Jesus comes to the destination of his lifelong journey: Jerusalem (Luke 19:28–40; Matt. 21:1–11; Mark 11:1–11; John 12:12–19). Finally, in Luke 24 there is the story of the "road to Emmaus," where two disciples go on a pilgrimage with the risen Jesus, realizing his identity only after sharing their bread with him. Hebrews 11:13 (KJV) declares that our forebears of the faith were "strangers and pilgrims on the earth." Paul also lived a pilgrim life as a missionary. Paul and the apostles were bound to the life of pilgrimage, as recipients of the Great Commission, a call of pilgrimage: "Go therefore and make disciples of all nations, baptizing them . . . and teaching them to obey everything that I have commanded you. And remember, I am with you always, to the end of the age" (Matt. 28:19–20).

Pilgrimage in the Early Christian Church

According to John 14:6, Jesus said that he is "the way, and the truth, and the life" for all Christians. Jesus' self-designation as "the way" was picked up in the early church, as Christians were initially called people of "the Way" (Acts 9:2). Yet throughout the early history of the church there was much confusion about who was actually the first person to go on an intentional pilgrimage. Some argue that the first pilgrim was Melito of Sardis, who visited the city of Jerusalem in AD 170 to see the places spoken of in Scripture.[31] The writer Jerome later expressed a view that a visit to the Holy Land would make it possible for pilgrims to understand the Scriptures better. Modern-day pilgrims travel by the thousands to the Holy Land for that reason: to see the sites where the stories of Scripture took place.

Robinson and other historians write that it was after the recognition of Christianity as the state religion under Constantine that the status of these sites changed. Constantine's mother, Helena, also made such a journey herself. Robinson writes:

> Her reports of what she found drove Constantine to action. Particular excitement surrounded the rediscovery of the site of the burial place of Jesus, as well as remnants of the sacred cross. According to the accounts of the day, the Christian community which had remained in Jerusalem had remembered where Jesus' tomb was located. The city had expanded so that it was now within the city walls and it had become concealed under heaps of rubble and the construction of a city street. Once the Christians were in the ascendancy, it became possible to excavate the site. Constantine then ordered the building of a beautiful church—the Church of the Holy Sepulchre.[32]

There was an increase in the number of people who began to journey to Jerusalem on pilgrimage, which was accompanied by a growth in what is now called "desert spirituality." Wanting to remove themselves from the worldliness and growing material quality of Christianity, there were some who went into the desert with hopes of escaping the habits and conventions of the faith, which were being trivialized in the eyes of the early hermits. Thus, the hermitage in the desert became an archetype and greenhouse of the "raw, bare, primal, and bottom-line freedom that is but the absence of bounds," writes Zygmunt Bauman. The hermits' pilgrimage to God in the desert was an exercise in self-construction, outside the boundaries and habits of the worldly Christians.[33] Belden Lane writes that "certain monastic communities in the history of Christian spirituality have developed rules for the ordering of life 'on the edge,' physically removed from the influence of a dominant culture."[34] This was the rise of Christian hermitage and a new movement in which people escaped "the world" in order to pray for the world. The center of this new movement was Egypt, which became part of the trail for those going to Jerusalem.

One of the best-known pilgrims in the fourth century and early fifth century was Egeria, a Spanish nun, who wrote *Diary of a Pilgrimage*. This form of literature is the *itinerary,* an ancient travelogue, in which the religious motivation of the traveler is known. Egeria is seeking out the monks in remote areas of the Sinai peninsula. In her diary Egeria records the liturgical accounts of life among Christian communities she visits, including services attended especially by the monks, such as the nocturnal offices. The text is filled with many references to devotional acts, which emphasize the spiritual purpose of her pilgrimage.[35] In looking at the life of Egeria as a kind of pilgrim exemplar, Robinson states that a pilgrimage to Jerusalem would not necessarily induce holiness where none existed before. Rather, the pilgrimage was seen as an aid to those who were already devout. Then who would be the primary candidates of pilgrimage? Those living in monasteries and convents.[36]

Pilgrimage in the Medieval Church of Europe

An interesting turn of assumptions about the value of pilgrimage took place during medieval times. Robinson writes that with an increase in individual pilgrims, there was an equal insistence that one need not go to a certain place for such a spiritual journey. While there was a connection between the spiritual life and pilgrimage, the monasteries, which did not want to lose monks to the travels of pilgrimage, insisted that the monastic life was superior to pilgrimage, to the point that some orders, such as the Cistercians, did not permit any monk to go to Jerusalem. They could imitate Christ within the monastery and travel to Jerusalem in an interior or spiritual sense.[37]

The medieval period also saw the rise of the use of labyrinths. These mosaic-tiled labyrinths with inward-spiraling circles in a sanctuary provided people who were not able to afford a trip to the Holy Land, or who were eager to have an experience of pilgrimage nearer home, a way to practice the art of pilgrimage. A labyrinth is circular in shape, usually twelve feet in diameter if not bigger, and is set into the floor. People would slowly and intentionally walk around the circular pattern, coming closer to the center of the labyrinth and thus drawing closer to the heart of God.

Robinson also writes of the rise of Celtic pilgrimage in what we now know as Ireland and Scotland, which was a combination of pilgrimage, spirituality, and mission. The monks of Celtic heritage would leave their homeland by setting sail in their coracles, or small boats, and allow the "wind of the spirit to take them where it would. The place where they landed would become their new, albeit temporary mission field." Other Celtic missionary monks, such as St. Cuthbert and St. Aidan of Lindisfarne, England, the "Holy Isle," would be in a specific area but would move around in the area, evangelizing. This was known as "travel[ing] for Christ, the *peregrination pro Christi*, to take the message of the cross to shores and lands which had never heard the gospel proclaimed."[38]

In the Russian Orthodox tradition, pilgrimage is captured well in the book *The Way of a Pilgrim*, in which the destination is unimportant compared to the journey within the pilgrim. The wandering is from one holy place to another, in which the primary intention is not the preaching of the gospel as much as the taking care of the spiritual life, thus imitating Christ.[39] The pilgrim is intent on learning how to pray constantly, finally doing so in reciting the "Jesus Prayer," which is simply "Lord Jesus Christ, have mercy on me," handed down by generations upon generations of Russian Orthodox believers.[40]

During the medieval period, many of our ideas of what is pilgrimage were born and embodied. Anthropologists Victor and Edith Turner identified five characteristics that seem to capture many pilgrimages.[41] The first is the belief of all pilgrims that the place where people are going is a place where miracles once happened, are continuing to happen, and might happen again. Such places hold out the hope that they are "hotlines to God." For example, people make a pilgrimage to Santiago de Compostela (St. James of Compostela) because of the supposed miracle of finding the relics of St. James (St. Imago) the Apostle in Spain, where St. James is said to have preached. People go to Oviedo, Italy, because the wine turned into blood, to Lourdes, France, because of the visions and healing stories of Mary took took place there, or to a building in a city in New Jersey or Florida because of a vision of Mary. Thousands descend upon Esquipulas, Guatemala, to venerate the wooden sculpture of Christ on the cross known as the Black Christ, *El Cristo Negro*. Yet what I was told in Esquipulas holds for the other places of pilgrimage as well: While one can pray and hope for a miracle, one cannot make the assumption that a miracle will occur. The pilgrim is not to expect any bodily, cognitive, emotional, or spiritual remedy to a problem, because that would be an act of pride. If anything, pilgrimage takes the pilgrim along the pathway of living humbly. If a miracle occurs, then the pilgrim is to attribute it all to God's grace. As they say in Esquipulas, "The Christ you seek you will not find unless you bring him with you." In other words, don't expect the Black Christ to automatically bring about a miracle in your life. Rather, the potent miracle already resides within our hearts, minds, and bodies, as we reside in Christ.

Second, the purpose of pilgrimage is to get out and away from a place in which there are the occasions of sin that make up so much of the Christian's experience of life. Geoffrey Chaucer's pilgrims going to Canterbury were getting away from where they lived, away from the problems of home, "to see the holy, blissful martyr [St. Thomas à Becket], who helped them when they were sick."[42] Or consider Bunyan's *Pilgrim's Progress*. Christian is leaving the City of Destruction for the gate that leads to the Celestial City because the City of Destruction is the place in which one will "sink lower than the Grave, into a place that burns with Fire and Brimstone."[43]

The third characteristic of pilgrimage is penitence. There is a connection with the imitation of Christ, with sacrifice and exile, with the development of the spiritual life, and with a contemplation of the inner life, all pointing toward the time of pilgrimage as a period of penance, "even if that penance is not related to a particular act of wrongdoing." Sometimes indulgences were attached to pilgrimage; other times self-flagellation was required, visiting physical suffering upon the body; at still other times, people would walk partially or totally naked as part of their offering of penance.[44] (Today pilgrims at St. Patrick's Purgatory walk for two days on the rocky island with bare feet.) In meeting the hazards along the way, such as robbers, these pilgrims were released from the illness of sins associated with their respective homes. The journey itself was one in which the Almighty tested one's very character. By entering the journey, the pilgrim was initiating and entering a level of existence deeper than what the pilgrim had known in the past or in everyday life. After completing the pilgrimage, a person was not expected to be the same as before. The journey was of greater importance than the destination.

Fourth, the pilgrim is never alone. There are no "Lone Rangers" on pilgrimages. For example, consider Bunyan's pilgrim, Christian, who from time to time meets someone on the crossroads of his journey or travels a distance with another pilgrim, for example, "Faith." Chaucer's pilgrims in *Canterbury Tales* form a community of Christians who go together to Canterbury and back home. Because the communion of saints gathers around us wherever we as pilgrims may be, any sense of isolation or loneliness is in the mind of the pilgrim. Indeed, if all of creation is molded by God, then in the shadows, in the gaps of the cliffs, there is God. Annie Dillard writes, "The gaps are the cliffs in the rock where you cower to see the back parts of God; they are the fissures between mountains and cells the wind lances through, the icy narrowing fiords splitting the cliffs of mystery."[45]

Fifth, pilgrims leave a certain place and go to a specific destination, though they may not know exactly what to expect at the point of arrival. There is a purpose to the journey that helps pilgrims especially in times of great trial or trauma on the road or sea. For Moses and the children of Israel, the goal was the "land of milk and honey"; for Bunyan's pilgrim it was "the City beyond the Wicket Gate." For Chaucer's pilgrims it was Canterbury Cathedral, to worship at the place where St. Thomas à Becket was martyred and his relics kept, while Lindisfarne and Durham Cathedral called forth the pilgrims to St. Cuthbert's tomb. In Ireland pilgrims go to the places where St. Patrick himself traversed, such as St. Patrick's Purgatory, while in New Mexico people travel miles by foot to touch the holy soil of El Santuario de Chimayo. Pilgrimage is an act of an entire community, though sometimes the pilgrim travels alone, in search of God, and in the process comes to know the self better. In seeking this relationship with God, the pilgrim will be irrevocably changed.

Granted, there are hucksters who use pilgrimage as a way of making money quickly. In medieval times not only were there robbers and criminals along the way, but these were also prostitutes, swindlers, and conmen and conwomen. During the eleventh and early twelfth centuries, the increasing attention on Jesus' human qualities spurred interest in devotion to Mary, the Mother of God. According to Rosemary Mahoney, such interest in the devotion to Mary also brought forward a surge in the number of miracles because of Mary's influence and authority. At the same time, the Muslim occupation of the Holy Lands, of Jerusalem and other sites, along with the Crusades, made going to the Holy Land on pilgrimage dangerous and nearly impossible. Mahoney writes, "Christians began creating safer points of pilgrimage closer to home. Unable to travel to the Holy Land, they simply brought the Holy Land to Europe. Across the continent shrines began to spring up boasting relics from Palestine," such as pieces of the cross of Christ, a bone of a saint, or other body parts.[46] In Spain, Santiago had pieces of St. James, while Walsingham, England, had St. Peter's fingers.

Pilgrimage and the Church Reformers

Under the influence of the Protestant reformers, devotion to pilgrimage waned. For example, in 1562, the Dutch reformer Erasmus published "A Pilgrimage for Religion's Sake." According to Mahoney, he mocked "the religious excesses of the Middle Ages: the superstition, the fixation on relics, and the hypocrisy and corruption of the clergy. Singling out the pilgrimage to Walsingham, Canterbury, and the Compostela, the colloquy contains a letter from the beleaguered Virgin Mary, who professes herself 'all but exhausted by the shameless entreaties of mortals.'"[47]

Martin Luther wrote that "all pilgrimages should be stopped. There is no good in them: no commandment enjoins them, no obedience attaches to them. Rather do these pilgrimages give countless occasions to commit sin and to despise God's commandments."[48] Because pilgrimage included the practice of indulgences, Luther believed that pilgrimage was as heretical as other practices of the church in those days.

Nevertheless, the period of pilgrimage has often been seen as sacred time, as the pilgrim is on a mission, has been sent by God, and is thus living a sainted life. Furthermore, Diana Webb writes that to be on pilgrimage in medieval times was "accepted as a meritorious, though not obligatory, Christian practice; the *bone fide* pilgrim was entitled to the protection of the law and the support of the faithful."[49]

Mahoney has noticed that at the beginning of the twenty-first century there has been a marked resurgence in pilgrimages, and many pilgrimage sites are thriving. She writes, "With the modern corrosion of organized religion and the emergence of quick spiritual fixes and alluring self-help seminars now available in exchange for little more than money," religious pilgrimages are booming.[50] There is something behind the transformation or change wrought by a physical journey with a faith-filled intent.

Martin Robinson suggests that pilgrimage may be a metaphor within the Christian experience:

> Some describe themselves as pilgrims in relation to a particular quest, journey or difficult experience within their Christian life. . . . Some who have been missionaries refer to their whole missionary experience as a pilgrimage. Others use the term to describe their ecumenical journey or their work for peace or reconciliation.[51]

In the next chapter I lay out a "map" for understanding growth and change in our lives through pilgrimage practices in the Christian experience of life.

Chapter 2

Growth and Change along the Pilgrim's Way

Transcendence has to be understood as an expansion of your being, a pushing back of the frontiers of your limitations.

(John Main)

For pilgrims through time, the truth is elsewhere; The true place is always some distance, some time away. . . . Judeo-Christian culture is, at its very roots, about experiences of spiritual dislocation and homelessness. . . . Our faith began at odds with place.

(Richard Sennett)

A Human Developmental Portrait of Jesus

In discussing change and growth in the church, it is important to understand that in the past century the American church has adopted theories of human development in framing change and growth in human life. These theories are in the curricula of the educational programs of the church, its pastoral counseling services, and other areas. These theories are based upon social science theories that were constructed by human beings in order to better understand our past actions, control our present behaviors, and predict future dealings of any group of people.

These theories can help us understand much about ourselves. For example, Sigmund Freud's theories of psychosexual development enable us to see how childhood experiences continually shape adult attitudes and behaviors, whether or not we are conscious of this. Jean Piaget lifts up the intricacies of life as a child, in which children are no longer seen as immature or little adults, as they were prior to Piaget's developmental schema. Erik Erikson calls us to focus on the social relationships that influence our sense of trust with one another in our modern society. Lawrence Kohlberg and Carol Gilligan encourage us to take seriously the moral life of individuals. And James Fowler directs our attention to the stagelike development of human-based faith.

While each theorist has given us a new appreciation of the intricacies of being human, each had his or her own shortcomings in religious matters. For example, Freud considered God a figment of human imagination; Piaget shrunk the importance of lifelong religious instruction to only the first four years of a child's life; Erikson outlined the importance of faith as another form of trust, and only important in the first stage or age of life, "trust versus mistrust"; Gilligan and Kohlberg failed to connect morality with faith, leaving faith to Fowler, who recast it as a human activity rather than a gift of God's grace.

To underscore the problems posed by these theories of human development, consider some developmental profiles of Jesus in his early thirties, the years that he was active in his earthly ministry. After all, the Council of Chalcedon in AD 451 stated that Jesus is unchangeably, indivisibly, and inseparably *human* as well as divine. Since theories of human development are universal and foundational, applicable to any person, that would include Jesus. According to Erikson, Kohlberg, and Fowler, Jesus would fit their descriptions of a young adult (ages 21–35) who was not quite a full adult. According to Erikson's typology, Jesus would be at stage six, "intimacy and solidarity versus isolation," a young man needing and searching for intimacy and candor within himself and his peers, able to form important relationships with the opposite sex during this time, dating actively, if not already married and raising a family, holding friendships with other men. Because Jesus did not marry, Erikson might say that Jesus retreated into a zone of isolation, where relationships are cold and empty.

In Kohlberg's system, Jesus is not quite postconventional in his understanding of the world, but still lives in the realm of conventionality, supporting and upholding the current social system in which he is a member. Of course, we know the opposite is true: Jesus challenged the orthodoxy of his day, even suffering death at the hands of the prevailing system. According to Fowler, Jesus should have been at the stage of "Individuative-Reflective Faith," struggling between his individuality and being defined by the group.[1] But what does Fowler make of Jesus' independence from the Jewish religious system, his making statements regarding ascending to the Father, or his sending the Paraclete on our behalf? Is this simply believing in a myth, or Jesus embracing his full individuality?

As we can see in this short examination of Jesus' life through the lenses of human developmental theorists, Jesus fails to live in the normative framework of these theories, as, I would suggest, he does in any of the other theories that are currently used in society and the church. More importantly, Jesus' life fails to be adequately understood or described by the norms of our human theories. Is it because Jesus is divine? Or is it because these theories fail to take into account an authentic sense of spirituality?

Herein lies a critical problem for the church when using these theories: At best, developmental psychologists relegate the practices of the church, through which we know God, to the role of aiding human beings in achieving or getting to various stages of development. The church serves a utilitarian role, a helper for the greater good of human development. Thus, at worst, the church is a relic of a bygone era, as other social systems can probably do the same work in aiding our development, with the goal of each person reaching full human actualization.

But what if the church is not a relic of a bygone era, or one community support system among many others in our world, but is a living inheritor of the true story of God's Son, a story that is learned best within the life of the church? And what does it mean to be part of a faith community that is concerned not only about the individual and the personal but the communal, the greater good, in and of the body of Christ? After all, Jesus is not the only one who does not necessarily fit the normative descriptive patterns of growth as described by human developmental theorists. Our daily life is complex, with neither rhyme nor reason to it most days of the week. When we reflect upon our lives, we can all discover ways that our lives are lived outside the normative description of these theories.

For example, Roberto Unger explains a number of characteristics to keep in mind when considering the changing, growing lives of people, and the impossibility of categorizing or creating stereotypes, as is our inclination. First, people have continually changing identities. We do not rest in one way of being in the world for an eternity. To this end, Erikson is more or less correct: Our search for or creation of our identity is ongoing. Second, we share a common humanity with others, and in so doing, we keep changing over time, whether that change is an internal desire to be like others, or a desire to stand out and let others know we are different from them. Third, the ends or purposes of our lives continue to change over time. Fourth, there is within us a desire to be unique individuals, despite our membership in a species of like-minded beings.[2] Or to consider this from a Christian perspective, God in Christ has given us different gifts, talents, and services in the body of Christ that take form or manifest themselves differently in each person, making each person invaluable to the ongoing life of the body of Christ. But Unger also rightly reminds us that because of our consciousness and free will, we differ from the other animals that follow their way in the world through instinct and a short range of learned acts. Instead, we live a life that is often bound by indeterminacy and consciousness, which means that our relationship to nature is either a problem to be solved or an unanswerable question in which we live. Our being in the world, though some would profess is predestined by God, is not foreordained according to the theories of human development. It is because our relationship to nature and to each other is not given an assured "and they lived happily ever after" ending. At any period in time, we understand that life is filled with opportunities and shifting alliances within the body of Christ and with others in this world, with whom we live, with certain limitations, and against specific odds.[3]

I raise these issues out of my own studies, experiences of life, and observations. Consider the numerous stories on television and radio, in magazines and books, of people whose life experiences defy theories of human development—for example, the ten-year-old boy who lives as an adult in a village in Africa, caring for his siblings as a parent after all the adults in his family died of AIDS. Or consider the story of *Rabbit Proof Fence*, in which a young girl becomes an adult at fourteen when she escapes a camp in which Aboriginal children are kept in order to breed out the blackness of their race. She travels hundreds of miles in order to be with her mother.[4] Neither of these children fits the human developmental norms of childhood, even though chronologically they are quite young.

I will now look at what it means to change and grow as Christians, based on the presumption that, first, we are members of a particular social system, the body of Christ; second, that this body, and us in it, is in constant motion—on pilgrimage—and third, that this body-on-pilgrimage is inclusive of people of all ages, abilities, genders, economic classes, ethnicities, national heritages, races, and sexual orientations.

Changing and Growing

To change and to grow is to become more like Christ in our daily lives. In other words, the "I" in "my" life is transplanted by the Christ who lives in us, around us, and in whom we reside as members of the body of Christ. John Main writes that such a journey of change and growth is an expansion of each person's capacity to touch God, who is infinity. Our life goes through a series of progressions, from the limitations of the self into the limitless life we experience in God in Christ.[5] Living in Christ will call upon us to live lives of discipline, concentration, and devotion.[6]

Transmutation means a radical change of one thing or being into another, and this occurs to us as Christians. There is the dying of the "old self," followed by a rising anew in Christ. For example, in baptism, Christ takes hold of our old life, which Paul refers to with the imagery of "Adam and Moses" (Rom. 5:14), embracing us in a love that knows no end. We join Christ in our baptism in a kind of death, so that just as Christ was raised from the dead by the glory of God, so we too are raised from the dead so that we might live in the newness of life (Rom. 6:4, 11). Thus, in our growing in Christ we are doing more than amassing or accumulating intelligence or knowledge as a form of power over other people. We begin with the recognition that we are in Christ and becoming more like Christ in all the challenges of our complex, earthly lives. In a sense, we are called to live more fully into our God-created humanity, to see the world with courage and hope, and to accept our limitations as we turn to others who help expand our capacity to be more present with one another in the context of the body of Christ.

Social theorist Saul Alinsky writes that "change means movement. Movement means friction."[7] By clinging to the present, or holding on to the memories of the past, we are liable to cut off opportunities to grow in the Spirit. Though it is hard to understand that holding on may stop us from making the necessary changes for the better in our lives, it is nevertheless true that, more times than not, the spirituality of change begins with the decision either to grow or retreat. We either live a little more or die a little more each day. This is a decision of great import that we make at those infrequent forks in the road of life.

So the choice, made possible by free will, is as follows: Either we choose the ancient Stoic model in the face of change, holding a stiff upper lip while enduring changes, thus growing smaller rather than larger and wiser, or we choose to change and grow. If we choose the latter, the break from our old way of life gives us an opportunity to explore the ways that God is doing a new thing in our lives. Octavio Paz says, "Wisdom lies neither in fixity nor in change, but in the dialectic between the two."[8] The growth we experience in the body of Christ on pilgrimage is most likely found and nurtured in Paz's dialectic. There can be no growth without change. We can never forget the past, but we have the choice of how to live with memories of the past in our present and future life.

In terms of growth, the world uses other measures for growth, such as academic credits and intelligence test scores, based upon an individual model of achievement. These measures are based upon performance, upon doing, upon levels attained. They are based upon a capitalistic economy of education in which we are clients and consumers who are buying the "best education money can afford."

In the body of Christ on pilgrimage, the way to assess or evaluate and acknowledge one's growth is to realize what really matters in life. The pilgrimage is about losing oneself, expanding from one's concerns about "me" and "mine" into the life of God in Christ and the ever dawning awareness of life as "us" and "we." It is learning to listen with the heart of Christ; it is to see with the eyes of God; it is to attend to the movement of the Holy Spirit in life all around us; it is to seek God when God seems to be hidden. Joan Chittister writes that such a life entails seeing life through

> a wider angle lens. The spirituality we develop affects the way we image God, the way we pray, the types of asceticism we practice, the place we give to ministry and community in our definition of "the spiritual life." It is spirituality that draws us beyond ourselves to find significance and meaning in life. It is our spirituality that defines our life (values): self-abnegation or self-development; community or solitude; contemplation or evangelization; personal transformation or social justice; hierarchy or equality. The spirituality we develop, in other words, is the filter through which we view our worlds and the limits within which we operate.[9]

On pilgrimage, growth calls us to be like Benedictine monks, writes John Main. We carry the past with us, collecting it on our pilgrimage. Thus, we change our lives and the world around us as we are being changed by the deeper knowledge of God's love, by the radiant presence of the new creation being born in our world today.[10] Our entire sense of self and awareness of our connections with others and ourselves in the body of Christ, with our connection to the earth around us, *expands,* pushing past our limitations as we enter into a creative, deepening, dependent relationship with God in Christ. As members of Christ's body, we are part of something larger than we are by our lonely selves. We are *in* Christ, in the *body* of Christ, as Christ *dwells* in us, working within us and others as we make one another, by the Spirit, more like Christ.

As our body, mind, and spirit grow as Christians on this pilgrimage, we are moving toward embodying in our lives the characteristics of God's realm. This occurs as we strive, by God's grace, to be and become more like Christ in our very lives. As we become more like Christ, who is closer to us than we are to ourselves, we grow into our flesh, our woundedness, our heart, our sense of powerlessness, our place. Columba Stewart captures this understanding of growth well as a constantly dawning awareness of the presence of God. It is not a cozy intimacy per se between equals; it is a relationship of amazement and dependence upon God.[11]

Our growth does not end or begin with us, but it begins and ends with God. We are part of the body of Christ, and because we are part of this body we continually grow and change as we live our lives next to each other in God. This growth causes us to go beyond our individual lives as we begin to understand and appreciate the ways we are connected to the lives of others. All this takes place within the context of the real world in which we live, yet also in the hope of the transcendent life that is to come. We exist in a world shaped by the visible yet invisible church.

Our growth is communal as we "grow up in every way into him who is the head, into Christ, from whom the whole body, joined and knit together by every ligament with which it is equipped, as each part is working properly, promotes the body's growth in building itself up in love" (Eph. 4:15–16). Sown within the fabric of life in the body of Christ is a vision of God's realm in which Christ has gone before us all: "In my Father's house there are many dwelling places. . . . If I go and prepare a place for you, I will come again and will take you to myself, so that where I am, there you may be also. And you know the way to the place where I am going" (John 14:2–4).

This way of understanding change and growth is inclusive. It sets no one aside and makes no one "disabled" or "delayed." Why? Because there are no foundational or universal markers, steps, or levels along the pilgrimage that denote if one is further along than others on this pilgrimage. While such markers and labels can help identify problems some people may have experienced, markers and labels of human developmental theories become stereotypes that pigeonhole people. The theories of human development can have the power to predetermine how one will live, putting one on a track chosen by one of the human developmental theorists.

Oftentimes, what is most important about being on pilgrimage is being conscious that we exist among others in the body of Christ, and that being and becoming a Christian among Christians involves a growing into the name that we have been baptized into. All who are filled with God's grace, who are baptized, are members of this pilgrimage. This includes those who are able-bodied (what some call "temporarily able-bodied," or TAB) and those considered by the world as disabled; those who are wealthy and those who are poor; women and men; those who are old and those who are young; and those of all races, ethnicities, heritages, sexual orientations, and denominations of the Christian faith.[12]

Understanding Growth and Change Anew: Expanding into God

One way to think of Christian growth and change is not as growing "up" in a vertical movement but as growing and changing as expansion from self to self-in-God-with-others. I borrow this phrase from John Main, who writes that all human growth is an expansion of one's being as we are pushed beyond the frontiers of our limitations and dead-ends. The sense of growth and change feels like a force that is within us, pushing us to go beyond our individual selves as we grow in learning to live in community and thus in relationship with God in the body of Christ. Main writes that we no longer understand ourselves in terms of our limitations, of what "I can or cannot do" in comparison with others' abilities. Rather, we focus on our capacity to grow or expand from the idea of "the world revolves around me" to a place in which I am a member of a body—both visible and invisible—in which God has revealed God's self in the person of Jesus Christ.

Paul says, "It is no longer I who live, but it is Christ who lives in me. And the life I now live in the flesh I live by faith in the Son of God, who loved me and gave himself for me" (Gal. 2:20). In Christ, we live in the topsy-turvy, paradox-driven world of God—in which the last will be first and the first will be last, in which one finds one's life by losing it for the sake of Christ. In Christ, we grow in our understanding of ourselves and the ways of God. This means that our human consciousness or mindfulness is always opening up to God. And when we try to close ourselves to God in times of doubt and despair, the Spirit reopens us through grace and faith.

A way to understand this growth is to compare it to the adult toy known as a Hoberman sphere, which was invented by Chuck Hoberman in the 1990s. The toy is described as a "transformer that changes its shape as it expands, from a sea-urchin-like bundle of hinges into a sphere of delicately attenuated struts." As it expands, "each hinge unfolds while at the same time pivoting, so that its relationship to the other hinges remains the same. The struts inscribe a series of triangles and pentagons that intersect with each other, and the points of intersection form geodesic circles that are similar to the shapes described by Buckminster Fuller, who was an inspiration for Chuck."[13]

A system of many links transforms a small sphere to one that is ten times larger, based on a mathematical principle that allows a structure to mechanically expand while keeping its shape. When it is contracted inwardly, it is a sphere of spines, yet each spine is connected to a neighboring spine. The volume inside the sphere is small. When it expands, the spines bend outwardly so as to make a larger sphere, with the inside of the sphere greatly expanded. The sphere comes in all sizes, from a small one that is able to be tossed around a classroom or outside on a playground, to a large sphere into which two people can enter and move!

What does it mean to change and grow on pilgrimage via this sense of expanding into God? Consider the following descriptive characteristics of change and growth. Craig Dykstra writes that the life of faith is

> a living, moving, dynamic existence that takes place in the environment of the Spirit. This existence includes the experience of growth in the manifold aspects of our nature: our bodies, minds, feelings, judgments, social relationships, imaginations. In the Spirit we come to recognize this growth as God's gift. We come to see that "God has made us and not we ourselves," and this frees us to allow the Spirit to work in our growing, rather than to struggle against the Spirit by trying to control it through our own powers. This is part of what is involved in growth in the life of faith.[14]

What is faith? "Now faith is the assurance of things hoped for, the conviction of things not seen" (Heb. 11:1). The writer of Hebrews tells us to understand or be aware that faith is often best understood retrospectively, as we cannot necessarily see it in action before we act, and we cannot control it because it is not of human origin but is God's gift to us. Paul says, "For by grace you have been saved through faith, and this is not your own doing; it is the gift of God—not the result of works, so that no one may boast" (Eph. 2:8–9).

Because of God's gift of grace, through faith, and the gift of the love of God which envelops us, we are always in the process of growing, a process that is in and beyond ourselves, in which we leave limitations behind and enter a creative growth of our entire being. John Main writes that this growth is a "deepening of the integral harmony of heart and mind," and I would include the body. Such awareness of the fullness of our being results from our awareness of God in Jesus and thus God in us and each other. That is *our* consciousness; we are now open to the human consciousness of Jesus himself, a consciousness which is already dwelling in our heart of hearts. Every one of us is called to the fullness of being, into the fullness of God, and we are called to this by the same process of transcendence as we go beyond our limited life experience by experiencing the life and love of Jesus in our daily lives.[15]

An image for describing this ever dawning awareness of the holy is a flower in a 1960s Walt Disney film in which the growth process is speeded up, showing us the graceful, balletlike movements of a flower moving from bud to full bloom, frame by frame. Grace and faith in God are already planted and sown within us, a gifted part of our fabric of life within Christ. In our budlike form, we are also being drawn open by God's love, in which we experience the expansion of these gifts in our daily life.

Early in the Christian life we may be aware of our limitations, along with a certain degree of self-centeredness, but not necessarily selfishness, that is part of life. As we grow in Christ, we become aware of the changes and alterations that are going on in our immediate lives as we attempt to live life as Christ would want us to live. When Paul considers what it means to be an "infant in Christ," in which we are fed with the "milk" of faith but not solid food, is this not because we cannot handle the larger course of theological "meals" (1 Cor. 3:1–4)?[16] In the earlier stages of our lives in Christ it would be too much to expect us to be aware or to be able to explore the parts of the self that are more demanding and difficult. This is because we are too busy trying to comprehend the magnificence of the mysterious gift of grace in the first place, regardless of our intellectual capabilities or cognitive limitations.

However, in due time in the course of the pilgrimage that is life we move from a place of self-centeredness or self-focus to a place of self-abnegation, a place of giving in to the love of God, thus giving our life for the common good, which for Christians is the body of Christ. In Christ, we are invited to see life differently than we ever thought possible; we are no longer living life for our own dreamy endings but for the good of the body of Christ. Our vision of life changes as we open our lives to what we could not see before we were put in the middle of life in the body of Christ. Our narrowness of perspective that trapped us in the smallness of our former life now moves to a more expansive, flexible state in the body of Christ and thus in the world. This change and growth along life's pilgrim way is not a matter of our own being or doing but is God's gift, because it is the grace of God in Christ through faith that opens our hearts, our minds, our bodies to the imaginative God who lives us into being and gives us life.

As we grow and change, we experience a love of God that floods our being. This love makes it possible for us to move from a sense of self-centeredness to a sense of loving God as we love our neighbors. This is the joyous struggle we are part of in pilgrimage that soon may vanquish the individualism that is rampant in most theories of human development. In pilgrimage we experience the rise of intimacy, of candor, and of vulnerability. We realize that we were created through the relationship of two people, and we thirst and hunger for relationship with others with whom we experience the fellowship of God, who resides in the lives of others as well.

Henri Nouwen writes of the "wounded healer" Christ and how we can be like Christ in recognizing the wounds we embody in life. He observes that those who are most comfortable with their wounds, wherever they received them, may become like a magnet, drawing others to their side as people want to share their hurt, woundedness, or brokenness of life. Such growth in the pilgrimage of life cannot come without some resistance.[17] As we move from living life in order to get what we want out of it to living life with the thoughts, concerns, and agendas of others in relationship with our own, we might find some resistance among those who are hungry to live out the American dream. Change and growth involve trying to ascertain the will, the mind of Christ, enabling grace to break through our stubbornness as we live life with others in the community to which we have been called. When we are striving to live more like Christ, the impossible (living in genuine community with others) becomes possible. As Dorothy Day and Jean Vanier state, the only antidote for hyperindividualism is the community where the bread of Christ is broken and distributed with others.[18] To grow as a pilgrim is to grow in our relationships within the body of Christ.

What pilgrimage provides for us in this life with Christ is an opportunity to bring body, mind, and spirit together as one, unitary, dense, rich, whole fabric of being. It is impossible to separate or to educate one part of this integrally related trio (body, mind, spirit). William Poteat writes against the Cartesian dual paradigm of mind-body tension, which "conceptually estranges thought about our minds from thought about our bodies." Poteat brings together the awkward creation of "mindbodily rootedness" in attempting to mix together concepts such as reason, logic, body, and mind. He believes that language is claimed first by the sinews of our bodies, followed by the rhetorical engagement with the world and with meaning itself.[19]

What Christian education in particular and the church in general have failed to address for generations is the centrality of the body in the act of educating Christians. With much focus on educating the mind, especially in Protestantism, the body, let alone one's spirit, has been relegated as "has been." It is important to understand that one does not *have* a body—one *is* a body. It is impossible to separate "me" from my body. The body is nature in its physicality. The body is cosmic as we are part of the universe, and the body is made up of the same elements that make up this planet and the rest of the planets in the universe. Thus, the universe is injected into our very being, our very body. The body is a fundamental functioning symbol of all that is human and of our life experiences as well.[20]

Both an intentional pilgrimage and the pilgrimage of life connect mind and body, which modern society once divided. A pilgrimage is a journey that is known and experienced with this "mindbodyspiritness." Christian pilgrimage involves more than mental or cognitive acuity and development. It involves more than what is mapped out in theories of human development. What is important to learn on pilgrimage is the integration of mind, body, and spirit, an integration that is summed up in the nature of "mindbodyspirit" in

Christ. This is where the miracle of life as pilgrimage lies: We learn through trial and error that we are more than bodies, minds, and spirit. Rather, our being is an integration of all three, located in one person. With our minds we are able to think, to observe, and to draw conclusions as we process the way of pilgrimage. With our feelings we act and respond to the feelings and actions of others, and we are able to reflect with others about the travails and high points of life's pilgrimage. With our bodies we are able to experience all the human senses along life's pilgrimage.

While the developmental psychologies construct a time in a person's life to oppose authority, usually adolescence, pilgrimage teaches us the importance of obedience to authority. Indeed, the novice pilgrim needs to lean upon the veteran pilgrim to make sense of the changes and growth she or he experiences in life. For example, in order to get from the beginning point of the journey to the telos, the destination of the quest, the pilgrim needs to be obedient to the authoritative knowledge of the pilgrimage that is held by those who have been on the pathway before. Invariably, trouble looms when the pilgrim opposes or resists the authority of those forebears. Pilgrims who forget or abuse knowledge about the journey face tremendous problems. Pilgrims need to be observant of those in authority.[21]

Chittister says that in living in the community of the body of Christ, the goal should not be conformity and control but becoming a community of heart, soul, mind, and, I would add, body. It is in the body of Christ that we realize and begin to work on the gifts, services, abilities, and talents we bring, for the good of the other members of the body of Christ and to Christ himself.[22]

Many of the theorists of human development have reached their conclusions through research methodology that is based upon a subject being able to speak, read, and hear. However, not everyone communicates in this way. Pilgrimage opens us to learn the multiple ways of knowing and learning in this world, be they through the multiple intelligence work of Howard Gardner, or earlier educational research studies that suggested that learners were simply oral, visual, or kinesthetic learners.

I propose that we consider the many-faceted ways we learn, regardless of what the world would say are our abilities or limitations. There are some on this pilgrimage who are artists, others who serve God in compassionate acts, and still others who are prophetic in the music or dance that they perform.

I will now focus on variables or factors that, together or independently, may provide reason for growth and change in the life of the Christian.

Chapter 3

Gestures of Christian Pilgrimage

[God] all powerful, let your radiance dawn in our lives, that we may walk in the light of your law with you as our leader.

(The Liturgy of the Hours)

If a man wants to be sure of his road, he must close his eyes and walk in the dark.

(St. John of the Cross)

Along the pilgrimage of the Christian life, we get a brief glimpse or a surprising discovery of the metaphorical footsteps of God in the mundane moments. Henri Nouwen writes that the God of all life is present among us even in the most humdrum tasks and chores and in the long, barren stretches of pilgrim paths where the Holy Spirit moves in the small events of a day.[1] John Spalding, like Søren Kierkegaard before him, reminds us that Jesus looked so much like every other Joe on the street, in the mall, in the school that his divinity was often unrecognizable. That was precisely why his claims to be God were considered an offense to reason and demanded a leap of faith.[2]

It is in the mundane moments of life that we are most apt to engage in Christlike gestures of God's serendipitous love. Joan Chittister says that we are to live ordinary lives with extraordinary awareness and commitment. God is not only to be found in the thrilling moments of emotivist appeals, like a weekend gathering of like-minded believers, but in our common, ordinary, day-to-day pilgrimage. The trick or the habit we need to learn is to keep living our common life on pilgrimage with uncommon conscientiousness, open to the movement of God's Spirit.[3]

This idea of discovering the holy in the common life of our daily pilgrimage is also captured well by Maria Boulding. She writes that in the walk or movement of pilgrimage, we are only given brief glances when we can make our way in the light of grace. She reminds us that often we are the ones to whom the faith is most hidden. What is hidden often in our life is the Christ, who is the source of life. That is why we will be revealed in glory with Christ in the age to come. How do we know of this life if it is hidden most of the time? Boulding writes, "At certain privileged moments—maybe once in five years—we know this for a split second. And then we do not again. It is so near that we can touch it all the time, but we do not see." Then she tells this poetic parable:

> You have to walk across a moor. You set out from a well-lighted house in which you have looked at maps and been given instructions. You start off on the track. As you walk on, dusk falls and it is more difficult to see the way. Then it is completely dark. You cannot see your direction and it is so cloudy that you cannot even see whether you are still on the path—or even whether there is a path. But you stumble on, hoping you are going in the right direction. Then a thunderstorm comes on and the going is even rougher. But just now and then there is a flash of lightning, and though it lasts only for a fraction of a second it is just long enough for you to see that your feet are on the track.[4]

Such grace-inspired revelatory experience and practice are often revealed on intentional pilgrimages. Throughout our lives, we can point to moments in which insights into the nature of the realm of God seem to break into our ordinary lives, illuminating, if only briefly, God's omnipresent love. Likewise, our daily pilgrimage is filled with ordinary gestures, such as walking in the dark by faith. God is in the habit of changing and causing growth in the life we live in this Christian pilgrimage. The importance is tied to our dependency upon life's gestures in general and Christlike gestures in particular.

For examples of God breaking into our practice of the ordinary gestures of life, consider the following pilgrimage stories.

Stories of Christlike Gestures on Pilgrimage

On my first pilgrimage in northern New Mexico, I remember the tender sole of my foot in a comfortable shoe, heel rolling to toe and then off the earth, leaving an imprint upon the brown, dusty soil. The overtly physical education of this novice pilgrim excited the web of nerves that stimulates the muscles of my shins and calves. The neural system enlivened, my knee began to bend, and my thighs tightened to move forward. Energy shot up my torso, zooming along my spinal cord as I consciously told myself to move forward, following another pilgrim right in front of me. Because I was intentionally on a pilgrimage, I found myself thinking only of the pilgrimage, the uniqueness of the experience, and what was coming next. In the first few days I did not know what to do with my hands. My arms would swing forward, or I would hold my hands behind my back. When it was cold in the early morning I would put my hands in my coat pockets and move forward quickly, trying not to step on the heels of the person in front of me. The only prayer that came to me most mornings was simply, "What, God, am I doing? And what am I doing here specifically, among these strangers?"

On the first morning of my inaugural pilgrimage, I remember being overwhelmed by the understated simplicity of pilgrimage—it was just moving forward, by foot, in my case behind and among a group of thirty-five pilgrims on a cold June morning in the foothills of northern New Mexico—all made complex by the momentousness of the occasion among the other pilgrims. People had worked all year in preparation for this particular pilgrimage, whether they had met in small groups to talk about the pilgrimage they would be on, or were raising money and volunteers to support the pilgrimage. The other thirty pilgrims had taken vacation time to walk this road, as had other bands of pilgrims who would meet us at roughly the same day and hour in Chimayo, having walked a similar distance of over one hundred miles. There were the complexities of arranging this time: the emotional struggle with deciding to go or not to go, planning for the care of my children at home in North Carolina, going on a venture I knew little about and with a group of people I had never met. I remember looking up to the dark blue sky of a New Mexico morning, uttering prayers of hope for the trek before me and thankfulness for the awakening of the day as I heard more chirping, scurrying, and throbbing of life before me.[5]

This pilgrimage was from Costilla to El Santuario de Chimayo in New Mexico. I had been on plenty of travels in my life and had visited plenty of historic places on the East and West Coasts as a child. I enjoyed hiking in and around the Pacific Northwest Cascades when I was an adolescent, and I am always thrilled with walking and seeing the sights of new places in different countries as an adult. Cintra Pemberton says that tourists like to take in the sights, learn about something, buy a souvenir, and then move on to the next place on the itinerary.[6] Tom Wright claims that it is easy to be tourists of Christianity as well, enjoying the music, saying a quick prayer, and shaking ourselves free of the cultural traps we find ourselves in daily.[7] It is also easy to take a weekend pilgrimage, such as Cursillo, De Colores, or Emmaus Walk, only to have the energy that was stirred up during this event dissipate within a few days or months. Likewise, pilgrimage is open to abuse; it can be treated as a magical event, as though there were a chance to get a brownie point or medal of valor from God for going on such a trek.

This pilgrimage was unique, not only because of where I was headed but because of the devotion of the brothers I was with. I was impressed by the planning and preparation that had gone on, including the people praying for over a year about this pilgrimage and the possibility of it changing one's very life. We were offering ourselves to the greater community of Christians in this part of northern New Mexico as we were taking the prayers and concerns of the people with us, offering our time, energy, and personal resources, furthering not only our spiritual growth but also praying daily for the growth of all of God's creation. As Pemberton reminds us, while tourists go to get something from where they are visiting, pilgrims go in order to offer themselves to others, sharing personally with people in order to further spiritual growth among many people. We search for God on pilgrimage because God is constantly and endlessly searching for us.[8] But this is not the only pilgrimage in which this could happen. Each pilgrimage is different because of the season of the year in which one goes, the group one goes with or meets along the way, the sights, the sounds, the smells, the miles on the road, the destination of the pilgrimage itself. But it is also different because of the kind of persons we are at the time, and because of the events going on in our lives when we go on pilgrimage.

On this pilgrimage I was part of a group of thirty-five men between the ages of thirteen and sixty-two. It was early June, a warm month in most parts of the country, though at three o'clock in the morning it dipped into the forties. Why go to Chimayo? Because the sanctuary in this little town of Chimayo is built over a spot of sacred soil, *el pocito*. People had come to this place on pilgrimage for over three hundred years, as the soil was known for curing people of their wounds, whether the wounds were physical, emotional, or spiritual. I kept being reminded that it was the *soil*—not to be confused with "dirt"—the gritty yet silky Mojave colored earth that held curative processes. Some compare Chimayo to France's Lourdes Cathedral.

For me, the pilgrimage began not only at the moment that I was traipsing off to a small chapel in Costilla for a grand worship service, or walking early that cold June morning, seeing parts of the Rockies of Colorado captured by the full moon's rays. In some ways it began with being told to go on this pilgrimage by friends who had told me about Chimayo some months before. There was a sense of beginning the pilgrimage when I began planning. In other ways, the pilgrimage began when I walked onto the airplane.

In retrospect, it was one thing to *think about* going on pilgrimage, but it was a wholly, and holy, other thing to *be on* pilgrimage. Reading about the pilgrimage of another person or the historical or anthropological study of pilgrimage keeps it at arm's length as an abstract, historical artifact or a quaint, cultural custom. I was not going to have the privilege of an anthropologist's perspective on this pilgrimage. Instead, I was going into this pilgrimage living a story first, as a story listener and later a story-teller. I went "native," a cultural anthropological "sin." I became immersed in the multitude of gestures and all their layers of meaning as I slipped off my watch—a gesture—on the first day and put it in my duffel bag, thereby giving control over my life and schedule to the veterans of this specific pilgrimage to Chimayo. In doing so I embarked on a journey in which I would be irrevocably changed. I was going to break away from stultifying habits of home, perhaps being able to see the world anew. Walking in the dry and arid American Southwest, I was exposed to my own anxieties that were fed a steady diet of the incautious, the unpredictable, the unexplainable, and the unavoidable God in my life. Yet at the same time, I learned to live, to breathe deeper, to walk with more confidence of faith and grace as a member of Christ's body, while being exposed to the uncertain wonder and broadening mystery of life in God. And this experience of pilgrimage began not with being forced to sit down and read yet another book on pilgrimage but with setting my foot on earth in New Mexico and walking.

After this inaugural gesture of a footstep, I was inundated with a host of gestures that I either knew well but not in this pilgrim context, or had to learn, and quickly. For example, on my way to Chimayo I learned I was the lone Protestant, the lone Presbyterian, the only one who spoke English and little Spanish (everyone else was bilingual, speaking Spanish as a second or first language), and the lone white Anglo-Saxon, as the other pilgrims were either Native American or Mexican American. I learned quickly how and when to cross myself, genuflect, and kiss the larger-than-life crosses in many churches, including a life-size statue of Jesus who was carrying a cross in one small church. I learned when or when not to kneel in prayer; how to massage the foot of a newfound friend after walking over twenty miles in one day. I learned new songs, prayers, and short phrases in Spanish. I prayed the Angelus at twelve noon and six in the evening every day.

One gesture that surprised me was taking off my baseball cap as a sign or gesture of respect whenever I walked past a church, a cemetery, or a roadside cross. I learned to take off my hat in front of Roman Catholic churches and cemeteries while keeping it on for Protestant churches and mission projects. After questioning the gesture with the other pilgrims, we soon began to take off our hats at *all* churches.

I learned the gesture of holding the cross on a busy roadway, being sure not to tip it one way or another, as one brother had shouted to me, "Don't put

Jesus asleep," when the cross had tilted in my hands. I learned the gesture of lancing blisters and applying moleskin so it would not rub off easily during the day, both on my feet and on the feet of my friends. I learned the gestures of walking on the side of a highway without running into the person before me, and pacing my walk, my life, with the company of the other pilgrims I was walking with. I learned how to pray for more than five minutes, even thirty minutes, and get lost in the prayers. Many of the new gestures were specifically part of being on a pilgrimage sponsored by the Catholic Arch-diocese of Santa Fe; others I carried along to other pilgrimages.

Christlike Gestures on Our Daily Pilgrimage

On pilgrimage, intentionality is everything. If a trip is going to be sacred, then it needs to be seen, heard, felt, and experienced as different and extraordinary. That intention is incarnated or made manifest in the gestures of pilgrimage. It is one thing to believe that in each one of us dwells a pilgrim, but it is another thing to actually live and practice the gestures of pilgrimage *as a Christian pilgrim among other pilgrims.* A pilgrim constantly discovers on pilgrimage the importance of the gestures of the body of Christ: the actual embodiment or ensoulment of the gospel in the art, practice, and daily devotional exercise of living the Christian faith in the ordinary or mundane moments of the day.

The importance of gestures cannot be overstated for the purposes of this book. Fenton Johnson writes that the first purpose of gestures is to interiorize holiness—wholeness—through a kind of discipline.[9] Though grace is the ini-tial reason to practice the gesture, we pray also that God will not only help us in disciplining our minds and bodies but will renew our spirits through the gesture that embodies the faith that we believe. Marilynne Robinson writes that the women in her book *Housekeeping* had been made to "enact the ges-tures and attitudes of Christian benevolence from young girlhood, until these gestures and attitudes became habit, and the habit became so deeply ingrained as to seem to be impulse or instinct."[10] The constant, repetitious use of gestures in our lives, which begins as novel, soon after becomes more or less a part of our lives.

To engage mind, body, and spirit is an imaginative act, providing a means by which the Spirit of Christ, the Word who became flesh and dwelt among us, is known to us. Jesus practiced many gestures in his life, which we are to prac-tice as his followers. For example, consider the list of gestured actions we are to perform according to the Beatitudes (Matt. 5); consider from Jesus' para-bles the list of gestures to be learned and performed; or consider the lifting up of the commandments to love the Lord our God with our entire being, and to love our neighbor.

In order to do what Jesus asks of us, our gestures require imagination. Fenton Johnson says that through imagination, which is expressed in the gestures we use daily subjected to the disciplines imposed by the limitations of our bodies, we become larger than ourselves.[11] For the purposes of this book, in the exercise of gestures of pilgrimage, we experience what John Main calls this expansion of our lives, our awakening to the fullness of being, realizing that God in Christ is dwelling in our hearts, our minds, and our bodies. By performing certain gestures, gestures that Christ himself may have performed, we may also discover the Christ who is within us. For example, by performing the gestures of baptism or Holy Eucharist we are reminded that what we are doing in the present are gestures of the sacred as first shown to us by none other than Christ. We perform the sacred gestures of these sacraments in Jesus' name because Jesus told us to do exactly what we are doing, "in remembrance of me." In doing so, we touch something, or someone, larger than ourselves by realizing and becoming more aware of how we are embedded in God, members with one another in the body of Christ, with the Holy Spirit residing among us. The goal is to imagine the community of human beings in this body of Christ, interconnected and sharing together a healthy dependence upon God, who unifies us even in all our diversity and ways of being in this world in a unifying force—love—that transcends our apparent loneliness or sense of being disconnected.

We know we are Christ's through the gestures we perform and that are performed around and among us. This is only natural for the church because we are instructed by Scripture to be "doers of the word, and not merely hearers who deceive themselves" (Jas. 1:22). Johnson rightly states that faith incarnates itself not only in beliefs per se but in acts: "not in what I believe about God but in the moment-to-moment decisions I make in choosing how to live this day, how to be one with myself, and to love and respect and forgive myself and my neighbor. In this it is a necessary condition for wisdom." Wisdom, after all, is "not a pearl to be found after constant searching, but rather the search itself. [Wisdom] begins in an act of faith. Like faith, it is a process, not a product."[12] Faith and wisdom are not only a process, but they are evident in the very act of being on pilgrimage and in the gestures we perform on pilgrimage.

What characteristics of gestures are central in the act of pilgrimage?[13] First, gestures include performances of our body, mind, and spirit that Christ first performed and charges us to follow and perform in our daily lives. As pilgrimage involves our entire being—mind, body, and spirit—so too does the practice of Christlike gestures. An example of how the mind, body, and spirit are caught up in the act or practice of a gesture is found throughout

Paulo Coelho's semi-autobiographical book, *Pilgrimage*, in which Coelho describes a pilgrimage to Santiago de Compostela in Spain. Led by Petrus, his pilgrim guide, Coelho writes of various gestured activities that he is to practice along his pilgrimage. Petrus reminds Coelho that the way to move forward on pilgrimage is by paying attention to the road and not always focusing on the destination; it is the road that teaches us the best way to get to where we want to go, and the road enriches us as we walk its length.[14]

For example, Coelho is told by Petrus to practice the so-called Speed Exercise: "Walk for twenty minutes at half the speed at which you normally walk. Pay attention to the details, people, and surroundings. The best time to do this is after lunch. Repeat the exercise for seven days."[15] Or there is the Cruelty Exercise: "Every time a thought comes to mind that makes you feel bad about yourself—jealousy, self-pity, envy, hatred, and so on—do the following: dig the nail of your index finger into the cuticle of the thumb of the same hand until it becomes quite painful. Concentrate on the pain: it is the physical reflection of the (mental and emotional) suffering you are going through spiritually. Ease the pressure only when the cruel thought has gone."[16] Petrus explains that in ancient times a golden pin was used for this exercise. Then Petrus tells Coelho to think of a time when he was cruel to himself that day and to perform the exercise. Unable to think of a time, Petrus tells him that that is the way of life: "We are only able to be kind to ourselves at the few times when we need severity."[17]

The second characteristic of gesture central in the act of pilgrimage is corporate in nature. These gestures are patterned, learned, practiced, and performed by members of Christ's body. The community of Christ is re-created by the gestures that embody the story of the gospel. Some gestures are particular for an individual's grace-given gift and service in Christ's body; others are performed in common and in coordination with other members of Christ's body; still others are performed within the context of worshiping God.

A powerful example of teaching and learning the gestures of prayer is told in the story of the Russian Orthodox pilgrim in *The Way of a Pilgrim*. In the introduction to this book, translator Helen Bacovcin reminds us of Gabriel Marcel's observation, that to be human is to be a pilgrim, which in Latin is *Homo Viator*: "Perhaps a stable order can be established on earth if man remains accurately conscious that his condition is that of a traveler," writes Marcel.[18] We do not have a lasting city on this earth, says Bacovcin, but our stability and our security consist of being rooted in God. This is because truth is not a thing but a person, and not a building or structure but God.[19]

The pilgrim in this tale is in search of the Jesus Prayer, or the Prayer of the Heart, in which the summary of the gospel is embodied. By saying this prayer, the Pilgrim hopes to satisfy his longing for uninterrupted communion with God. In this simple recitation of the prayer, the Pilgrim believes that it will reach beyond the intellect and human knowledge and beyond all efforts of people seeking to find some kind of meaning in life. The Pilgrim knows how absolutely wonderful God is: "By the grace of God, I am a Christian, and by my deeds a great sinner, and by my calling a homeless wanderer of humblest origin."[20] The Pilgrim says that he has heard enough homilies or lectures about prayer. They have all been instructions about prayer in general—what is prayer, the necessity of prayer, the fruits of prayer—but no one has spoken of the way to succeed in prayer.[21]

To the Pilgrim, the gesture of prayer learned in community is the source of all good actions or gestures and virtues. Prayer is wrongly seen as the means and method to the fruit of prayer. Rather, the Pilgrim understands that to use prayer as a means or method to get to the good life of Christian existence is to depreciate the power of prayer. Without prayer, it is not possible to do good. Only fidelity to prayer will lead a person to enlightenment and union with Christ.[22]

The Pilgrim goes on pilgrimage, learning both the gesture of the Jesus Prayer, "Lord Jesus Christ, have mercy on me," and the *Philokalia*, the narrative or commentary on the prayer itself, which awakens the Pilgrim to God's special power present in the gospel. The simple gesture of repeating this easy prayer becomes the portal through which the Pilgrim experiences the fruit of the Spirit. Spiritually, he tastes God's sweetness. Emotionally, he experiences pleasant warmth and revelatory moments in which he experiences true enlightenment of the mind as the light of Christ breaks through the darkness of life.[23]

But the gesture of the prayer does not stop with the Pilgrim. The Pilgrim believes that the results of prayer, contemplation, and the other methods should not be kept to the self but should be written down for the good of all.[24] The Pilgrim, who learned the gestured words of the Jesus Prayer and who was given the *Philokalia* to interpret the revelatory moments surrounding this prayer, returns the gifts of the fruits of the Spirit to the rest of the community of Christians, thus making this gesture of prayer truly a Christlike one. In sum, the Pilgrim of this story reminds us all that we are to pray and do what we will, and our actions will be devout, fruitful, and beneficial for our salvation.[25]

The third characteristic of gesture central in the act of pilgrimage is a story being performed or a theological conviction embodied, by which we impart or communicate what we believe. The narrative or story that we communicate or express by the gestures we practice is an affirmation of what we believe and who we believe. Consider the story of Coelho on the way to Santiago and the gesture of carrying and collecting scallop shells, the sign of pilgrimage for Santiago de Compestela. Coelho deposits the shells on a table. A monk then prays over the shells, which glow with a light, and the monk says, "Wherever your treasure is, there will be your heart . . . and wherever your heart is, there will be the cradle of the Second Coming of Christ; like these shells, and the pilgrim is only an outer layer. When that layer, which is a stratum of life, is broken, life appears, and that life is comprised of agape."[26] In the gesture of carrying and collecting shells is a story of greater meaning:

> Wherever it is that you want to see the face of God, there you will see it. And if you don't want to see it, that doesn't matter, as long as you perform good works [gestures]. When Felicia of Aquitaine built her small church and began to help the poor, she forgot about the God of the Vatican. She became God's manifestation by becoming wiser and by living a simpler life—in other words, through love.[27]

Or consider the story that Petrus tells Coelho of the man who said that he did not believe in God yet every night said three Hail Marys, on his knees, as a gesture of faith. Even though the man did not verbally acknowledge God, he believed that the tradition of uttering the three Hail Marys, even in his darkest days, was enough of a gesture of faith to bring him salvation. No matter how grand or simple the gesture may be—whether it is complex and involves one's whole being, or is the simple use of lips, or involves the making of the sign of the cross on one's forehead, lips, and heart—there is a greater story that is being embodied and performed through each gesture on the pilgrimage of life.

The Gestures of Pilgrimage in the Church's Daily Life

We are members of the body of Christ on pilgrimage, which means that in each one of us dwell the heart, soul, mind, and body of a pilgrim. On the one hand, our pilgrimage is toward becoming more like Christ as our understanding, comprehension, and awareness of God in life grows. On pilgrimage, we begin to take notice with all our senses of the places where God's presence is tangible. Likewise, on pilgrimage we learn gestures in the Christian community that indicate where God's presence may be located. In gestures enacted in baptism, with the water bubbling and trickling, we mark those baptized with the gesture of the cross upon their foreheads, publicly welcoming them to the pilgrimage that they are now entering. These gestures may also be enacted in the Eucharist, as we eat and drink as a way of seeking and becoming united as a tribe or band of pilgrims seeking God.[28]

On the other hand, pilgrimage is about more than self-knowledge and being more like Christ; it is a journey toward what Augustine called the City of God. We are part of the earthly city, making our way to the city created by the true God, where true love, which goes beyond oneself, reigns.[29] The earthly city is marked by conflict and war, and any peace that is possible is only temporary and even then fragile.[30] The task of the pilgrim church—what Lohfink calls "God's contrast-society"—is to identify not with the "earthly city *per se*, but to more closely identify with the City of God." Lohfink writes that the pilgrim church is not necessarily a glorious one, as we deal with many of the trials and temptations of the age. Rather, the age of the pilgrim church is an "obscure time in which there is little joy . . . [for where] joy does exist, its origin is hope," which is Christ.[31] The city of the saints that Augustine refers to is "above, though it brings forth citizens here below in whose persons it sojourns as an alien until the time its kingdom shall come. On that day it will assemble them all as they rise again in their bodies, and they will receive their promised kingdom, where with their Prince, who is king of the ages, they will reign for all eternity."[32]

I propose that we remember concretely that we are this pilgrim church, moving toward the City of God while learning more about ourselves in the context of the body of Christ, through the gestures of pilgrimage itself. In the gestures we not only live out our faith, but by the grace of God through the performance of the gestures we witness to others and ourselves what we believe and in whom we believe. Our gestures become a living, breathing sign of the pilgrim church, moving inexorably toward the City of God.

Baptism Gestures   Tom Wright says that when we sign on for our earthly pilgrimage, or if we are infants and our parents or guardians sign us up for the pilgrimage, we either commit ourselves or are committed to periodic sojourning in the wilderness, but also for the "Galilean battle for the Kingdom: You commit yourself to words and deeds [gestures] which say—as Jesus did—that there is another Kingdom, another King." Wright understands that in baptism we commit or are committed to doing the gestures not as our grand social action, implemented by our initiative, "but in the power of the Holy Spirit, and by the Word of God."[33] He believes that baptism is a way of ensuring that disciples will take seriously the journey they are on in this life. On this lifelong pilgrimage, baptism reminds us that we are more than cheerful, shallow, flippant pilgrims going to Jerusalem, with hands in pockets and whistling a tune.

We are to arrive on our pilgrimage with the pain of the world, so that our tears of the desert may be presented in the temple of our God.[34]

Holy Communion Gestures   The other set of complex gestures are part and parcel of Eucharist or Holy Communion and begin with the words of the Great Thanksgiving. We watch and then partake in the gestures of eating from the broken loaf of bread and drinking from the cup of salvation, being told to do so "in remembrance of me." The gestures of taking the bread and the cup become a physical, cognitive, and spiritual act of remembering Christ and what Christ has, is, and will do as the one who sits at the right hand of God Almighty. Such knowledge is so great—cognitively, emotionally, and spiritually—that people *have* to respond with a word of thanks, "Amen," with prayerful hands, mind, and spirit.

Other Christlike Gestures   In the church, we are to practice and perform gestures on this earthly pilgrimage as an attempt to invite into our hearts and bodies what we know in our heads. We know cognitively so much *about* God and *about* the Christian life, given the plethora of books and other resources that are in the church today. But the trick is to find a way to bring our thoughts and ideas—the theological, biblical, historical, and pastoral knowledge that we hold—to an understanding that such knowledge also has spiritual and physical implications and connections. Sitting down and learning such material, whether we learn it through writing essays, taking a test, memorizing it, or discussing the truths of the Scriptures in a small group, is filled with gestures that enable us to communicate with one another. Seeing, hearing, talking, touching, moving, and tasting all involve human gestures of body, mind, and spirit. The next move on this pilgrimage as God's people in a congregation or parish is to make such knowledge part of the gestures we lean on and depend upon in our daily life as Christians. This may best occur by removing ourselves thoroughly from the conveniences of everyday life, such as the books we rely upon to make the case for our faith, let alone all the other trappings that get in the way of our being faithful pilgrims but that we take to be so necessary in life. We do this so that we may figure out or discern in what ways the ordinary things and the simple gestures of life fill us with pleasure. Such a stripping away of the matters of our life, like the gestured stripping of the altar on Good Friday, is a way to remember how—in the bareness of it all—we may better see, hear, or take notice of the presence of God. That spirit of being a pilgrim is within each and every Christian and may begin to awaken us, to arouse us from the stupor or the neglect in our very lives. If we are baptized into the act of pilgrimage, then we must cultivate and nurture the wanderer within and among us. Otherwise, it will soon become a dormant figure, a relic, an antique way of talking about the Christian life.

The gestures of pilgrimage that we may perform in our daily life as members of the church are what Flannery O'Connor calls "gestures of grace." O'Connor writes that what makes her stories work is a gesture of a character that is unlike any other in the story, one which individuates where the real heart of the story lies. Such a gesture would have to be both totally

> right and totally unexpected; it would have to be one that was both in character and beyond character; it would have to suggest both the world and eternity. The action or gesture I'm talking about would have to be on the level which has to do with the Divine life and our participation in it. It would be a gesture that transcended any neat allegory that might have been intended or any pat moral categories a reader could make. It would be a gesture which somehow made contact with mystery.[35]

By this gesture we would understand that the grace of God has been offered, making it not so much our action but our discovery of God's love in the action of the gesture we are performing as members of the body of Christ, and "frequently it is an action in which the devil has been the unwilling instrument of grace."[36] Thus, by performing the gesture of God's grace, the devil himself is undone.[37]

But more than personal growth, what we can do as a church in learning the performance of Christlike gestures as part of our pilgrimage is to behold how learning such gestures will have a direct effect upon not only ourselves but on the entire community. When we perform these Christlike gestures, which are made possible by the gifts of God's grace, more than our individual or relational lives are affected. There is a radical social dimension to the performance of Christlike gestures. As we welcome the strangers, the pilgrims, into our midst, performing with them these gestures, then we too are building ourselves up as a society where the realm of Christ's rule of fraternal love is the law of our life together. As Lohfink duly notes, "It is precisely through the church's being what it is by virtue of Christ that the church will grow of its own accord in pagan society and that Christ will be able to fill all things through the church." By performing Christlike gestures on the pilgrim's way, we, the Church, the body of Christ, grow and change as we become an "efficacious sign of the presence of God's salvation in the world."[38]

Chapter 4

Discovering the Whole Person
on Christian Pilgrimage

*Bless to me, O God, the earth beneath my foot. . . . Bless to me, O God,
the thing of my desire. . . . Bless to me the thing whereon is set my
mind.*

(Anonymous)

*Pilgrimage concerns the body as much as the mind and spirit; it
bridges the concrete reality of physical life and the elusive abstraction of
the holy.*

(Shirley Du Boulay)

*Pilgrimage was an attempt to invite into our hearts what we know in our
heads.*

(Tom Shaw)

*I*n the previous chapter on pilgrimage's gestures, my hope was to recover
what has been diminished in Christian education: the importance of the mind,
spirit, *and body*. In pilgrimage, the body is important. In pilgrimage, the life
of the foot, leg, knee, thigh, back, shoulders, hands, neck, head, and face matters, as pilgrimage is about Christlike gestures. It is hard to think when my
foot is hurting due to the small pebble that has snuck inside my shoe. It is
hard to contemplate spiritually when my body is exhausted from walking
twenty-five miles in a desert on a day in June.

This is not a chapter on body language, as neither was the chapter on gestures, and I am not advocating an anti-intellectualism or "dumbing down" of
religious instruction. Rather, educating Christians as lifelong pilgrims requires
shaping and nurturing them with a balance of attention to the complex needs
and demands of their bodies, minds, and spirits. It is a balance that comes into
full play on pilgrimages.

Stories of Body, Mind, and Spirit on Pilgrimage

On the border of the Republic of Ireland and Northern Ireland there is a large lake known as Lough Derg (the Dark Lake). In the middle of the lake is Station Island, and for over one thousand years it has been known as the pilgrimage site of St. Patrick's Purgatory. For the hundreds of pilgrims who make it to St. Patrick's Purgatory during the summer, the focus is on the foot as well as the heart and mind.

Legend has it that St. Patrick himself came to this place and saw purgatory itself in a secluded cave on the isle. It is because of this legend that pilgrims began to come to this desolate, rugged, yet beautiful place. According to Pete McCarthy, the earliest pilgrims to come and tell of their experiences were medieval knights and monks from England, France, Spain, Hungary, and other parts of mainland Europe:

> They wrote of spectacular and miraculous visions experienced in the cave in which pilgrims were then confined. . . . In 1353, the cave was recorded as being nine feet long, three feet wide, and high enough for a grown man to kneel, but not stand. The pilgrim was required to carry out a twenty-four-hour waking, praying, non-eating vigil in the cave, having previously existed for fifteen days on bread and water.
>
> From the earliest days until as late as the eighteenth century, the pilgrim, on entering the cave, was laid out as if dead, ready to confront the pains of purgatory and the judgment of the Creator. Although this cheery practice has since been discontinued, and the fifteen-day fast reduced—first, in 1517, to nine days; then, in 1804, to three—the form of prayer and ritual of deprivation to which the present-day pilgrim must submit is the same as it has been for many centuries.
>
> In 1200 Peter of Cornwall, a regular visitor, wrote: "Beware. No one leaves Lough Derg without some loss of mind."[1]

For centuries, people have made pilgrimages to this solitary isle that have shaped their bodies, minds, and spirits. What was novel for me was walking around St. Patrick's Purgatory for two nights and three days without shoes and socks. The island is strewn with rocks. One priest told me that he thinks the other priests go out in the middle of the night to sharpen the rocks, as they have not worn down much from the many feet, knees, and hands they have supported over the centuries.

Even though I went to St. Patrick's Purgatory in the middle of a July summer, I was told that I might experience all four seasons during my three-day stay, since it can get down to thirty degrees in July at three o'clock in the morning. Indeed, it did get chilly during the early morning of my twenty-four-hour vigil. In one of the houses near the basilica where people could rest up between saying the stations of prayers, people wrapped their bare feet in newspapers they had brought to the island. Others took their hats, muffs, or scarves and covered their feet.

For three days, the other three hundred pilgrims and I walked St. Patrick's Purgatory, following a prescripted ritual of prayer and fasting. We walked slowly on the island's memorial sites, supposedly and hopefully in meditation. We murmured a certain number of Hail Marys, prayed the Lord's Prayer, recited the Apostles' Creed, worked the beads of the rosary, and engaged in other Irish Catholic prayers and rituals while walking, kneeling, crossing ourselves, and on occasion kissing the cross.

Amid the flurry of repetitious activities, I was focused on our bare feet. It was amazing to see all of us pilgrims without shoes and socks on. There we were, walking the craggy boulders separated by dirt and gravel paths. By the water's edge there was an old pebble-strewn pathway that surrounded half the island. The entire time I kept looking at the feet of other people. On the first round of prayers—there are nine repetitions of the same cycle of prayers described above that took at least ninety minutes to finish the first time through—I was looking down at my feet so as not to stub my toes while walking the circuitous routes. At one point we were all in the lake, the cold water lapping upon our feet and knees as we knelt on wobbly stones.

At home I learn about people by looking at their faces, not their hands or their feet. We even talk about putting a "name to a face" if we are meeting someone we've heard about, talked to on the phone, or e-mailed but have never seen in person. Yet here on this isle I was cued in by looking at people's feet. I put people's names to their feet. Someone told me that this sort of pilgrimage was a great equalizer, as you could not tell who was rich or poor. There were some feet with painted toes; some feet had intricate tattoos on them; some feet were old and had purple veins sticking up in odd places; others had scrunched-in toes from wearing high heels or stiletto heels with pointy toes. All the feet were white from the cold night air. I was surprised after a few hours in this condition of walking and sitting without shoes and socks, however, that while my feet were never warm, it didn't bother me after awhile. As for the fasting, which also affected my body, I can say that I was never achingly hungry throughout the pilgrimage. We were allowed a meal of dry black toast, toasted oat cake, black tea or coffee—no milk allowed—which I made sweet with sugar, which was allowed. My body also had to get used to not sleeping. As a result, I was both hungry and tired throughout most of the walking prayers. I was reminded that the word "sacred" comes from "sacrifice," which means to cut up. To have a sacred journey one has to give up something, to make a sacrifice.[2]

Reflections on Pilgrim Narratives of Body, Mind, and Spirit

I have heard that the preacher Howard Thurman once said that the longest journey is between the heart and the head. After my pilgrimage to St. Patrick's Purgatory, I would add that the longest distance is between the heart to the body and the body to the head. Yet on such pilgrimages, the body, mind, and spirit are never able to be disconnected but are fused into one entity.

Imagine pilgrimage gestures being taught as if we were in a dance class or mime session, choreographing and patterning the gospel for one another rather than just memorizing it with our minds, or focusing our reflection with just our spirits. There is no mind or spirit without body. Likewise, there is not much awareness of spirit or the body without one's intellect. And the ability to name that which is spirit is made possible by the mind, which is located within the body.[3] Imagine learning the gestures as one would learn to turn a pot of clay, play the piano, paint a mural, scale a stone wall, cook a meal, bathe a child, or love an adolescent with one's whole being, bringing in whoever the prodigal is in our family or church. Imagine the members of the body of Christ being taught gestures of peacemaking, of charity, of hospitality, focusing on the bodily movements of a handshake, a hug, and a smile, along with the reasons for such movements. The focus is on the entirety of one's being—body, mind, and spirit. After all, we worship God with our bodies as well as with our minds and spirits. So too we educate with our bodies, minds, and spirits.

I propose that this trinity of body, mind, and spirit is not a set of three parts of the self that can be independently examined, but that these parts are fused as one.

The physical body is the conduit of knowledge and experiences of the holy. The experience of pilgrimage is an outward physical experience of movement and motion toward a place or a people that others have determined as sacred or holy. In moving to this place or people, our bodies are marked, strained, aching, sore, and yet strangely revived by the physicality of the movement over the geographical terrain. Indeed, some parts of our travel-as-pilgrimage challenge us physically as well as cognitively, emotionally, and spiritually.

But such movement is not helter-skelter. Before I had any thoughts *about* pilgrimage, I was physically *on* a pilgrimage with my body. Huston Smith writes that pilgrimage becomes transformed into an art form of sorts, as our physical or bodily movement becomes the poetry of motion: Pilgrimage is "the music of personal experience of the sacred in those places, where it has been known to shine forth. If we're not astounded by these possibilities, we can never plumb the depths of our soul—or soul of the world."[4] Such an ability of hearing pilgrimage in the music of personal experience is made possible by seeing pilgrimage as an art of the body, shaping or nurturing how we walk, talk, listen, write, see, and hear.[5] I have heard others refer to pilgrimage as a poor person's physical mysticism, as it takes no amount of money to walk or move forward to the place we are headed. Rich and poor alike travel on a pilgrimage.

Victor and Edith Turner understood it well, calling pilgrimage an exterior-ized or outward form of mysticism, in which the private mystical journey we are on is made public; it is a journey of the spirit physically enacted with our very bodies.[6] Michael Sallnow refers to pilgrimage as a kinesthetic experi-ence—meaning motoric and movement-based experience—mapping space and charting bodily movements of the contours of the religious or Christian landscape as it rises upward from the peripheral homeland to a sacred center, such as a shrine. Sallnow notes that many pilgrimage narratives point to the statement of Mircea Eliade: "Every shrine is an archetype of sacred center, marked off from the profane space around it, where heaven and earth inter-sect, and there exists the possibility of breaking through to the realm of the transcendent."[7] These shrines physically embrace the "thin places," where we can hear God with our bodily ears more clearly and feel God more closely with our hands and feet than we thought possible.[8] By walking or moving across the landscape, we come to know the land anew, whether we had been on this stretch of land before or not.

The pilgrim's body itself is a conduit of knowledge, a medium of commu-nication, a means of connecting with others as well as with ourselves. Pil-grimage involves the body as much as the mind and spirit, bridging the concrete reality of physical life and the elusive abstraction of the holy, which is most often attributed to things of the spirit. Eye, ear, nose, mouth, neck, shoulders, arms, hands, back, torso, thighs, calves, shins, ankles, and feet: each one of these parts of the body are imprinted by being on pilgrimage. By walking, kneeling, crawling, riding a bike, or moving in a wheelchair, we are protesting against the modern age, as we who are pilgrims pray with our feet.[9]

The long stretches of road before the pilgrim and the continuous movement required may evoke pain, boredom, or exhilaration, with people praying, thinking, meditating, singing, or telling jokes along the way. For some, the physical pain is a "cleansing of the spirit." Others feel strangely emboldened through such pain and fatigue, with a new or renewed self-understanding. Still others are amazed at the body's ability or limitations while realizing how for-eign our bodies can be, even to ourselves.[10]

The experience of pilgrimage stimulates one's thoughts.   My mind races and careens when I go on a pilgrimage, and staying focused on the task before me, silencing the other voices within me, is an act of intellectual will. To embody pilgrimage as a way of living the Christian faith is not only an act of the body but of the intellect, as the pilgrim integrates faith with the intellectual life during the physical motion of the pilgrimage. We may be pilgrims first by walking, but pilgrimage involves the mind, enabling us to consider theologically the place of God in the world in which we live. Since pilgrimage always involves at least two conversations or discourses—our life story and the story of the pilgrimage and those who preceded us—we depend upon our capacity of hearing and understanding the discourse, especially when the pilgrimage experiences may be so new or different to our ordinary daily lives that we need to think carefully about what we are experiencing in a marvelous yet decidedly different experience in the world.[11]

We have the capacity to ascertain and reflect on what is going on in a pilgrimage. Our minds are not computers or other machines that understand our wills and desires.[12] Through sensations, through our nervous system, because of our intellectual prowess, we all have the capacity to interact with the world, to know the world around us, to interact with other people, and to control or oversee our desires, our hopes, our thoughts, our feelings, and our dreams. And while there were some Enlightenment philosophers who tried to divide thoughts and feelings, nonetheless the two are inextricably bound together throughout the course of one's life. Our minds are capable of making choices that are consistent with the same understanding of the world shared with others.[13]

For example, choosing pilgrimage as a metaphor for growth and change is an intellectual or cognitive choice. Having reflected on the practice of pilgrimage, I made a choice in understanding change and growth in the Christian life as pilgrimage, giving rise to aims, questions, and methodologies. Making this choice involved a cognitive function. To better understand how pilgrimage is a way of understanding or approaching growth and change in the Christian life, by participating in the experience of pilgrimage and hearing the voices of pilgrims themselves, is to get a feel for the organism of pilgrimage and the many forms it takes.

Zygmunt Bauman observes that Protestants have chosen to be inner-worldly or intellectual pilgrims. Protestants invented a way of embarking on a pilgrimage without leaving home, and this has typically been through books and other reading materials. Protestants could be on pilgrimage in this way without reaching out of their hometown or beyond their front doorstep.[14] This pseudointellectual pilgrimage is praised in theological seminaries where more time is spent in libraries and classrooms than in the pilgrimage of life occurring around the minister in training. This is why it comes as a great shock to many when they leave seminary to come into a congregation or parish that has not had this luxury of pilgrimage of the mind.

But being created in the image of God, as God took on the human condition, through imitating consciously the gestures of Jesus Christ, we are able to intellectually as well as spiritually and bodily grasp the hope that through Jesus' faithful pilgrimage to us, healing and restoring our broken humanity unto death and raising us to new covenantal relationship with God, we begin to see how pilgrimage becomes a time of greater change and growth than we ever thought possible.[15] In the end, reason or knowledge alone cannot help us choose an action simply because it is worthwhile or should be chosen, nor can it prohibit us from some new activities.

The experience of pilgrimage is of the heart and the Holy Spirit.   Oftentimes the point of pilgrimage is to improve ourselves by enduring and overcoming difficulties, whether those difficulties are cognitive or spiritual. Usually if the journey we are on is a pilgrimage, it is seen or approached as a soulful journey that will at times be rigorous. Joan Chittister writes that spirituality is the way in which we express a living faith in a real world: "[Spirituality] is the sum total of the attitudes and actions that define our life of faith."[16] Pilgrimage is a spiritual practice writ large as we who are on pilgrimage move through the world in which we live. For St. Paul, spirituality meant giving oneself over to living in Christ, seeing the gifts of the Spirit as gifts meant to build up the body of Christ in the here and now.[17] As pilgrims, we embrace this description of spirituality as we give our lives to Christ, depending upon God in Christ for our well-being as well as for seeing us through the joyful times and periods of challenge. It is in such times on the pilgrim's way that the fruits of the Spirit matter most. What comes to the surface of our consciousness, what we see and hear, receive and share, in times of great growth and change in our personal and communal lives are the gifts, the talents, and the services of the Spirit that would have remained dormant or hidden if there were not the occasions for the fruits of the Spirit to appear and matter. Prayer and solitude become filters through which we learn to see the world aright and anew, without which we would live a life without a kind of spiritual consciousness and thus fail to grow and change according to the movements of the Holy Spirit.

Most importantly, it is with the power, presence, and grace of the Holy Spirit that we see or comprehend the fullness of our lives coming to birth the only way it really can: through the labor, distress, challenges, joys, sorrows, and trials that we face and endure on pilgrimage. Chittister observes that it is when we are least prepared, when we find ourselves lost on the pilgrimage and unsure of the next step, that the Spirit arrives and guides our unsteady feet. When it seems most unlikely, the "Great Hiatus" comes, and life as we know it changes in the blink of an eye.[18] The change in our life is a shock as we grow in our awareness of God and deepen in our spiritual maturity. After all, says Jean Vanier, "to grow" is the theme of our journey of life.[19]

Michael Casey writes of an interesting movement along life's pilgrimage. While many of us may go on pilgrimage bodily, without necessarily thinking about why we are doing it, we progress to a point on the pilgrimage where the pilgrimage itself reveals the subjectivity of the Christ in our collective lives. This move is from the physicality of pilgrimage to thinking about the very physical act of pilgrimage. For St. Theresa of Lisieux, as well as for many Reformed theologians, the expression or manifestation of faith that is known by and to us—or its outward expression as spirituality—depends not on a fleeting experience per se but on praxis; not on emotions but on human will and human knowledge. Faith is revealed to our minds (thought), sealed in our hearts (spirituality), but is also made manifest in the world through human gestures (body).[20] The heart of faith, of spirituality, is a willed obedience, with an array of Christian disciplines as the only way to survive faithfully through life's long deserts as we seek God.[21]

As we move along the pilgrim's way, we become more transparent, vulnerable, and open with one another and to ourselves, as Christ becomes more transparent to us.[22] This is not merely an experience or an occasion to be put in the box of "spirituality," for it spreads beyond such a metaphor. Being on a pilgrimage is a time and an opportunity to connect with the core of our very lives; the body reconnects with the mind, the mind with the soul, and the soul with the body. True pilgrimage thus changes our very lives, whether we go halfway around the world or merely to our backyards, as in each of us dwells a pilgrim who desires to be on her or his way to God.[23]

There is no moment that one's body, mind, and spirit are not engaged simultaneously during a pilgrimage. While we may not be conscious of what is going on in our very own lives—whether it is because our feet hurt, or our thoughts are wandering, or we are buoyed by a sense of God's Spirit on pilgrimage—nevertheless, the outer experiences or physical moments of pilgrimage, and the internal or not necessarily visible parts of our being, are shaped and nurtured by the experiences of being on pilgrimage. Much of the pilgrimage literature talks about the kind of inner or interior growth (spirit and mind) that is stimulated through the exterior (bodily) aspects of pilgrimage.[24]

Body, Mind, and Spirit: The Pilgrimage
of the Whole Person in the Church

Wendell Berry has been quoted as saying that the pace by which we walk is about the pace or speed by which we think or reflect upon life. This seems highly appropriate for this discussion on pilgrimage as the way of being church together. Because of the beauty and restlessness of our hearts and the wanderings of our thoughts, I believe that we go on a physical pilgrimage in life. The challenge before Christians is to maintain the connection between mind, body, and spirit. Christians share the same fate as poets: We live in a fallen world, yet we are to refuse to surrender our vision to an alternative, less compromised realm of existence, namely, the body of Christ.[25]

Below are some ways we may partake in pilgrimage in our ordinary lives:

Going on Small, Daily Pilgrimages   The poet Wordsworth thought our identities are malleable according to who we are with and where we walk or move to. Because of this malleability, Wordsworth recommended traveling through landscapes in order to feel emotions that may benefit our souls. In order to feel small in the world, some go to the desert or the edge of the seashore and stand amid the vastness of the world. In such places we may see, feel, and think. We may be reminded that we are frail, temporary, and have little to no alternative but to accept some of the limitations imposed on us in this life.[26] I would suggest that one way for people to get the sense that they are on a pilgrimage in their daily lives is to intentionally walk or move in a certain pathway, or perhaps to take a small hike each day. I have seen couples walking and talking with each other in many locales in the middle of a beautiful day as a form of physical exercise. This can be a deliberate time for pilgrimage.

Designing a Labyrinth   Labyrinths were first created as a means of offering people an experience of pilgrimage, especially those who would never be able to afford a pilgrimage to Jerusalem or another holy shrine or site. This is an excellent way of bringing the pilgrimage into the very structural or architectural heart of a congregation. I have witnessed people walking a labyrinth, moving a wheelchair along its path, and even slowly crawling along it.

Participating in Drawing or Sketching or Some Work of Visual Arts   By focusing on the world around us, or focusing on one part of the vastness of this world, our previous blindness to the true appearance of things may disappear or lift for a moment. From such artistic forms of expression as drawing or photography, painting or sculpting, turning a clay pot and firing it in a kiln or making jewelry, we also derive a conscious understanding of the reasons behind our attraction to certain landscapes, people, and views of life.

Composing and Performing Music   My children are in awe of the drums that are now sometimes brought into a church's sanctuary, providing a rhythm that I never heard in the church where I grew up. I am reminded of hearing drums in marching bands and sometimes in church processions and pilgrimages, usually Catholic, in which the figure of the Christ or of the Virgin Mary (Our Lady of Guadalupe) is carried on a stretcherlike platform by twenty men and boys.

Choreographing a Dance   Just as creative visual arts connect mind, body, and spirit, the movement of dance, of arms and legs in syncopated movement, is a way of connecting all three aspects in one motion. This may be done with young and old, women and men. Likewise, pantomime is a similar kind of movement that may be used for teaching and learning anew the gestures of the body of Christ.

Writing Poetry   On pilgrimage, we find poetry in places we least expect it.[27] Poetry is that rare blend of looking and seeing, of listening and hearing with our entire lives to the movements of God. Searching for metaphors for talking of God—who is beyond our simple language—is the task of the poet. Such a task takes the body, mind, and spirit of an artist in painting with words the movements, the nature, of God.

While there is an awakening of the fusion of body, mind, and spirit in a person's life, this conversion leads to turning from ourselves to others in our community of Christian faith, and thus to God. In the next chapter, I will explore the communal nature of Christian pilgrimage.

Chapter 5

Companions and Community on Pilgrimage

Leader: *You guide your pilgrim Church on earth through the Holy Spirit.*
People: *Lord, be the companion of our journey.*
("Prayers: Archdiocesan Pilgrimages for Vocations,"
Archdiocese of Santa Fe)

*C*onsidering the gestures of our body, mind, and spirit that are aspects of Christian pilgrimage, we learn these gestures from our friends, families, and the acquaintances that we meet along the pilgrim's way. For example, consider the gestures of passing the peace during worship. We shake the right hand of or hug another person nearby, and with our lips and larynx we say, "The peace of Christ be with you," or "Christ's peace be with you." By such a physical connection with another person who likewise expresses peace, we hearken back to Christ, who calls us to share God's peace. This is a peace that surpasses the enmity and strife we may feel or bear toward one another. This peace is a virtue that we yearn for in our prayers and desire to spread in our Christian pilgrimage.

Passing the peace reminds us that Christian pilgrimage is not a "Lone Ranger" practice. Pilgrimage is an act of Christian companionship and community. Companionship and community may come through a relationship with one other person we are walking or moving with (companion), with a community of like-minded others (the church), through the people we meet along the way (strangers and acquaintances), or through the silent witness of the communion of saints. We are never alone but are part of a body that is inexorably moving toward God's realm.

Martin Robinson proposes that if we think we are alone on pilgrimage, we fool ourselves. We undoubtedly have those "chance encounters" that may turn out to be *a*, if not *the*, significant element in the overall experience of pilgrimage. Meanwhile, even if we think we are alone, the Holy Spirit accompanies us on our quest, along with the communion of saints. It is among the friends as well as acquaintances we meet along the way that we may learn best the art, the act, the skill, the joy, the performance of the gestures of pilgrimage. Relationships in general and friendships in particular—which compose a school of the virtues of the Christian life—may be the primary context in which we are most engaged in the practices of the School of the Pilgrim. Because there exists no systematic way of teaching pilgrimage or of being a pilgrim per se, save for actually immersing oneself in a pilgrimage, it is in the conversations and interactions we have with strangers, acquaintances, friends, and enemies that we discover the way of the pilgrim.

John Dunne writes that we can know God by learning from the friends of God. The friends of God "walk and speak with God, experience a love that is 'from God and of God and towards God.' The to-and-fro with God in which they live seems to be the only real knowing of God that man has reached. To actually know God ourselves we will have to enter ourselves into the to-and-fro. . . . it too has to do with experiences: floods, storms, earthquakes, afflictions, and in fact everything that happens whatsoever."[1] Such a discovery is based upon the model of Jesus' ministry: Jesus bestowed on us the name "friends," bringing us closer in love to the one who is on pilgrimage with us, before us, behind us, and always among us. In friendship Jesus teaches us of God, of the Holy Spirit, of life in God, and of the nature of grace by joining us in the pilgrimage of life and calling us his friends.

Stories of Pilgrimage Companions and Community

On the second day of my first pilgrimage to Chimayo, my companions and I were moving from Questa to Taos in northern New Mexico. We arose at the seemingly incredibly early morning hour of three o'clock. It was still dark—dark as night. By four o'clock we were on the road to Taos. The previous day's walk was on relatively flat terrain as we hugged the side of the mountain ridge that was east of us. This day's walk was more or less on a gradual incline with an unexpected decline followed by another incline, testing our already sore feet and aching legs. We walked out of the artificial glow of streetlights into the dark maw of the cold night before us. I heard someone quietly utter the word "spooky" behind me, capturing the dark, still-air quality of the early morning's walk to Chimayo.

By 7:30, the vehicle traffic, made up of trucks, vans, RVs, and now and then a car, increased dramatically. It is hard to walk on the road with such traffic, as the air sucks you close to the vehicles when they speed by and then pushes you away once they pass. Suddenly, an old white-haired man with an angry scowl on his craggy face drove up to our line of pilgrims and then slowed down his 1980 white Oldsmobile Cutlass sedan. He was now traveling the same speed as our walking, snaking line of pilgrims. He rolled down the passenger-side window, stuck his finger out at us as he leaned forward, and shouted angrily, "He ain't on the cross anymore!" With that said, he jerked his head forward, put both hands on the steering wheel, and, looking nervous and upset, stared straight ahead and gunned the engine of his Cutlass. It was as if he were afraid we would run after him, catch up with him, and beat him up with the cross, the flag, and the heart of Jesus.

All our heads turned to the insulting driver the minute he shouted at us, and our eyes turned to follow his tire-peeling departure, our mouths open slightly in response to the angry comment hurled at us all. On the first day of the pilgrimage, we were explicitly instructed not to wave or engage drivers in conversation while walking, for fear that we would or could be the cause of an accident. A growing murmur arose among the pilgrims during a stretch of road in which we had been instructed to remain silent and in prayer, as this angry outburst broke the trance of prayer. "What did he say? Did he say what I *think* he said?" asked the younger pilgrims. As the lone white Protestant gringo, I was equally stunned by the vitriol of the driver, even though such anti-Catholic sentiments are not necessarily foreign in parts of North Carolina. Clearly, this driver was a Protestant like me. Yet amid my Catholic brothers, one of the pilgrims, a *peregrino* among others in this context, I was not only one of "them," but one of "us." I had discovered community.

Theological discussions arose quickly around me, more ferocious, impassioned, important, and much more critically insightful than I typically found in any seminary or divinity school classroom. In most introduction courses in seminaries, the students sit in a large room, with the professor in the front of the room lecturing, using the "chalk and talk" method of instruction while the students sit and absorb the knowledge dispensed to them in spoonful dollops. On the open roads of New Mexico, theology was a miracle elixir, needed in earnest to unpack the overflowing pot of feelings that were causing chaos in the lives of the young people. Within the next twenty-four hours we conducted a dialogue about the differences between evangelical Protestantism and Catholicism that challenged my knowledge base as well. We covered the differences in our sacraments, the life of the Protestant Reformers, and the role of icons and pilgrimages in Protestantism and Catholicism. There was no test at the end of this day. The knowledge that was shared was quickly absorbed and taken to heart by one and all.[2]

While the company of others can insulate us from an actual journey, I found it reassuring to know that no matter where I was on this earthly pilgrimage, whether on an actual, intentional pilgrimage or engaged with the pilgrim life of the church, I would be cared for through the kindness of strangers and the discovery of friends in the context of the community of Christ. I discovered people living these words from the Rule of St. Benedict: "Let all guests who arrive be received like Christ, for He is going to say, 'I came as a guest, and you received me.' And to all let due honor be shown, especially to the domestics of the faith and to pilgrims."[3]

Pilgrimage Companions and Discovery of Community

I am not a Christian or a pilgrim by myself. I am a Christian and pilgrim by the grace of God, which I know through faith, a faith that is made manifest in the storied lives of the people with whom I worship, work, pray, play, serve, and study. These two truisms were never as real to me as they were after I had been on several pilgrimages. Being a Christian is not something of my own doing, machination, or production. I simply cannot make myself into a Christian. It is because of God's divine invitation and calling that I am a Christian. This has all been made possible because of the sacrificial love of God in Christ, a love which I know of in my mind, body, and spirit because I have been told and shown this through the gestures of others in the body of Christ.

But equally true is this conviction: I am a pilgrim because of God in Christ, who is the reason for the journey in the first and last place. Pilgrim is not a name I call myself but is a name given to me and us so that we may understand the greater relationship we find ourselves in with the risen Christ. Central in my understanding on this pilgrimage is the realness with which I understand that Jesus is the Christ *and* my companion on this journey. God in Christ is, by God's own decision, the true companion of our journey: "Lord, be the companion of our journey."

The definition of the word "companion" is rich with meaning for the pilgrimage we are on. "Companion" comes from the French *compagnon*, with *com* meaning "with" and *panis* meaning "bread or food." In French, the word *compagnon* means either "a bread fellow" or a "messmate," one with whom we break bread. The importance of this word is given a rich overlay when we read the story of the disciples on the road to Emmaus. Jesus the stranger is revealed as the Christ in the breaking of the bread among the disciples.

But these relationships, whether with strangers or companions—both of whose good company we profit from richly—are part of the fabric of living and being a Christian community.

Strangers

On his way to Santiago de Compostela in Spain, John Spalding wrote that there was a kind of otherworldliness on the way—*el Camino*—in which there was a startling candor among pilgrims who, like strangers at a bar, opened up in ways that they could not with others in their everyday life. "I knew more about my fellow pilgrims than many of the colleagues I worked with for years," wrote Spalding.[4]

"Stranger" designates one who is foreign to us, and comes from the French word *estrangier.* The stranger is the one who does not know or is unaccustomed to or unacquainted with someone, a group of people, or a place. Sometimes we are the stranger; at other times, we are the ones in the "know," as it were, and our task as Christians is to perform the gesture of welcome, of hospitality, to those who are strangers in our midst.

Tolstoy understood that to live meant seeking God, for there can be no life without God: "Our spirits develop in strange, unexpected ways; it helps to know we are not alone on the journey."[5] On pilgrimage the stranger has become a saintly figure, especially in light of the story of the road to Emmaus in Luke 24. In this story, the risen Christ comes upon the disciple Cleopas and his friend who are on the road to Emmaus, seven miles from Jerusalem, having left the place of Jesus' death. Hidden from their recognition, Jesus comes upon them and asks, "What are you discussing with each other while you walk along?" Cleopas answers, "Are you the only stranger in Jerusalem who does not know the things that have taken place there in these days?" After Jesus asks, "What things?" Cleopas shares all that has happened in Jerusalem during the past few days. Cleopas calling Jesus "stranger" highly exalts the stranger in our midst as possibly Christ. Similarly, in Matthew, in the judgment of the nations, the Son of Man declares, "I was a stranger and you welcomed me" (Matt. 25:35). Jesus names himself the stranger among us, exalting those who welcome the stranger while condemning those who fail to welcome the stranger as Christ: "I was a stranger and you did not welcome me" (Matt. 25:43).

This close association of Christ with the stranger among us is at the root of the Benedictine habit of welcoming and receiving guests: "As soon as the arrival of a guest is announced, the superior and members of the community should hurry to offer a welcome with warm-hearted courtesy. First of all, they should pray together so as to seal their encounter in the peace of Christ."[6] Furthermore, rules of fasting may be broken by the superior (abbot, prior, or prioress) to entertain the guest, and the superior pours water for guests to wash their hands and then washes their feet, with the whole community involved in the ceremony. As the stranger, the pilgrim, visiting the Abbey of Christ in the Desert Monastery in New Mexico, I was always seated next to the abbot, a place of honor, and not among the brothers, for "the superior's table should always be with the guests and pilgrims."[7]

In this act of praying together and sharing in the life of the community, the body of Christ—be it a monastery, an intentional Christian community, or the church—is working from two main axes of faith, which are the values the pilgrimage strongly emphasizes: praying and sharing. Brother John of the Taizé Community writes that by praying and sharing life together in this way we are "enlarging to the scale of God's people the experience which many are already living, and have been living for years. To go out to one another, beyond the barriers which usually separate us, and to go forth together to encounter God in prayer—is this not the true meaning of the Christian pilgrimage?"[8]

In a sense, by welcoming the stranger among us, we transcend our own needs and wants by putting them aside in welcoming Christ in the stranger, and thus the community becomes the very living sacrament of human fulfillment and discovers a purpose in life: being and becoming a pilgrimage community.[9] By welcoming the stranger, the community broadens and stretches its soul, mind, and body, for we are not necessarily in control of what will occur in community when we welcome the stranger, who is Christ among us and who in turn enables us to be about something greater than ourselves.

Brother John notes that the very word "parish" comes from the Greek *paraikos*, which means "pilgrim, passing stranger." He then writes:

> Is not every Church, in fact, called to be the "pilgrim's house," centered on prayer and sharing, a place of welcome and communion for everyone? In so far as [the Church] fulfills that vocation, keeping nothing for [itself] but living, in the image of [its] Lord, as the servant of universal reconciliation, the Church gives us a glimpse of the goal of the pilgrimage, the future city already breaking into our present life (Heb. 13:14).[10]

What the stranger—the one who is foreign to us and our gathering—does in effect is a very human thing: The stranger may be the stimulus for growth and change in a community's life. God may very well bring the stranger among us as we try to cling to old ways, knowing our propensity to change at a snail's pace as we cling to the sidewalk and stones on the pilgrim's path. Strangers call us to listen to one another, to sit silently and take in the stories of another, thus taking in the stories of God's people. The stranger, the pilgrim who visits—which may be us in a new setting—causes a ripple effect of change, calling a Christian community to truly be the body of Christ in ways that those who are already members no longer can do because of the stability, or the ruts, we have become accustomed to in community life. The stranger also reminds us how we can be strangers to ourselves, pointing out parts of our lives that we fail to care for or tend to in our daily pilgrimage.

In welcoming the stranger—be it in a church or other intentional Christian community—we welcome him or her into our lives and make space for that person to grow. Jean Vanier writes that welcoming the other person is to give space in our heart, where people know that they are accepted just as they are, with their wounds and their gifts. In welcoming the other, we no longer live in fear and insecurity, unclear about who we are and what our vocation in life is. It means to take time for all aspects of a person's life.[11]

Jean Vanier also cites Jesus as the paradigmatic stranger, coming to us as an alien, as an other worldly presence of sorts:

> The stranger is a person who is different, from another culture or another faith; the stranger disturbs because he or she cannot enter into our patterns of thought or our ways of doing things. To welcome is to make the stranger feel at home, at ease, and that means not exercising any judgment or any preconceived ideas, but rather giving space *to be*. Once we have made the effort of welcoming and accepting the disturbance, we discover a friend; we live a moment of communion, a new peace; a presence of God is given. The stranger is frequently prophetic; he or she breaks down our barriers and our fears, or else makes us conscious that they are there and may even strengthen them.[12]

After some time a surprising change happens: Soon the stranger is no longer the stranger, the foreigner among us, but becomes a companion. It may be as a friend or acquaintance joining together on the community's collective pilgrimage toward God's domain.

Companions: Friendship and Acquaintances on Pilgrimage

Jesus is the pilgrim whom we follow and model our life after. In Mark we read that soon after Jesus called his first disciples he began a "preaching pilgrimage" in Galilee: "Let us go on to the neighboring towns, so that I may proclaim the message there also; for that is what I came out to do" (Mark 1:38). Jesus went with his disciples on his earthly pilgrimage, "proclaiming the message in their synagogues and casting out demons" (1:39). When he later sent the twelve disciples out on their own, he instructed them not to go out by themselves but two by two, and [Jesus] gave them authority over the unclean spirits. He ordered them to take nothing for their journey except a staff; no bread, no bag, no money in their belts; but to wear sandals and not to put on two tunics. He said to them, "Wherever you enter a house, stay there until you leave the place. If any place will not welcome you and they refuse to hear you, as you leave, shake off the dust that is on your feet as a testimony against them." (6:7–11)

The disciples did as Jesus instructed, casting out demons and anointing and healing with oil, curing many. This is a prototypical example for us on our pilgrimage. Jesus called his disciples to go on the pilgrimage of their earthly ministry in paired relationships. Again, it was Cleopas, a disciple of Christ, and another disciple who were walking toward Emmaus from Jerusalem after the crucifixion. In a sense, they carried on with a pattern or partnership with one another after the crucifixion.

During certain stretches of an intentional pilgrimage or actual pilgrimage there are times in which we find ourselves walking or moving as if we are by ourselves. Of course, we are never alone as Christians, for it is the Spirit of Christ who resides in us. And our intention for being on pilgrimage is because of God in Christ who calls us to a certain place or group of people on our earthly pilgrimage. It is a manifestation of what Martin Buber calls the "I-Thou" relationship.

But in walking with another pilgrim, pilgrims enter a "We-Thou" relationship, as wherever two or more are gathered in Jesus' name, Jesus is present as well (Matt. 18:20). John Dunne writes that we have a choice in our learning process of knowing God. Dunne prefers to learn from the

friends of God, who walk and speak with God, experience a love that is "from God and of God and towards God." The to-and-fro with God in which they live seems to be the only real knowing of God that man [and woman] has reached. To actually know God ourselves we will have to enter ourselves into the to-and-fro. Maybe from that vantage point we will be able to [understand that which we hold in common]. It too has to do with experiences: floods, storms, earthquakes, afflictions, and in fact everything that happens.[13]

Various dyadic relationships can form while on pilgrimage. Sometimes the ones we walk with will never form a relationship deep enough for friendship to occur. Such are the partnerships of acquaintances. Along the pilgrim way we will meet many such people, with whom we shall share names and a few pleasantries but little more than that.

There are different kinds of friendships that we will experience during a pilgrimage. Aristotle and later Aquinas identified several kinds of friends:

There are some friends with whom we share a great end or goal; with them we may share a bottle of water and food, or we may stop in a place for a glass of wine and a good meal. There are friends of great usefulness who enable us to advance in life. Then there are friends with whom we know and share the moral life. We are shaped by such friendships in many ways, such as learning goodness and other virtues of the moral life.[14]

This third kind of friendship is the one in which we share lives and discover the community of which we are already members. It is this friendship where we grow in the virtues of the pilgrim life. This friendship is based upon the love that God has given to us. Such friendship is possible not because we are coequal with God in Christ, but because God in Christ has deigned to befriend us, calling us friends. Paul Wadell writes that each and every friendship needs the love and affection exercised between friends, but especially in the love God has for us, a love that expresses itself in and through friendship we have with God, known in our friendship with one another.[15]

Community on Pilgrimage

The idea of a community of pilgrims comes from the Gospels. Jesus chose twelve primary disciples to go with him on his journey. One of the later "Ur-texts" of pilgrimage is Geoffrey Chaucer's *Canterbury Tales*. Chaucer's merry band of pilgrims engages in a competition to tell the best story, all for a good meal and a place to sleep. Sharing lodging, a meal, and traveling is all a meaningful act of these pilgrims as they journey toward the common goal of the shrine of St. Thomas à Becket in Canterbury Cathedral.

To imagine that the church is actually on pilgrimage as the body of Christ is the penultimate understanding of this pilgrimage we are on as a communal one. In the early days of the Christian church, entire communities might go on pilgrimage. The pilgrims would approach the shrine as an act of corporate devotion, thanking God for salvation from a plague, a war, a natural disaster, or as a communal act of tribute and devotion. On difficult days the community might go on pilgrimage to seek deliverance.[16]

Even today when individuals go on a pilgrimage, they do so representing in a sense the cares of the community. For example, when I was on pilgrimage to Chimayo, from each place we stopped to eat, to rest, to pray, and to sleep, we would take two items: a sample of soil and the prayers of the community. We carried the soil and the prayers with us to Chimayo. On the day that all the pilgrims met in El Santuario de Chimayo, all the pilgrim groups gathered at one point and poured together in a circle all the samples of soil that had been gathered from the various locales along the pilgrimage route, and we blessed it. Likewise with the prayers: we prayed the prayers of the communities that we passed through during the pilgrimage. During my pilgrimage at St. Patrick's Purgatory, many pilgrims told me they were there representing a family member or friend who could not attend. In the name of a brother or a sister, these pilgrims would then fill up bottles of "holy water" that poured freely from some walls of the island. In Esquipulas, Guatemala, bands of pilgrims line up in a straight line at one side of the basilica and put their recently purchased trinkets and tokens of remembrance before them. Then a priest comes by with blessed water, and with a sprinkler the priest blesses the items. The pilgrims then go home, sharing the items that they purchased and that had been blessed that day.

Why do they come as a community? Martin Robinson has written that bands of pilgrims come to search for God, and in doing so, they hope to find themselves. We are all drawn to leave home to find ourselves or reconstruct our lives in a place that does not know our past. Often the familiar obscures the eternal, not because the eternal is not present but because it cannot be recognized without the experiences that occur on a broader canvas of pilgrimage. Writes Robinson, "We cannot find the 'I' within until we have found the 'Thou' without."[17]

When a *community* goes on pilgrimage both the individual persons and the community will grow. While an individual or a couple may focus on the ways that they come to know their lives in a deeper, more meaningful way through the practice of pilgrimage, likewise the community, the body of believers, not only comes to know themselves individually or personally in a deeper and more profound way, but their relationship to and with God is made richer. More profoundly, a body of believers on pilgrimage open themselves up to knowing the inner life, the system, the gifts and challenges of a community's life in the presence and arms of a loving God who created the Christian community—the church—in the first place. The community will draw out of this experience a sense that the God of Israel, who moved with the people in the ark of the covenant, who walked among the people of Galilee and Jerusalem, is still present with us, in the form or shape of the Spirit who accompanies us on this communal pilgrimage.

An interesting aspect of early Christian communities was that when a community, such as a monastery, grew too large or large enough, either the original founder or followers of the original founder would leave in order to begin a new community. Monks and nuns in these early orders were keen evangelists as well, with a strong inner vision and with outward mobility and a commitment to bring Christ to others.[18] St. Patrick of Ireland (d. 461) was such a pilgrim, as were St. Brendan, an Irish monk who traveled as a pilgrim (d. 575), and St. Aidan, who left the Iona Community off of Scotland's coast to begin a community in the far reaches of the British northern coastland in Lindisfarne, now dubbed the Holy Isle, at the invitation of King Oswald in 633.[19] To this day, pilgrims-as-missionaries are sent out from their respective faith-based Christian communities to spread the good news in other lands, among people who are themselves called to be on pilgrimage.

Companions and Community: The Church on Pilgrimage

The chief lesson learned from considering the importance of companionship and community on Christian pilgrimage is the realization that *the church is moving too.* For example, in reading the parable of the Great Banquet (Luke 14:15–24) recently, I was amazed at the last lines of this story, in which the slave (Jesus) is sent by the master (God) to go out into the roads and lanes and compel people to come in so that God's house may be filled. Nowhere in this parable does it say that the slave comes back and the place is filled. Instead, I have come to understand these last lines to be a calling of the Christ, now in the form of the body of Christ, to be on pilgrimage, sent from the master's house to bring others into relationship with God.

In several places (1 Cor. 12, Rom. 12, Eph. 4, Col. 1), Paul writes that we are the body of Christ, with Christ as the head of the body, and that we take various places and roles in the body: eyes, hands, nose, ears, mouth, arms, hands, legs, and feet, to name but a few. This organic sense of being a particular community—the body of Christ—lends itself well for discussions of Christian pilgrimage as the way we may approach growth and change in the context of the community itself.

Furthermore, the New Testament itself is a letter to the church today, calling, cajoling, and instructing us to be a people who should be eager, if not anxious, for the coming days. The church in Paul's time awaited the imminent return of Christ, and the sense that the church is a moving, dynamic, and flexible organism is not lost in any of the books, from the Gospels to the book of Revelation. The creativity evident as churches tried to be house churches, alternative communities, or "contrast societies" to use Gerhard Lohfink's term, was a result of a church in which the Holy Spirit was not only talked about but believed to be almost corporeal in nature, manifested in the living life of the church. God's love is not static, writes Vanier; a human heart is either progressing or regressing. Life brings new life, and a church in which there is no sense of life is not about growth but is regressing.[20]

If we know that growth and change may occur on pilgrimage, then the question for the church today is this: What pilgrimage gestures could we do in a parish or congregation to reveal the moving, dynamic nature of our pilgrimage today?

Welcoming Strangers   It is helpful for us to look at ways we welcome strangers and pilgrims among us. As I shared above, it has been my experience in visiting various Benedictine communities, as well as L'Arche communities, to be treated as a royal guest in such lovely and warmly welcoming places. But do we do this in the church?

Vanier writes that one of the signs that a community is alive is how we welcome people: "To invite others to live with us is a sign that we aren't afraid, that we have a treasure of truth and of peace to share. If a community is closing its doors, it is a sign that hearts are closing as well."[21]

Welcoming people to our communities is not just something that happens when they cross the threshold. It is an attitude of the heart, mind, and body—constantly opening our hearts to say to people every morning and evening, at every moment of the day, to come in. It is to give people space, to listen to them attentively.[22] Sadly, I have attended churches where I was late and the ushers refused to give me one of their seats. In one church, the usher gave me a bulletin, then sat back down in the last remaining visible seat.

Pairing Up of Pilgrims   Pilgrimage is not an isolated practice. We learn so much about life on pilgrimage that we need to share it with others, and vice versa. We might write in journals, record songs, paint, sketch, and otherwise record our experiences of pilgrimage alone, but others around us are eager to hear about the joys and challenges of life together.

Some Christian communities practice placing people together in a kind of spiritual accompaniment. In this lifelong pilgrimage we need people we can talk and share with from time to time about our respective lifelong pilgrimages. Being sojourners together on this pilgrimage of life is a gift and a requirement of sorts, so that people understand they are not alone.

Processions to Worship   A sense of movement of God's people coming to worship is a most powerful way to begin worship. At St. Benedict's Monastery's Sacred Heart Chapel on special occasions, people gather together in "The Gathering Space," a large hall outside of the sanctuary. Certain people are given items to carry in: the cross, poles with streamers on them, flowers, water, the elements for the Eucharist, and the Scriptures. Led by a group of the Schola, the choir of sisters, we walk into the sanctuary. It is a truly awesome event to move in a group, as if we were one body in Christ.

Churchwide Pilgrimages   Many Protestant and Catholic churches partici-pate in pilgrimages, though they may not call them pilgrimages per se but a CROP walk, for example. There are moments throughout the church's sacred year when we may choose to go on pilgrimage together from our home con-gregation to another sacred space, for a holy purpose, with hopes of building up a congregation in the love of Christ. One such pilgrimage in my experi-ences occurred with St. Matthew's Episcopal Church in Hillsborough, North Carolina. One Sunday morning, a group of pilgrims from St. Matthew's walked as a pilgrimage group to the various churches near this Episcopal church. We had prepared prayers to be prayed in front of each place where we would stop. In front of the African Methodist Episcopal church we prayed a prayer from their tradition. We experienced a wonderful surprise when mem-bers from that church came out and prayed with us in a large circle. We sang a hymn with words by John Calvin in front of the Presbyterian church; in front of the United Methodist church we prayed a prayer of John Wesley; and we sang a good Baptist hymn in front of the Southern Baptist church, con-cluding with a solemn ritual welcoming pilgrims upon their return at the Episcopal church.

There is a difference between traveling on our own and in the company of others, but change happens either way. In the next chapter, the focus will be on the actual people who are responsible for the growth and change in the lives of pilgrims and on the process of learning the pilgrim's life via the process of conversion.

Chapter 6

The Saints and Memory on Pilgrimage

Therefore, since we are surrounded by so great a cloud of witnesses, let us also lay aside every weight and the sin that clings so closely, and let us run with perseverance the race that is set before us.

(Heb. 12:1)

(Listen) to the saints—to the gossip of the ages.

(Patricia Hampl, Virgin Time*)*

Pilgrimage is not a modern invention—it's as old as Christianity.

(Zygmunt Bauman, Life in Fragments*)*

*I*n the Apostles' Creed, Christians say what we believe: "in the Holy Spirit, the holy catholic church, the communion of saints." In the Nicene Creed, Christians say the same and that we "look for the resurrection of the dead, and the life of the world to come." Both creeds affirm the hope of the writer of the letter to the Hebrews: that we are surrounded by a great cloud of witnesses, and that we look forward to the resurrection of the dead and the life of the world to come.[1] I began repeating these words as a child of the church in Maplewood, New Jersey. My children have grown up in churches reciting these creeds as well.

But what does "the communion of saints" mean for us today in the life of the church on pilgrimage? This acknowledgment of saints is clearly a Christian designation. Non-Christian traditions do not have the practice of honoring saints. For the purposes of this book, the communion of saints is the living memory of the church universal, throughout time, including the living saints among us today. The way of the pilgrim is made clearer by seeing where other people's feet have trod before us. Their very lives are like footsteps or trails on a map, where we see the way others have gone before us. We are merely the latest generation of pilgrims who will one day be considered part of the communion of saints.

69

For many pilgrims, the sense that we are walking on ground made holy by past events is crucial. Martin Robinson says, "The sense of the holy is gained first from an awareness that great events, especially the miraculous, have taken place in a particular location." Places mentioned in Holy Scripture, such as Jerusalem, as well as far-flung places like Santiago de Compostela in Spain and Chimayo in the United States, become important places. Robinson continues, "The original import is reinforced by an awareness that the pilgrim is part of a previous multitude, a community of saints, who have added their testimony of prayer to that which originally took place. . . . The witness others give the actual route as well as the destination [is of] a particular importance. Walking in the footsteps of Jesus, the saints of old and the community of the faithful helps the process of reflection," and, I would add, education, in the church today.[2]

We remember the saints reciting the liturgies of old and by reflecting on the stories of these saints, such as Luther's nailing the ninety-five theses on the door of the Wittenberg Cathedral, or El Salvador's Archbishop Romero celebrating the Eucharist before being gunned down by an assassin. We read of the Canterbury pilgrims who flocked to venerate Thomas à Becket at Canterbury's Cathedral, "the holy blessed martyr there to seek, who gave his help to them when they were sick."[3] We pilgrims today then reappropriate those stories, making them our own: "The past becomes present. The experience of the pilgrim in actually walking in the way of others enables them to become a participant in all that has happened. The pilgrim becomes one with all who have gone before."[4]

But pilgrimage is not about walking in the past but about moving forward into the future. When I have found myself wondering what is my next step in the pilgrimage of this life, I turn and listen to the stories of others who have had similar problems or been stuck in comparable situations. Yet even in doing so, I know that what I am about to do is at least new for me, if not for others around me. Knowing what the pilgrims did in the past enables us to learn from their lives what we are to do in the circumstances we face today. After all, we share a common search for a place and a time that always seems distant, in the future, as we yearn to discover what Augustine called "the kingdom of eternity."[5] This is the realm that determines our gestures, causing change and growth in our lives. It is also summed up well in the Second Helvetic Confession of the Reformed tradition:

> We acknowledge [the saints] to be living members of Christ and friends of God who have gloriously overcome the flesh and the world. Hence we love them as brothers [and sisters], and also honor them. . . . We also imitate

them. For with ardent longings and supplications we earnestly desire to be imitators of their faith and virtues, to share eternal salvation with them, to dwell eternally with them in the presence of God, and to rejoice with them in Christ. . . . They are to be honored by way of imitation.[6]

In the following section I will explore the importance of the communion of saints and the stories that they lived or live and pass on to us. The saints and their stories can become a treasure chest of memories and a repository of fresh lessons for the church to learn today.

Pilgrimage Stories of the Communion of Saints

On pilgrimage I came to a profound appreciation for the way that my parents taught me the history of a people: by immersing me in the very place where the story, where history, took place. The history of my forebears took on a new life during the first pilgrimage I took to Chimayo. When we pilgrims were in Penasco, New Mexico, we were told that the chapel where we rested one morning was built around the same time that the Declaration of Independence was written. I had not remembered that Catholic missionaries had helped to colonize this part of the world for Spain at the same time as England had established its colonies in the East.

When we reached El Santuario de Chimayo, we heard the story of a man who discovered the cross of Christ coming out of an earthen hole. Overwhelmed by this miracle, he carried the cross to the nearest sanctuary, waiting to show the priest the next morning. But the next morning, he found that the cross had mysteriously appeared again at the very same earthen hole. This place, which is marked now with an adobe chapel, was considered the place of a miracle.

How do I know this story? It was told to me as it has been for generation upon generation. Later I came face to face with some members of the cloud of witnesses, the communion of saints, when I was on Lindisfarne, the Holy Isle, located in northern England near the border with Scotland. Lindisfarne is famous for once housing a Benedictine Abbey, which was home to St. Aidan and St. Cuthbert, real-life characters and now saints whom the Venerable Bede wrote about. I walked the shores of this isle, drank its famous mead, and tried to stay out of the way of the many bird watchers who now visit this once-upon-a-time pilgrimage retreat.

Earlier in this journey to England I had gone to Canterbury Cathedral, where I found not pilgrims but tourists. As I walked around the cathedral's large interior space, I heard voices not only from the United States but also from France, Germany, Spain, and the Netherlands, for many of the tourists had come through the "Chunnel," which connects England with the European continent. I found the cathedral beautiful and mammoth, with magnificent soaring arches and huge columns grounding it to the earth. When walking around the cathedral I found this sacred space a pale imitation of what it once was, due to the reforms of Henry VIII and later the Reformation that swept through England. Though many come to worship on Sundays, and a few gather for evensong during the week, I found the palatial grounds almost haunting, part of a life long gone.

One evening while in northern England, I followed a strange impulse to go to the Holy Isle's graveyard. The rickety, wooden, fenced gate that is usually open was closed and, curiously, locked. It was spring 2001. Mad cow disease was all over England and Scotland, and the places where sheep, cows, and horses were kept were now cut off from any human contact for fear that the disease, which can ride on the bottom of shoes, could be transmitted to other places.

I sat on the gate itself, swinging my legs to and fro like a small child, peering into the darkened cemetery until my eyes became used to the murkiness. Pale light from the milky white moon gave the cemetery a glow. A small blue searchlight from a fishing boat in the harbor swung around the cemetery, casting a steady blue beam every twenty or thirty seconds that glanced off the cemetery's tombstones. For a moment I felt like I was an audience member in the middle of the cemetery scene from Thornton Wilder's *Our Town*, awaiting Emily Webb's first steps among her dead relatives, friends, and acquaintances. I decided to talk to the saints and souls, inquiring as to why I had to come all this way, and for what reason. "Thanks for bringing me here, Aidan, Cuthbert, and King Oswald," I said with a matter-of-fact tone, assuming all the while that they were listening and hearing my voice.

Hearing nothing but silence in response to my word of thanks, however, I thought it only fair to follow up with a note of gratitude to God for each saint's life and what he had given to the life of the church, both visible and invisible. Then I started an inquiry, asking for someone to explain why I had felt this strong intuitive yearning to go to Lindisfarne. It wasn't close to home. And where were all the other pilgrims on this sandy and rocky spit of land, cut off each day by the incoming tide? Feeling braver, my voice grew louder as I asked each saint to make sense of what I was doing in this spot. "Why'd you bring me up here? I've been to a lot more active places of pilgrimage. The only possible pilgrims I can find are the people in the pub, and possibly two women who look like Catholic nuns from some order I know little about."

Silence. I listened to the silence and beyond it, leaning in, reflecting, pondering, meeting nothing else but solitude. It began to dawn on me that this incredible impulse to get out of a warm bath—where I had been less than an hour ago—only to sit on a rough wooden fence along the chilly northern England coast was either irrational or a genuine stirring. Here I was, listening for God, with only the full moon hovering overhead and cold white, age-worn tombstones as sentry.

I sensed a movement from the inside, like water gushing forward, pushing me, flooding over me, as my frustrated, benign inquisition gave way to a startling discovery. Christian pilgrimage is not something we can or have to create; it is a gift of time, of patience, of love. Pilgrimage is a repertoire of gestures that sets the stage where we inherit the tales of others who have and are traveling with us as members of the communion of saints and whose stories lead us to the ways of Christ. We try to follow their footsteps, not only as an outward sign of interest but also inwardly; we try to walk in their faithful footsteps.

I remembered reading the stories of Cuthbert seeing the angels take St. Aidan to heaven and of Cuthbert's miracle cures, as told by the Venerable Bede.[7] Throughout the isle, I saw images and heard stories of other momentous miracles and journeys of Aidan, Cuthbert, and Oswald, now recognized saints in the communion of saints. The next morning I awoke, took up *The Age of Bede*, and reread several stories, remembering that it was here, on this very isle, that these stories took place.

Invigorated by the discovery that I am to learn from these people the way of pilgrimage, and to live my life as if pilgrimage mattered, I was eager to find out more about St. Cuthbert, especially after his death. The story is told that St. Cuthbert's body itself became a relic that was venerated by many. Because the body did not decompose after his death but remained in good shape for years afterward, many believed this was a sign of Cuthbert's sainthood. In order to keep Cuthbert's body away from the marauding Norse forces who it was feared would desecrate it, the Benedictines hid Cuthbert's body between Lindisfarne, York, and Durham in northern England.

As it so happened, I was on my way to Durham the next day. I got in my car and drove straight to Durham, ran up to the cathedral's door, and grabbed a map of the interior of the cathedral. While I had been to the cathedral before as a tourist, this time I was going as a pilgrim with an insatiable need to see where Cuthbert was buried. I walked quickly down the length of the chancel, went behind the altar to an area with a large wooden canopy overhead, and found the large stone slab in the floor marked "CUTHBERTUS" in medieval script. I fell on my knees and prayed the prayer engraved on his tomb. I whispered, "Happy Feast Day," for this day in March was Cuthbert's feast day. Giddy, I went to the small museum in the same cathedral and found two women who ran the museum operation. They gave me a free pass to go and see the actual intricately carved coffin (or reliquary) of St. Cuthbert that traveled around England. It was small, with scenes from the Gospels carved on the side and on the top.

Behind the sanctuary in a cloistered setting, I paid my respects to the Venerable Bede by saying a prayer on the side of this black marble tomb. It was Bede's storytelling ability that drew me to the life and times of Cuthbert and Aidan. I left Durham with a satisfied smile as my pilgrimage had brought me to the resting places of these pilgrims. I had gone from head and book knowledge to bent knee and soul knowledge.

I then traveled to Caythorpe, outside of Nottingham. Walking with a friend, we passed a small, antique metal church. And the name of this Anglican chapel? St. Aidan! I started to chuckle and then let out with a rolling laugh, explaining to my friend what a day I had had in discovering all these places that, thanks to the Venerable Bede, are rich in the living memories of the Lindisfarne duo of Sts. Cuthbert and Aidan.[8]

Reflection on Pilgrimage and the Communion of Saints

We are forever on the edge of hubris when we think that our story, our generation, our country is the best, or the favorite one of God. Anti-intellectualization has often been seen as the great evil in modernity, for it threatens the knowledge found only in learning and knowing the stories of people long gone. We are but the latest link in the clinking, clanking chain of life, the most recent turtle on top of a long line of turtles on each other's back. We are related to a web of people who may or may not seem related to us, but because of our human heritage are. We are related to the slave woman in the South known as Sojourner Truth, as well as the slave owner by the name of Allston (or Alston) in my part of Chatham County, North Carolina.

The communion of saints gives us footsteps or markers that we can detect in moving onward in our pilgrimage of life.   The footsteps of those who have preceded us in this pilgrimage may enable today's pilgrims to get a sense of where we are on the trek. We can get a sense of where we are going, and whether or not we are closer to our destination, thanks to the saints' experiences before us.[9] But the trick is discerning both where their metaphorical footsteps or imprints of their lives are in this world, and then what lessons we are to learn from their lives on our stretch of this Christian pilgrimage.

It was one thing to read the Venerable Bede's account of the storied lives of St. Aidan and St. Cuthbert, but it is a wholly other thing to go to the actual place where they lived and died. In *English Medieval Pilgrimage*, D. Hall describes the Holy Isle of Lindisfarne as "the crouching village of Northumbrian stone" which is barely visible among the windswept trees. I saw and walked that spit of land reaching out into the ocean where there is the sixteenth-century castle of Beblowe, which interestingly enough was built with the very stones that used to be the monastery where St. Aidan and St. Cuthbert lived.[10]

England is a land crisscrossed with pilgrimage trails, but alas, many of the sites and places where pilgrims would go in years past have been forgotten by the people today. There are some pilgrimage sites that are coming back to life, however, such as Dorchester Abbey near Oxford, in which the shrine to St. Birinus was once housed, though his remains are located today in a reliquary at Winchester Cathedral. In another part of England, Walsingham's small healing well is becoming a pilgrimage site again. On the other hand, Ireland is alive with pilgrimage, and there is an upturn in the number of pilgrims who are visiting Santiago de Compostela. The number of people who go to St. Patrick's Purgatory and Santiago, as well as Lourdes, amazes those who have studied pilgrimage.

The process of discerning the footsteps and meaningfulness of the pilgrimage we are on is always one of mystery and surprise. It is not always readily apparent what we are to learn from the lives of pilgrims before us, or for what purpose. For example, Shirley du Boulay tells the story of being on a pilgrimage to Canterbury Cathedral to visit the place where Thomas à Becket was martyred. On her way there, she and her group stopped at St. Martha's, a small, living church. Then the questions began: Why stop there? What is the history of the church? What is the mystery of St. Martha? Apparently, St. Martha's Church is not named after St. Martha of Bethany, sister of Mary and Lazarus, friends of Jesus. Instead, it is a corruption of "Martyr's Hill," for in the year 600, Christians were martyred on that site. Du Boulay was astounded to learn this while being on a pilgrimage towards another martyr's shrine.[11]

The communion of saints leaves a legacy of stories embodying the memory of pilgrimage's past. In human developmental psychology, a focus of most theories is on our memory. Freud depended upon the power of memory in shaping and releasing his patients from captive dreams. Piaget believed that the memory of what we have done or accomplished in the past is crucial in order to move forward. Erikson believed that memory and identity are intertwined, as you cannot have one without the other. Indeed, for all the theorists of human development, moving forward depends upon our ability to remember. Without a memory we are doomed to perhaps repeat past practices that may have caused pain in our lives.

In *Housekeeping*, Marilynne Robinson takes us on the "pilgrimage" of three women's lives. She writes that "memory is the sense of loss, and loss pulls us after it. God Himself was pulled after us into the vortex we made when we fell—and while he was on earth he mended families . . . being man he felt the pull of death, and being God he must've wondered more than we do what it would be like." Robinson continues, writing that there is so little to remember of anyone when they are gone: an anecdote, a conversation at a table. But every memory is turned over and over again, every word, however chance, written in the "heart in the hope that memory will fulfill itself—and become flesh—and the wanderers will find a way home, and the perished whose lack we always feel, will step through the door finally and stroke our hair with dreaming, habitual fondness."[12]

We can keep the story or memory of the saints alive through oral, written, and visual methods of communication, as well as through the liturgies and other rituals we perform in this age and the monuments and relics that dot the pilgrimage landscape. The methods of communicating stories are many. Howard Gardner presumes that due to biological and cultural reasons, we have seven, if not eight, intelligences or methods of communication. These include linguistic intelligence, mathematical intelligence, art or spatial intelligence, physical intelligence, musical aptitude, and inter- and intrapersonal relational skills. Gardner and those who follow this approach are also interested in a spiritual way of knowing and a certain kind of sensitivity to the land.

As Gardner and those who follow his work are quick to point out, there is always a mixture of these intelligences, which I believe is manifest in the way we tell stories or in the way pilgrims leave their mark upon this world. Walter Starkie, in writing about his pilgrimage to Santiago de Compostela, says that the names of modern pilgrims are written with water, a visual or spatial intelligence. Starkie also notes the work of the masons who built the cathedrals: "Those anonymous masons and stone-cutters of eight hundred years ago, when they tarried in this narrow street where I linger today, left as a token of their passing some tiny individualized figure or ornament, which, in a flash, illustrates the universal significance of the pilgrimage."[13]

Or consider the importance of reliquaries and relics, fragments of people's very bodies, as another way of causing people to stop in their tracks and ponder the lessons of the past. Some of the reliquaries that hold bodily fragments of saints, and the shrines that entomb them, help us remember what lessons we need to learn from the past, calling us to consider the stories of other pilgrims who may have faced the same conflicts we face in our pilgrim lives today. For example, the stories of Archbishop Romero of El Salvador continue to reverberate in other tales of oppression today, both in Latin

America and beyond. Romero, who has become a saintlike figure in that part of the world, learned his story of standing in solidarity with the poor from Jesus Christ but also from other saintly figures of his lifetime and of the past.

The stories of the saints before us are often communicated not only by the pages of a library book, a theological citation, a historical examination, but also through art, as in stone cuttings, stained glass windows, music, drama, and in visiting the very spots where the pilgrim's life took place. These are all ways that change and growth may be stimulated in our lives today. For example, to get an impressive view of the lives of saints in works of art, I visited the "basement" of the Abbey Church at St. John's Abbey in Collegeville, Minnesota. Not only is there a reliquary with a saint's relics entombed in gems, but there are bits and pieces of other saints in another portion of the basement.

When it was common practice for each priest of the abbey to celebrate Eucharist daily, he was assigned a small chapel in the basement. To this day, in each chapel there is an icon or work of visual art, either contemporary or old, of a saint's life. There is a carving of a stout St. Thomas Aquinas in one chapel, and some beautiful images and icons of Mary in others.

The communion of saints reminds us that earthly life is but a brief overture to the eternality of the soul.   What is it that the saints are trying to tell us today in the songs of their lives, their reliquaries, their chapels, shrines, basilica alcoves, the stained glass windows, the music, and the dramas written about their lives, and the stories or the theological tomes they wrote? What the saints have to tell us is something about the way they lived faithfully both in great or momentous times and in ordinary times.[14]

In *Little Saint*, Hannah Green tells the story of St. Foy. Green and her husband did not know the story of this young woman until they visited and then moved to Conques, in south central France. They heard about the story of this "little saint" through the stories of those who knew her. In the village's yellow stone basilica is a gold reliquary, in which the relics of St. Foy are held. St. Foy was a girl of twelve who was beheaded in the fourth century because she refused to deny her faith before the Roman consul who ruled that part of France. "So they sang of her in sacred canticles, for so she answered the Proconsul Dacien, though she knew that she would die for it: 'My name,' she said, 'is Faith. And I am a Christian.' That was at Agen in the year 303 in the reign of the Emperor Diocletian, at the time of the last of the terrible persecutions—the Great Persecution it was called."[15]

The basilica and the reliquary of St. Foy is a shrine seen by some as a kind of "transformation station" between earthly and heavenly realms. Shrines have a kind of thaumaturgic effect, bestowing healing power upon those who are ill.[16] St. Foy's shrinelike reliquary is no different, as it gives people the possibility of healing wounds that are physical, emotional, or spiritual.

What is intriguing is that this story is of a "little saint," a brave young woman, who showed a kind of faith that "is a great tree, an oak tree rooted deep in the heart of France," writes Green, quoting the poet Charles Peguy from this very same area. The roots of this tree of faith reach back to the fourth century and the life of this young woman.[17] There is no doubt that for Green and others the story of St. Foy became a story of faith in the pilgrimage of life that others can learn from as they face the challenges and calls of faith in today's world.

But even more powerful or dramatic is this idea: By praying, by being in solidarity with the communion of saints of old, by living in those places where a member of the communion of saints once lived and affirmed the gospel, we too participate in the communion of saints.[18] The stories of the communion of saints are still open; it is not a closed archive or a locked treasure chest of old memories. By participating in the way of the pilgrim, by seeking out the members of the community of saints past and present, we too become part of that community. No longer is it "their life" versus "our life," but we get a glimpse and a taste of our life together as members, one of another in the body of Christ, a body made a holy gathering by God's divine gestures in the life of Christ.

The Communion of Saints in the Church's Pilgrimage

Bruce Morrill writes that the church is a "multiplicity of bodies and histories as the very 'place' of humanity's redemption on the basis of the Gospel, wherein the Holy Spirit creates, guides, and raises up the body of Christ, animates the Church as the body of Christ for the life of the world, and sustains believers with the Eucharistic body of Christ at the center of all ritual sacraments."[19] One part of that "multiplicity of bodies and histories" is the communion of saints in the life of the church today. Perhaps the reason that there is interest in pilgrimage today is because the Holy Spirit is animating the church to learn about its roots and the stories of its past. Perhaps like the men and women who were monks and nuns in the past, we can collect the stories of pilgrimage and transform them into the radiant present as we move into new territories of our collective life as the body of Christ on pilgrimage.[20] As God's word was addressed to the communion of saints of old, God's word is still addressed to us today for the change and growth of our lives into salvation's story.

As Thomas Gillespie has stated so well, our lives are overtaken at any minute by the unforeseen and unforeseeable events and circumstances that direct us into paths never imagined, much less planned. Life, writes Gillespie, is what happens to us while we make other plans.[21]

What do we do in these situations when our life takes unexpected turns? Again, one of the best and most reliable resources for us as a church is the lived stories of those who today compose the communion of saints. This is more than collections of historical facts or abstract discussions of lives once lived. One way to make the stories of the communion of the saints *matter* for the church is to remind the people of God daily that we walk in the shadows of the past and that the past matters.[22] One time in which these stories are best remembered and celebrated is when we celebrate baptism or Holy Communion. In baptism, the minister or priest reminds us of the significance of water in the history of God's people, Israel.

In Holy Communion, we celebrate a family or household of God in reunion, for we who are alive are not the only ones present. The members of the communion of saints past and present are praying for and with us. The gestures of Jesus at the Last Supper and the words of institution are reminders that this meal is a connecting thread for all who have participated in it before we came along and gathered around the table.

Another important ritual in the life of the church may be around the days of All Hallows' Eve (Halloween), All Saints' Day, and All Souls' Day. During these holy days, a congregation, parish, or other intentional Christian community may remember the lives of those pilgrims who preceded us, recounting the stories of their lives as they live on in our lives. I have visited many Catholic cemeteries on these days, remembering the candles burning brightly on individual gravestones. In Guatemala, the small shrines where the bodies of the beloved are buried are usually freshly painted for these holy days.

Another way of remembering the stories of God's people before us, now part of the communion of saints, is by intentionally visiting a cemetery. While serving various congregations as an interim minister in North Carolina, if there has been a cemetery on the church grounds, I have spent an afternoon visiting it and reading the various names and dates. In one church I served, early on Easter Sunday morning we gathered around a large oak tree in the middle of the cemetery to celebrate Holy Communion with all the saints. It is customary among Moravian congregations to gather outside in a cemetery on such occasions as well, oftentimes singing hymns with a brass choir.

In one church on All Saints' Day we remembered those who had died by writing down their names on a piece of poster board and reading them aloud during the worship service. I remember telling the congregation that one day, all of us gathered that very day would have our names on the list as well. It is our future!

Among the Benedictine communities where I have stayed, during the morning prayers there is a reading of the names of community members who had died on that day. At St. Benedict's Monastery, it is not unusual to find on a dining room table a small framed photo of a member of the community who had recently died, with a votive candle nearby, which is lit as that one person is remembered. While we who are alive today in the body of Christ are all members of the communion of saints, those who have died surely have a renewed and clearer understanding of what it is to be part of this awesome gathering of saints.

The communion of saints is one of our resources for our earthly pilgrimage of change and growth. Yet we do come to places on this pilgrimage in which the words of Antonio Machado are apt: "Traveler, there is no path. Paths are made by walking."[23] The stories found within the Bible and the saints' stories have taken us to a point, and we have no choice but to walk forward, thus blazing new trails for others who will follow our metaphorical footsteps. Philip Cousineau makes this comment: "All journeys are the rhapsodies or variations on the theme of discovery."[24] In the next chapter, the focus is not only upon the story of the saints who have gone before us, but the guidance of those who are walking with us. These guides are also pilgrims, though they are a little bit ahead of us in their experience of the pilgrimage of life. While such guides are still learning, nevertheless, their place in the body of Christ is to be teachers of pilgrimage, showing us how best to make sense of the pilgrimage we are on.

Chapter 7

Teaching and Learning to Be a Pilgrim

Make me to know your ways, O Lord;
  teach me your paths.
Lead me in your truth, and teach me,
  for you are the God of my salvation;
  for you I wait all day long.
                        (Ps. 25:4–5)

*B*eginning a pilgrimage and learning the pathway and gestures of pilgrimage are first taught to the beginner by a guide or a teacher who is a veteran of pilgrimages and who accompanies the beginner on the journey. In the process of teaching a new pilgrim the way, the veteran pilgrim is reeducated as well, becoming reqcquainted with the gestures of pilgrimage and relearning the lessons learned along the pilgrim's way. After some time, through multiple pilgrimages, when the novice pilgrim becomes a veteran, that person may then teach others who are new to the way of the pilgrim life.

Sometimes the veteran pilgrim teaches a cluster of people who are beginning a pilgrimage for the first time. The schooling of such novices takes place on the pilgrimage path itself, rather than in a room set apart from life's pilgrimage where an instructor talks about pilgrimage as if it were something that could be known objectively through an anthropological, historical, sociological, or theological lens.

Nevertheless, should one study the anthropological, sociological, theological, and historical characteristics of pilgrimage in a modern-day classroom, Sunday school, or seminary setting? Can pilgrimage be conveyed in lecture format with multimedia presentations on the facts and history of pilgrimage? Or does one learn the practice, art, or act of pilgrimage from a person who knows it firsthand and who lives pilgrimage in the here and now? To learn from the viewpoint that Christians live a pilgrim life means to learn it *in a pilgrimage context.*

Along my own pilgrimages, I have experienced the wonderful, providential hand of God in bringing me to people who have led me, cared for me, and taught me the very acts, the art, of pilgrimage. There is no sign-up board or room marked clearly "Pilgrimage" in a church's educational wing where I could meet up with these guides. There is not even any necessary or obvious authority over the pilgrim guides. There is no paper curriculum for being a pilgrim that adequately covers the serendipitous moments of pilgrimage. This is because there exists no systematically controlled method of teaching the curious rationale of the pilgrimage of Christian life. Likewise, there is no way to fake or imitate a pilgrimage and still discover the authentic, genuine nature of the Christian life as pilgrimage. People who can best teach us pilgrimage appear unannounced, often coming out of nowhere. These guides appear at the right time and place, during the right circumstances, when we are most open, vulnerable, ready, and eager to learn.

Likewise, these pilgrim guides depart at the right time, not a moment too soon or too late, in just the right circumstances—that is, when we would like him or her to do "it"—whatever "it" is—on the pilgrimage, rather than doing it ourselves. Having no other option, we press onward and do what is required of us in this pilgrimage that is life. Call it the unexpected, the unplanned, the spontaneous moment, all the right circumstances for epiphanic revelations from the Holy Spirit. The timing is up to God, or so it seems—much like Christ revealing himself and then disappearing before the two disciples on the way to Emmaus (Luke 24).

Pilgrimage Stories of Guides and Accompaniment

Consider the roles and functions of the pilgrim guide and the pilgrim disciple:

Pilgrim Guides   When I arrived in Taos, New Mexico, and knocked on the door of the Catholic Church's rectory, the spiritual director of the pilgrimage, Father Ed, greeted me warmly, as if I were a long-lost relative. Father Ed had walked this pilgrimage trail several times over the past twenty-five years, though this year he was not going on pilgrimage because he was having hip surgery. Even though Father Ed drove his car throughout this year's pilgrimage, he would take me aside from time to time and teach me about the land of northern New Mexico, the indigenous population, the local historical lore, the current problems facing many at Taos Pueblo, and the story of this specific pilgrimage experience which had been resurrected by the Archdiocese of Santa Fe over twenty-five years ago. I was reminded along the pilgrimage that while the Catholic missionaries came to this area over four hundred years ago, the people who lived upon this land had been here longer.[2]

One morning outside of Taos, Father Ed brought all the pilgrims together outside of the National Guard armory where we had slept the previous night. We gathered in a large circle around a patch of earth that was largely void of the thick, brown stalks of prairie grass. Father Ed told us, "The earth is the Lord's," a belief that the psalmist as well as Father Ed's ancestors, who were people of this land, firmly believed. (Father Ed had several different tribes that he "hailed" from.) Father Ed then deposited on the ground a leather pouch full of tobacco as a gift to the earth. With a clay bowl full of water he blessed the earth as God's good creation, sprinkling the brownish-red soil and leaving dimpled marks upon it. Then, placing the large bowl of water in the center of our circle, he scooped water from it, wetting his large frame by touching the areas of his body that included the five senses. Next he wet each limb. Finally, he drew a ladle of water from the bowl and drank. Each of us participated in the same ritual as Father Ed prayed, "The earth is the Lord's, and all its fullness, and all who inhabit it. Thanks be to God."[1]

Another unexpected guide was Mary, whom I met on my pilgrimage to St. Patrick's Purgatory. Mary ran a bed and breakfast in her old farmhouse outside of Pettigo, Ireland. The farmhouse was called "The Carne." Mary was a widow who lived most of her adult years in this large house, raising four children without a father. The house was no longer surrounded by cows but by large trees, wild green grass, and a magnificent garden in full summer bloom, with snapdragons reaching their summer growth heights. Mary had just returned from a pilgrimage to Lourdes, France, a place of healings. Despite this, she managed to make a breakfast of Kellogg's Corn Flakes, Wheatabix cereal, fresh milk, sausage, ham, fried tomatoes, bacon, eggs over easy, tea, toast, and jam at ten o'clock in the evening! Our nighttime conversation focused on pilgrimage. Living so close to St. Patrick's, Mary told me that she had been on pilgrimage there twelve times. She told me the legend that "if you go on pilgrimage three times, then you don't have to go to purgatory, but go straight to heaven." I told Mary that she had been to St. Patrick's enough that she could just slip around purgatory right into heaven, bringing a few people along with her! I found in Mary's stories of pilgrimage a great window and preparation for what I was to encounter in my own pilgrimage to St. Patrick's Purgatory the next day.[2]

Being a Pilgrim   I learned to be a pilgrim by a variety of ways. The most traditional way was by preparing to teach a course on pilgrimage in a seminary where it had been drilled into me that the one way to learn is through books, popular magazines, and peer reviewed journals, as well as movies, videos, and music. Through this method I learned a great deal about the practice of pilgrimage, but not what it meant to be a pilgrim of life.

To learn what pilgrimage means in the Christian life requires immersing oneself in the "culture" or context of pilgrimage itself, by taking part in an actual, intentional pilgrimage. I learned the basics by being on a pilgrimage in northern New Mexico with the other pilgrims under the leadership of Father Ed. The group took this novice pilgrim and carefully taught me songs, how to use the rosary and other rituals of life, the mysterious comradeship of the Penitentes, and the art of walking over one hundred miles in less than six days.

I learned cultural variations on pilgrimage through listening and participating in the pilgrim life in Esquipulas, Guatemala. With the help of the Capriel brothers as my translators, I learned that the reasons for going on pilgrimage are as numerous as there are pilgrims. Watching the fervent faithfulness of the many pilgrims from the point of view of those who lived in the monastery gave me a front-row seat for watching the performance of faith in the flesh. But it was not just the basilica in Guatemala that made the impression; it was visiting the other shrines near the basilica, visiting the other churches in the area, with their respective black Christ figures, then going back to the basilica while hearing and watching a large woman from Belize cry for a blessing on the small T-shirt that she was holding up before the statue of the Christ. She was praying for a blessing for her grandson.

Conversion: Learning to Be and Become a Pilgrim   On the one hand, discovering that I am a pilgrim within the body of Christ is still a truth I am wrestling with, even as I write this book. Tom Wright says that once we sign on for pilgrimage at our baptism and in the subsequent conversion process, we commit ourselves to periodic sojourning in the wilderness.[3] Later in life we are given the option of choosing to live as a pilgrim in order to avoid being lost in the deserts of this world. It is better to walk with a purpose while wandering over this earth than to meander through life with no destination.[4] We commit ourselves to doing these things not as a grand social act of our own initiative, but inspired by the Holy Spirit, the living Word of God among us. Without God we can do nothing. God's Spirit, who alone can help us to know what is right, gives us the impulse to be eager in doing God's will, so that on this earthly pilgrimage we will help the weak with loving care, serving them as we serve Christ. We will forgive others as we turn to Christ for forgiveness, building one another up with deeds done for the love of God.

On the other hand, this is a process that takes a lifetime to learn. We may begin each day by struggling to deal with the injustices in this life, creating beauty and truth and challenging unworthy claims that try to win our heart, mind, and body. Tired of trying this approach after only a few weeks, we may feel like quitting. This is when we learn that being a pilgrim of God is life-long. There is no quitting, and we learn best among other pilgrims.

For example, one place that I have come to understand the act of conversion is in moving from being only a pilgrim to teaching others the practice of pil-grimage in seminary courses. For four years I have taken students on a nine-mile pilgrimage. Each time the pilgrimage was a wholly—and holy—different experience, and I drew a variety of lessons from each one of the experiences. What I have learned through looking at pilgrimage education as conversion over the years of being on intentional pilgrimage, as well as discovering that the Christian life is a pilgrimage, is that growth is not necessarily comprehen-sible at the time it is occurring but only after a period of reflection. The journey does not end; it is continuous, sometimes along a straight path but oftentimes circuitous and difficult to discern given the complexities of life.

Pilgrim Guides, Being a Pilgrim, and the Process of Conversion

I am reenvisioning the church as a place and people who teach one another to be the pilgrim church. I challenge the presumption that any warm body can teach the gestures of pilgrimage. In the context of the body of Christ, such a thing is impossible. Pilgrim guides are not aware they are guides until they go on their second pilgrimage, bringing others along as novice pilgrims and teaching them pilgrim gestures. It is in the teaching of pilgrimage that the veteran pilgrims learn something new. For the pilgrim, the classroom for learning pilgrimage is life on the road; the pedagogy is found in using the gestures learned through rituals and relationships, and the process is lifelong.

Pilgrim Guides

Consider "Petrus," in *The Pilgrimage*, a pseudofictionalized story of a modern-day pilgrimage to Spain's Santiago de Compestela. Paulo is eager to begin pil-grimage but cannot begin until someone shows him the way. As if out of nowhere, Paulo begins to talk to a figure hiding in the dark. Petrus, a "man about forty, in khaki Bermudas and a white, sweaty T-shirt [arrived]. . . . He was gray-haired, and his skin was darkened by the sun."[5] All that Petrus knows is that he was told by others to wait for Paulo at this certain place, but he does not know whom he is going to meet. (In real life, Petrus is a prize-winning Euro-pean industrial designer.[6]) Petrus tells the pilgrim Paulo, who has lost his first bid to obtain a certain sword as an award for finishing the pilgrimage, that the true path to wisdom can be identified by three things. First, it must involve agape, and I'll tell you more about this later; second, it has to have practical application in your life. Otherwise, wisdom becomes a useless thing and deteriorates, like a sword that is never used. And finally, it has to be a path that can be followed by anyone. Like the road you are walking now, the Road to Santiago.[7]

Petrus reminds Paulo where evil is located on the trail, where they may rest, and what are the practices of pilgrimage needed to gain insight into the nature of the mysteries of life, love, God, and himself. Petrus reminds Paulo who and what matters most in life, guarding him each time he stumbles on the pilgrim's way. Petrus's job is to lead the pilgrim Paulo along the road to Santiago while at the same time teaching him not only the practices of pilgrimages but practices that will put Paulo in good stead for life. At some point along the journey Petrus will leave, and Paulo the pilgrim will become Paulo the guide, who will teach other novice pilgrims.

What credentials does Petrus have? Petrus tells Paulo that pilgrimage has to be experienced firsthand in order to be understood. You can't understand the secret of pilgrimage by reading it in an E-book in a library carrel, or through any other form of modern education; it must be experienced. According to Petrus, the secret of teaching pilgrimage is as follows:

> You can learn only through teaching. We have been together here on the Road to Santiago, but while you were learning the practices, I learned the *meaning* of them. In teaching you, I truly learned. By taking on the role of the guide, I was able to find my own true path. . . . Life teaches us lessons every minute, and the secret is to accept that only in our daily lives can we show ourselves to be as wise as Solomon and as powerful as Alexander the Great. But we become aware of this only when we are forced to teach others and to participate in adventures as extravagant as this one has been.[8]

The true guide for our earthly pilgrimage is Jesus Christ. We look to the examples of Jesus' earthly ministry to discern where we are to go in this life, studying every detail in the life of Jesus in discussing and deciding the direction of life as Christians. We are accompanied on this journey by the Holy Spirit, God with us. The living God chooses to walk with and alongside us, whether we are rich or poor, male or female, able-bodied or disabled, from all countries and nationalities, young and old alike. In the guides of life's pilgrimage is the gift of wisdom, for wise direction is central to growth.[9] In these people is a love of God and love of neighbor, for without such love, there is a good chance that the pilgrim guide would grow so exasperated with a pilgrim that it would be easier to leave the pilgrim stranded rather than endure the conflict that the pilgrim faces.

Some characteristics of the pilgrim guide are as follows:

Notices footprints   The pilgrim guide helps us to study the footprints in the roadway of life to see that we are not necessarily the first on a pilgrimage but just the most recent travelers down this portion of the road.[10] Along the pilgrim road we will gather or collect stories, including our own, perhaps in journals or drawings, a photo album or recordings of sounds, as we move through landscapes and have the occasional odd encounter with others we meet on the way.[11]

We are not only to look at the footprints of others but at our own footprints as well. We are to look at ourselves from new or different angles and perhaps become judgmental aliens of our own lives.[12] While this is a daunting task at first, for living retrospectively is easier said than done, it is possible for us to taste freedom as we come to see what constitutes our lives and the lives of others.

The pilgrim guide, oftentimes having been on certain portions of the pilgrimage, may know where the troublesome parts of the road lie. When I have led pilgrimages with classes, it has been of great help to know the pathway well enough that I can help pilgrims anticipate what they may need to do for certain stretches of the road, or where we can rest before traveling onward. Likewise in life's pilgrimage, there are certain stretches along life's journey where we as teachers can warn novices or otherwise be useful in helping them. While there will still remain surprises in store for pilgrims and pilgrim guides, nonetheless, chances are that the experience of the pilgrim guide will be a great advantage for everyone.

Reflects on roads   One of the gifts of a pilgrim guide is stability, especially for the pilgrim who is anxious or upset.[13] This is where the lessons of life's pilgrimage take place best. On the road, immersed in a situation with time to reflect on what might have just occurred, is where we may learn best the lessons of life. For example, consider the "Evangelist" in Bunyan's *Pilgrim's Progress*. It seems like every time Christian gets stuck along the pathway, perhaps in the Slough of Despond, it is the Evangelist who suddenly appears. And what does the Evangelist offer Christian? The simple admonition for Christian to remember why he is on the journey in the first place, and where he is going. Christian is called to remember the story of his life. In Dorothy Day's pilgrimage of life it was her mentor Peter Maurin who almost miraculously appeared, taking the young Day's hand and teaching her the practices of the Catholic tradition. In Day's autobiography Maurin serves as the pilgrim guide, Day as the pilgrim.

Speaks of Progress to a Destination and of Saving for the Future   While we may feel like we are stuck with Christian in the Slough of Despond, we might also find hope through the aid of pilgrim guides who speak to us of the progress we have made on this pilgrimage so far. Oftentimes we can be stuck in the illusion that we have not advanced or moved closer to God. Growth in the pilgrim life is adopting a conscious "habit of being," to quote Belden Lane, or a habit of envisioning in which we work toward discovering God's presence in our weakness, renunciations, and even despair.[14] All of these produce a palpable pain which may lead to a sense of grace that is terrifying yet beautiful at the same time.

The progress, the future, that we all aspire to, is important for the pilgrim guide to enunciate throughout the pilgrimage. The pilgrim guide, with her or his knowledge of pilgrimage, may tell about the way the God of creation is living in us, not as our creator per se but as our true self where the hidden Christ lives.

More importantly, the pilgrim guide reminds pilgrims of what lies ahead in terms of our destination. While in the middle of the journey of the Christian life, it is easy to focus on where we are, forgetting what lies ahead. It is easy for us to start "pole vaulting over mouse droppings," as one friend told me on a pilgrimage, focusing on the small "molehill" problems and making of them mountains that are impossible to scale. Pilgrim guides enable us to keep problems before us in perspective in terms of the greater goal ahead.

Choosing who will be a pilgrim guide involves, as with most other leadership positions, the discernment of a community of other pilgrims and pilgrim guides. Because Christian pilgrimage is a communal venture, pilgrim guides will be called out to be leaders from within the community. They may be old or young, women or men, rich or poor, from any and all nationalities and ethnic heritages, gay or straight.

Being a Pilgrim

The primary thrust of this book is learning to be God's pilgrim, with our body, mind, and spirit as conduits of knowledge, whether it is a cognitive knowing or a deeper sense of knowing and being known by God. As we grapple with the question "What is faith?" our acceptance of faith is identical to our being incorporated into the life of the body of Christ.[15] If life is about God, things of God, and being created in the image of God, it follows that human life is a primary means of communication and of connecting with others in relationships. It follows then that by God's grace, as pilgrims we are agents of social change, regardless of our station in life.[16] Learning to live a life of pilgrimage cannot help but cause a stir among others in this world.

Nancy Louise Frey writes that there are three elements pilgrims carry with them that teach them to be pilgrims. The first is the scallop shell. The scallop shell comes to us from the traditional pilgrimage to Santiago de Compostela, which is close to the ocean. The scallop shell is symbolic of the good works the pilgrim is expected to perform. Note the shape of the shell, which looks like a baseball mitt or the back of one's hand, with the fingers extended outward.[17] On our journey we come into a sense of wholeness and limitlessness through relationship and service to, with, and from others. In this sense we are living out what Jesus calls the two great commandments: love of God with all our heart, soul, mind, and body, and love of our neighbor as ourselves.

The importance of loving God and neighbor, and the opportunity for such service or servant leadership, is something that I have treasured in my work with people with disabilities. For generations, one model of work with people with disabilities was doing things *for* or *to* them, seeing them as objects of missionary work. This robbed the person with a disability of being a whole person, a brother or sister in the body of Christ. Instead, the art of pilgrim service is learning to *be with* others and letting other people simply be with us. Through this we can understand how to live with each other in the body of Christ.

The second element pilgrims carry with them is a walking stick. Originally the walking stick was used for protection against dangerous animals like wolves and dogs, a possible threat on pilgrimage. Now the walking stick is used primarily for physical support, offering assistance when one's legs are weary. Interestingly enough, the walking stick is representative of the ascension of Christ from the cross of crucifixion, as the walking stick points to the heavens.[18] The significance of the walking stick as a tool of assistance was clearly lost on me for some time. I remember Deacon Don on the way to Chimayo with his old metal ski pole, which he used to move us faster but also to assist him in his walk. When I was given a beautifully carved walking stick from one of my students in a seminary pilgrimage class, I saw walking sticks in a new light. Yes, I was the leader, but I too needed assistance in the walk.

The third element is a backpack, which denotes that the pilgrim is transient, a stranger, and distinct from others who are "at home." The pilgrim serves as a herald of Christ, telling others the good news. The backpack is a place to store memorabilia from the pilgrimage's adventures.[19] One of the great activities to do at the end of a pilgrimage is to empty the backpack. I have been amazed at every pilgrimage reminder I have collected along the way: songbooks, written prayers, objects found on the roadway such as a rock, a sea shell, a leaf, a corroded coin, and so on. On one pilgrimage, one student has a game for the group in the evening. Our playing pieces? Bits and pieces we found along the roadway. In my time at the basilica in Esquipulas, Guatemala, I have gathered weavings, rosaries, coronas, unlit candles, and stone cakes that are reminders of the pilgrim life in that part of the world. I still use the book of prayers and songs I used for the first time on the pilgrimage to Chimayo.

In the pilgrimage of life, we are not only inheritors of stories, but we collect stories as well and other fragments of the Christian life. We need these reminders, or what I learned in Spanish as *recuerdos*, objects that remind us of where or what pilgrimages we have taken, which in turn remind us of our life as pilgrims.

Conversion as Growth and Change on the Pilgrimage

Learning to be a member of the body of Christ, and learning of God in Christ, is accomplished through *conversion*, which I mentioned in chapter 2, using the Hoberman Sphere for an example of growth on pilgrimage. Pilgrimage speaks to the times when our lives are overtaken by unforeseen forces in events and circumstances that direct us into certain pilgrim pathways that we never imagined, much less planned. God has a habit of leading us on an educational pilgrimage by taking us off our chosen or planned map of life.

Conversion is the way that many pilgrims talk about growth and change in their lives. Indeed, conversion is most appropriate for our way of talking about growth and change in the way of Christian pilgrimage in general. Conversion, like pilgrimage, is the continual dying to self, turning to God, becoming more authentically human. It becomes an unfolding, mutating, perplexing yet rewarding reality of pursuing both transcendent holiness and peace in the here and now.[20] Conversion, like pilgrimage, is lifelong, a continuing process. We always live in the possibility of conversion, often punctuated with more failures in life than successes. Like pilgrimage, where one *is* a pilgrim and always learning more *about* pilgrimage, conversion is affirming that we *are* Christians and that we are *becoming* more like Christ.[21]

Conversion as the process of learning to be God's pilgrim has the following characteristics:

Conversion and Pilgrimage: An Immersion Approach to Education   We learn to be pilgrims wherever we find human lives interacting with one another, immersed in the thickness of life itself. Consider this story of the famous African American photographer Gordon Parks, who was well-known for his black and white photographs for the Farm Security Administration (FSA) in Washington, DC, during the 1940s. The photographers for the FSA and their boss Roy Stryker documented the lives of farmers and workers, many of whom were mistreated because of their ethnicity and were thus displaced by the nation's economic situation. Parks was interviewed about why he thought Stryker hired him:

> "I didn't know much about Washington, so [Stryker] gave me my first assignment. I was not to take a camera out. I was to go to a big department store downtown and buy a topcoat, go from there across the street and have lunch and then see a motion picture. And he wanted me to give him a report on it."
>
> The day was emblazoned on Parks' memory: he was refused at all those places. "How did it go?" Stryker asked him when he returned to the office.
>
> "I think you know how it went," Parks said.
>
> "Yeah, I think I do," Stryker said. "What are you going to do about it?"
>
> "What can I do about it?"
>
> "Well, why did you bring your camera down here?" Stryker said, adding, "Talk to some older black people who have suffered all their lives what you suffered today."[22]

Conversion began when Parks went to the various places that Stryker told him to go to, where he encountered racism firsthand. This is the kind of education that takes place in the School of the Pilgrim; it is an immersion approach to education. By an immersion approach, I mean that one learns best in the very context in which we work, live, and worship, which, for the purposes of this book, is along the pilgrim's path. The teacher or guide may be a few steps ahead of the students, but we are all on pilgrimage as Christ's people, open to what comes our way along the path.

In the above story, Gordon Parks learns what he is to photograph not by Stryker telling him about racism in a context set apart from racism. Instead, Stryker immerses Parks in a racist environment where he learns the ugly reality of racism by being turned away from each place where he attempts a normal interaction—and only because of the color of his skin. In such a way, racism was "emblazoned on Parks' memory [as] he was refused at all those places."[23]

This leads to another point: The ideal place to learn is the context in which one is to practice a job, or learn a certain way of life. Parks learned about racism in a racist culture. The teacher and the student are both immersed, submerged by the active context itself. We learn best here, in the moment that a life lesson is to be applied in the rush of life. The more distant and disconnected we are from where we are to practice, to live, and to learn with others, the more uninteresting, artificial, and abstract the learning moment becomes. In the church, we have become accustomed to teaching others *about* but not *of* Christ and the ways of the body of Christ. We tell parishioners and congregants in education classes about God, about Christ, and about the Holy Spirit in a room that is set apart, away from the throbbing, pulsing life of the body of Christ in prayer, worship, or in fellowship with one another. We point to, refer to, and show computerized presentations about the life of the church —away from the life of the church. We make the life of the church something to be learned from or analyzed from afar, without the benefit of actually making changes or engaging in living interaction with the very people we are talking about. In church-based education and seminary education we are accustomed to preparing case studies, à la modern business schools, and bringing these case studies into the classroom to teach from, talking about life in the church without getting messy from actually interacting with life in the church.

In the 1960s Jerome Bruner wrote of the !Kung in Africa practicing such an approach to educating their young. The !Kung taught their young by immersing them in the context in which they were to live rather than taking them to a secluded location away from the action. The young were very much a part of community life, with constant interaction between young and old. They ate, played, danced, sat, and hunted together. Children are constantly using the rituals, tools, and weapons of the !Kung. Bruner wrote: "In the end, every man in the culture knows nearly all there is to know about how to get on with life as a man, and every woman as a woman."[24] Likewise, we learn piano best by being at the keyboard, we learn computer skills in front of the monitor, we learn painting by using paints on canvas, we learn pottery with clay in our hands, we learn to be a cook in a kitchen, and we learn pilgrimage best by being on pilgrimage with other pilgrims.

Creation Goes on Creating: The Dynamic Character of the Christian Life   There is a struggle of ongoing creation in our lives, whether we are aware of it or not.[25] This creative dynamism is driven by God's love. John Main writes that no one has ever seen God but that we can experience God whenever and wherever we encounter love.[26] It was out of love that God created this world, out of love that God led the people of Israel out of slavery, out of love that God gave us his only Son. It follows then that we may begin to see that the reason we change and grow at all in this life is out of God's love for us. In love God summons us into the fullness of life.

A Willingness to Let God Be God   We learn to let God be God in the context of our Christian communities.[27] God moves in these communities, enabling us to be someone greater than ourselves and see anew our relationship with one another and God. In part, stubborn as we may be, we need the gift of discernment. Chittister writes that discernment is based on an awareness that we cannot always have what we want but that there is hidden within us a value that is enduring: "Getting to the point of letting God's will rule our lives may plunge our lives into chaos . . . or into faith; a faith that can withstand the pressure, defying psychological and theological challenges."[28]

Chittister rightly reminds us that God is in the "dregs of our lives—that is why it takes humility to find God where God is not expected to be."[29] Self-revelation is necessary to growth. The struggles we hide and try to avoid are the struggles that most often consume us. There is a point, somewhere along the pilgrimage, where we must cease wearing masks, accept the graces of growth, and try to stop pretending we can be perfect. The dynamic nature of conversion lets us move beyond ourselves, leaving behind the limitations of our past, or what we thought were limits, in order to enter a creative space where our whole being—mind, body, and spirit—experience the love and life of Jesus afresh.

In order for these first three characteristics to be realized, there has to be a kind of "dying to self," which was the way of the monks in the desert. Belden Lane writes about the three spiritual lessons taught by the desert monks: dying to language, dying to self, and dying to neighbor.[30] There is, in a way, a self-emptying in which, by God's grace, there is a space in our lives that is hallowed by the Spirit of God. Only when we learn we do not need people can we love them.[31] There is a difference between *needing* to be with certain other people, as if one were addicted to being around the presence of another, versus *wanting* to be with someone in particular, out of choice and heartfelt desire.

Opening Up to New Questions   Chittister writes that life is a conversion from the chaotic to the orderly, from scattered thinking to more centered thinking, and from exploitative relationships to empowering relationships.[32] But throughout, conversion is the call for us to think of God, pondering who we are in Christ. God wants to guide us to new life, opening our eyes to possibilities and to find out for ourselves who God is in our life and who are we in God.

Opening ourselves up to new questions about God and ourselves in God may leave us feeling powerless. Chittister says that powerlessness is the grassfire of the soul, as we convert from leading a life that is less than authentic as we try to please others, to living a real, transparent life.[33]

A Disciplined Life   In the Benedictine *The Liturgy of the Hours* there is a prayer: "Lord, look upon us and hear our prayer. By the good works you inspire, help us to discipline our bodies and to be renewed in spirit."[34] The works that we aspire to or are able to do in this world are because of God's grace, which has already made possible our salvation. Because of God's grace, among the many gifts that we will receive along the way is gratitude for God's love. God is not to be "achieved," but is a presence we respond to, and without that presence we could not respond or have occasion to respond.[35] We need all of these gifts of God, without which we cannot possibly become fully ourselves.[36] That is why we ask for God's help to discipline our bodies, sharpen our minds, and renew our spirits. This process of conversion in the life of Christian community is to have the "edges of our life rubbed off," writes Chittister.[37] St. Theresa of Lisieux believed that the heart of faith is a willed obedience, learned by being with other disciples as the only way to survive faithfully through a lifelong desert.[38]

Pilgrims, Pilgrim Guides, and Conversion in the Church

The call for the church as the body of Christ is for us to be a pilgrim people. The journey began before we came into existence, but now we are part of it, committed to a progression from the limitations of the self into the limitless life of God.[39] John Main asks the important question for this chapter: In the face of the claims of the gospel, is this journey really possible for ordinary people?[40] With God's help, the answer is clearly yes. The God who is incarnate, crucified, resurrected, and ascended gloriously exists in our lives today.[41] In the next chapter I will explore this further in discussing the ritual life of Christians on pilgrimage, for it is in the rituals of the church that we learn best the work of the people of God and the true sense of the word "liturgy."

Chapter 8

Rituals of Christian Pilgrimage

Why are Christians not reminded more often that the Eucharist was born of a pilgrimage? It was born during the Passover pilgrimage to Jerusalem. . . . Jesus himself had come up to Jerusalem as a pilgrim for the feast of Passover.

(Francis Bourdeau)

Then they told what had happened on the road, and how he had been made known to them in the breaking of the bread.

(Luke 24:35)

*I*n the *Institutes of the Christian Religion*, Calvin writes, "Christ teaches us to travel as pilgrims in this world, [so] that our heritage may not perish or pass away." And what do we practice in the church to be sure that our heritage may not perish or pass away? We practice rituals. But what are the rituals, practices, or rubrics that remind us of our heritage? Obviously, Calvin is referring to the practice of pilgrimage to a holy site, a shrine perhaps, and to the eternal search for the holy. Both Catholics and early Protestants in Europe were aware of the practice and art of pilgrimage in Calvin's days.

Calvin is also referring to *us*—the readers and the writer of this book, to all of Christendom throughout time—as pilgrims. To be a Christian is to be a pilgrim who is called by God to be on our way to the Holy City. Through the rituals, sacraments, and other rubrics of the church, pilgrims and pilgrim guides experience conversion. The church is not a static entity—a passive, lifeless monument to God. Because the church is the body of Christ, it is alive, moving forward toward the in-breaking realm of God. To quote John, "Look! He is coming with the clouds; every eye will see him" (Rev. 1:7a). As Francis Bourdeau rightly observes in the epigraph at the beginning of this chapter, in Holy Communion (and baptism) we are given opportunities to remind one another that we are a pilgrim people.

Or consider the insight of Patricia Hampl on pilgrimage and sin:

Sin . . . is an incident along the longer, larger Way. Penitence is a trip toward life. . . . Sin needn't be a shaming public exposure, and expiation needn't be a private hair-shirt, a half-step short of neurosis. Certainly pilgrimage as a form of expiation underscores the liberation that is meant to be at the core of the sacrament, the radiant lightness of the shriven heart.[1]

For Hampl, it is in the Catholic sacrament and ritual of penance that she experiences the sense of pilgrimage. For others, it is in other sacraments, church rituals, and rubrics of a particular congregation or parish that the "we-ness" of pilgrimage is taught.

This chapter is on the necessity of rituals on pilgrimage. In Jesus calling us to follow him, it involves a sacrifice on our part: "If any want to become my followers, let them deny themselves and take up their cross and follow me" (Matt. 16:24). We have rituals to remember exactly why we are following Christ on this earthly pilgrimage. Rituals are necessary along the journey. They assist pilgrims in remembering where they have been and where they are going. Rituals help pilgrims to focus on and put into a theological context what is occurring at any moment along the pilgrimage. This is why the rituals we perform on pilgrimage become more intense than usual. No longer are rituals to remind us of where we are on the Christian calendar or season of activities. Instead, rituals become living markers on the pathway of life, showing us what we ought to do and be as members of Christ's body. The intensity of ritual is noted by Flannery O'Connor: "If Eucharist is a symbol, to hell with it. It is the center of experience for me; all the rest of life is expendable."[2]

Stories of Rituals on Pilgrimage

There is a difference between performing the ritual gestures of the Christian life as a frivolity and performing the ritual gestures of pilgrimage in which our very life depends upon performing the ritual rightly in order to get our bearings. After all, rituals and the sacraments of the church are not only windows or portals into the nature of the holy. In our rituals we come to realize that God is the beginning and end of our earthly pilgrimage. Likewise, this book is not about inventing pilgrimage as if it were a new idea; rather, it is to reclaim something quite old, older than the church itself, as it precedes Pentecost. Through the ages, one common thread is found among pilgrims: Pilgrimage is facing the right direction and moving toward God's realm, one step, one day, one place at a time, in life's rituals.

For example, it is five o'clock on a Sunday afternoon in Costilla, New Mexico, far from my home in North Carolina. "Formation!" is the word I hear being shouted above the rumble of boys and men getting ready to be on pilgrimage. I follow the slowly gathering group into a single file behind the three standards that will lead us in the next few days. The first is the *guia*, which is a cross with a wooden corpus of Jesus on it. It is dramatic; Jesus' head is bent downward, with his chin touching his red, beaten chest while his mouth is wide open as if in screaming pain. A crown of thorns is placed firmly upon Christ's head, causing a profusion of blood to cascade down from his brow and cover his entire body. The hands and feet are frozen in a spasm of pain from the nails going through them. This is followed by a large, colorful flag with the image of Our Lady of Guadalupe. At the tail end of this short line, a person carries a large, wooden puzzle piece that, when put together with other puzzle pieces, is the heart of Jesus.

As we walk single file to the small chapel in Costilla, we perform a ritual that will be repeated time and again through this journey. As we come closer to a chapel, singing a simple song—usually in Spanish—a band of members from the chapel we are going to visit are singing another song, carrying in front of them a large banner with an image of the patron saint of the chapel on it in bright, beautiful, and usually bold colors. Along this pilgrimage we will see banners with the images of St. Anthony of Padua, St. Joseph, St. Geronimo, St. Teresa de Jesus, and of course, Our Lady of Guadalupe. Once the pilgrims holding our *guia*, banner, and puzzle piece meet the members of the church holding their banner, the singing comes to a stop or softens as each pilgrim kisses and venerates the image on the church's banner, and the church members kiss and venerate what we are carrying. The church members then turn around and lead us into the smaller chapel, often an adobe structure with pink or white interior, with the banner and the people of God leading the way as we all walk single file into the building.

At the rough-hewn, wooden, arched doorway of each church, a curious encounter takes place: Parishioners line up and create a corridor that we pass between. They reach out and touch us gently while smiling and saying, "Bless me." For example, an older woman touches my hand and raises it to her wrinkled forehead in order for me to give her a blessing. I place my hand on her forehead, take my thumb, and make the sign of the cross upon her weathered, wrinkled brown flesh. She smiles and knowingly nods to me. Whatever worry she has is now gone for the moment. A holy blessing has taken place, but not by our own initiative. It is a holy moment, instituted by God in Christ. The pilgrim is considered "blessed by God" because of the sacrifice made to come on this pilgrimage. We are welcomed as blessed earthly saints, given small slips of paper with petitions that we pray for throughout the week. We are treated as a "chosen race, . . . God's own people" (1 Pet. 2:9).[3]

Pilgrimage Rituals

Rituals are those basic social acts, reeking of meaning, that depend on bodily gestures in specific, narrated contexts, with certain patterns of gestures that are often stereotypical in nature and are repeated time and time again. Catherine Bell writes that every ritual "comes fully embedded in larger discourses." These discourses may be rooted in myth, legends, religion, anthropology, sociology, psychology, or social psychology.[4]

The rituals we perform in the church reestablish our connection to the rest of the faithful with whom we are joined in Christ's body. Rituals are a way for us to embody the blessings of God while recognizing that blessings are themselves rituals. It is in the blessings of God—whether it is in the words spoken, the bodily gestures performed, or perhaps through other material objects used—that we are reminded of who and whose we are. Rituals have a way of nurturing or educating us as well, reminding us of the meaning of what we are doing on pilgrimage. It is in the sacramental gestures of baptism, or Eucharist, or washing another's feet that we remember the acts of Jesus.

Pilgrimage narratives have plenty to say about the centrality of rituals. One of the primary pilgrimage narratives in which the central theme is the investigation and exploration of the rituals of the church is that of Egeria. The book on Egeria's pilgrimage was written or recorded some time after 394, though she went on the pilgrimage earlier.[5] Egeria is a fascinating person whose story is a mystery to this day. The text is a diary of Egeria's pilgrimage, cast in the form of letters, in what is today considered the Middle East. She wrote these letters to a group of other religious people in her homeland of Galicia. This young, consecrated virgin traveled to monasteries and churches, investigating the ritual life of these places.[6]

Egeria's pilgrimage was thoroughly religious and not a tourist's adventure. She was interested in the relationship of humanity to God in both the Old and New Testaments and how that relationship is existentialized in and through the rituals practiced among religious people in these various locales. Through personal encounters with those places marked by the action of God and humanity, as well as in meeting and praying with those who exemplified best the Christian life she desired to live, she hoped to confirm her faith and the truth of Scripture.[7] So when she arrived at a place along her pilgrimage, she would follow this ritual: Say a prayer, read a Bible verse, sing a psalm, and say another prayer.[8] She took four journeys to places such as Mt. Sinai, Mt. Nebo (the locale of Moses' death), the tomb of Job, and the tomb of St. Thomas the Apostle in Odessa, along with a trip to Constantinople and the tomb of St. Thecla.[9]

What captivates most scholars in liturgical studies about Egeria's travels is both the earliness of this journey and the detailed records that she kept about the early church. Of particular interest to educators is her window into the early church's catechetical or religious instruction. She writes that in the process of catechesis, the young confirmands would be taught about the resurrection and the other theological tenets of the Christian faith. The confirmands would go through five weeks of instruction, and then they would receive the creeds of the church.[10] They were to take in the significance of the Old Testament. After evaluating the confirmands' knowledge and the life of the confirmand him- or herself, the church allowed the confirmands to hear the good news of the New Testament. This confirmation process concluded with baptism, often during the Easter vigil itself, as a celebration of the resurrection and new life. The rigors, the length of the process, and the kind of examination that went on in this process, as well as the centrality of rituals, captures the intricacies of educating Christians at a time before Sunday school and other modern forms of catechetical instruction. The Catholic Church has restored this ritual of confirmation in its Rite of Christian Initiation of Adults.

Egeria found rituals essential to what she learned on her pilgrimage. The importance of rituals in the life of the church on pilgrimage is also stressed by Tom Wright. Wright notes that going on an actual pilgrimage to a sacred place is not necessary or a sufficient condition for being a good Christian, especially since pilgrims always walk on a "tight rope" with the holy ideal of pilgrimage on one side and commercialism on the other side.[11] Wright understands that pilgrimage is like a sacrament, in which the act of pilgrimage involves "looking back"—looking back as an act of great remembrance—yet also looking forward to a time of final redemption. He cautions that, like sacraments, pilgrimage is open to abuse and being treated as if it involved magic, as though going to a place could gain a person grace or a "gold star" on a cosmic chart of good and bad deeds.[12] For example, in baptism we remember the importance of water in our collective past, with stories of Noah, the Red Sea and the great exodus, and the baptism of Jesus in the pilgrim-packed Jordan. Yet the waters of baptism remind us that we are baptized with Christ, which sets for us our life course toward God's kingdom, which is our future. Wright notes that in the waters of baptism, it is more than an allegory for our spiritual journey; it is the early stage in God's unfolding plan in this world.[13] In the Eucharist, we break bread and drink from the cup, remembering what Jesus

Christ has done for us, in spite of us, and through this holy meal we remember that our future is in God's hands.

There are four characteristics to consider in looking at the connection between rituals, especially sacraments, and pilgrimage:

First, in pilgrimage rituals we remember our pilgrimage on earth. Much of this tying in of the past, present, and future occurs through the sacred stories that are told, whether these stories are found in Scripture, in the history of the church, or in the local lore of the congregation or parish community. Ritual storytelling is every community's primal way of knowing, and the church itself is formed by the ritual storytelling that takes place in our communities.[14] The stories of the Christian faith community we are part of, and the stories of pilgrimage throughout the years, give us imaginative ways of ordering our life experiences as pilgrim Christians. The Christian faith is located and made manifest in the stories found in the life of the church. For example, the Canterbury pilgrims told stories on the way to the shrine of St. Thomas à Becket.[15]

A caveat: stories may be told and may be read, but these are only two modes of communication, or what Howard Gardner would call "two intelligences." There are many ways of telling, living, and regaling one another with stories of pilgrimage. For example, the visual arts are an important way of communicating the stories of pilgrimage, through painting or weaving, pottery, or sculpture. Or consider the great ballads that were first composed along the pilgrimages, especially in medieval Europe. Pilgrims depend upon language and stories as well as symbols and signs (e.g., glyphs), images and icons. These are not only along the pilgrims' way but also in the small chapels and large shrines that dot the landscape of pilgrimage, as well as in the larger churches that may be at the destination point of a pilgrimage. Several contemporary authors of pilgrimage narratives mention the work of Mircea Eliade, who observed that the raison d'être of pilgrimage to a shrine is based on an archetypal need. Deep in the human psyche there is a need to find the sacred center of our world, marked off from the profane space, where heaven and earth intersect, time stands still, and there exists the possibility of the transcendent breaking through.[16] The transcendent may break through a thin veil, a thin place, in which the holy may be best heard and witnessed to in this human life.

In a sense, the rituals of the church are helpful on pilgrimage as they mark off the path of our procession with ceremonies.[17] With music, words, drama, dance, banners, stained glass windows, sparklers, heavy cloth, vestments, pews, baptismal fonts, clay and metal chalices and patins, incense, food, drums, flutes, guitars, candles, circles of people gathered together, crosses, crucifixes, flags, and large puzzle pieces, we are provided with markers that let us know we are on a pathway to God. The rituals of pilgrimage provide us this pathway, until we miraculously enough become the path itself that others walk upon and follow on their pilgrimage.[18]

Second, on pilgrimage the rituals define us as God's people, as members of Christ's body.   We follow the steps of others before us who became the living pathway to Christ, who is the way, the "royal road" of Christian conversion.[19] For some time, pilgrimage was called a "poor person's mysticism," as the highest sort of mysticism would have been that of a monk. The physical journey of the pilgrimage is a ritual passage of peasant pilgrims across the terrain, but not only of the earth; the earth becomes symbolic of one's spiritual life. On pilgrimage, a person symbolically reappropriates the all-powerful, animated landscape by its now rightful denizens.[20]

Jean Corbon writes that the ritual of liturgy itself involves action and energy, and heavenly liturgy reveals and tells us who the actors are in the heavenly drama we are living. According to Corbon, the very heart of the liturgy—God the Father, Fountain of both this life and eternity—is adored, releasing the life that burst from the tomb itself.[21] In our rituals we learn to become neighbors to one another, especially to those who are wounded and broken, as we are all on a journey of transfiguration to a sacred center, namely, God.[22] Through the power of the Holy Spirit, the rituals of the church may find a kind of embodiment, especially as we focus on the gestures of pilgrimage that give life to human beings by bringing us all into communion with the living Christ.[23]

Third, on pilgrimage we perform the rituals as a way of following Christ, the Way.   One of the best ways that we can discern the ways of Christ is through the actions of Christ himself, whose earthly gestures have become our daily or weekly rituals.[24] For example, when Jesus gave his disciples the instructions on how to pray, saying, "Our Father," he did not do so with the knowledge that we would make that prayer the "Lord's Prayer" or the "Our Father." Did Jesus know that Paul would take the words he spoke at the last Passover meal and make them a central part of what we call the "Last Supper," or "Eucharist"? Did Jesus know his words of baptizing people in the name of the triune God would now be part of our sacramental repertoire?

We experience these ancient rituals and liturgies as reality, yet they create a transfiguration moment when we gather in the name of Jesus.[25] As Jesus roused faith in the heart of his disciples, uniting them to the body of Christ, Corbon writes that when we evoke the name of Jesus, whether it is with our lips or with sign language or other bodily gestures, we release the energy of the people of God with the energy that comes *from* God, to the church.[26] Our gestured rituals are energized by this very same Spirit.

When we gather as pilgrims, kneeling together with one another in worship or another ritual, we are validated by the gift of the Spirit. T. S. Eliot wrote that in church we are not there to verify, to instruct ourselves, or to inform our curiosity or carry a report. In the rituals of pilgrimage in a church, we are there to kneel where prayer has been made valid.[27] In these moments on pilgrimage, in the rituals we perform, in sacred places, we know who God is and discover whose we are.[28]

Fourth, pilgrimage rituals light the way ahead for us. Cousineau describes the art of pilgrimage as the art of reimagining or reenvisioning how we walk, talk, listen, write, see, and hear the world around us, especially in the relationships closest to us and in our journey with God in Christ. It was a tradition in some Christian pilgrimages to have portable lanterns lit along the way through the darkness toward the warmth of the pilgrim's inn. This tradition lasted for centuries. It allowed pilgrims to find their way and the host to provide safe entry to a place of rest.[29] Many churches continue this tradition with luminaries (paper bags with candles lit in them) dotting the way to a sanctuary on a holy festival day.

There is a sense of darkness in some stretches of a pilgrimage, and in life's pilgrimage as well. Maria Boulding writes of the chaotic storms of our lives that are enough to throw anyone off the way of pilgrimage. Rather than the neat pathways of life that we so yearn for, the chaos and conflict of life seem never ending. We forget too easily that the Spirit of God was in the wind on the first day of creation (Gen. 1:2). The rituals, and the prayers we pray in those rituals, are not within our total control, but it is the Spirit within us that prays in us and that leads us in our worship of God in Christ. The Holy Spirit, who is both comforter and discomforter of our lives, yearns and groans in the life of the church and the Christian as we stand and walk midway between what has been achieved by God and what is to come. Boulding, quoting George Montague, writes that the Spirit recycles the chaos of our life into praise and that the distractions of life are yet another form of chaos and can be expected to be exposed to the Spirit's actions.[30] It is in the rituals that we practice that we find some concrete footholds in the storm-tossed lives we live daily. Corbon writes that the celebration of liturgy in this time and place is the moment when the river of life, hidden in our world, penetrates the life of the baptized in order to divinize it, leading us to the Other who is before us, the God who beckons us home.[31]

Pilgrimage Rituals in the Life of the Church

The rituals that are performed on actual, intentional pilgrimages are the very same rituals that are first performed in the life of a church. This is because an intentional Christian pilgrimage is based upon the ritual practices of the church itself.

For those who have been on an actual pilgrimage, there is something strangely comforting about joining in the traditions of the church, wherever we may be. I have been told by Jewish friends that the sense of being part of a "Jewish culture" is strengthened for them because they share a common language together, along with the various rituals. One Jewish friend told me she could go to synagogue in Australia, in Japan, in Germany, in South Africa, and in Brooklyn and not miss a beat because of shared rituals and a common language read and spoken. Similarly, when I have been to other Protestant or Catholic churches on pilgrimages, I can usually figure out what is occurring within various parts of worship, although sometimes I stumble with the language since worship is in the vernacular.

What people who have not been on an actual pilgrimage miss while sitting in the pew is the very real sense that we are a pilgrim people wherever we live in this world and whatever our social class may be. For example, the place where we attend worship is not really the same week in and week out, though it may feel so at times. The Scriptures read quietly or spoken aloud change, the music is different, prayers are different, and the sermon or homily changes. Even the pastor, priest, or others of the religious life who are leaders in a faith community may change, and the people who gather as a congregation or parish are not the same ones who attended church a week ago. But none of us are the same people we were a week ago. In the span of a week, we have been on a pilgrimage in this world and have come back to find some sense of continuity and inspiration, confirmation, and affirmation in the ritual life of the church. Wright notes that baptism is the formal beginning of one's life on the pilgrimage that is the Christian life. Paul insists that baptism defines us as the renewed people of God in Christ—the only definition or description that matters to Wright—though we try to use other markers and rituals to identify ourselves in terms of our status in the life of the body of Christ. As we are defined and named as Christians in our baptism, we share in the life, death, and resurrection of Christ, who now gives us "food" and nurture for the way ahead.[32]

What Wright is doing is connecting the dots between an actual, intentional pilgrimage and our life in the ongoing pilgrimage as the body of Christ. Once we are signed on for the pilgrimage in our baptism and ongoing conversion, we commit ourselves to a periodic sojourning in the wilderness, as well as to taking the side of the Galilean in the battle for the kingdom, the reign of God upon this earth. Wright believes that we are committed to Christ by the act of others in our baptism, who use our words and other deeds which say—as Jesus said and did—that there is another kingdom, another king, to whom we have sworn our allegiance. Why and how do we do these things? We do these things with the power of the Holy Spirit, led by the Word of God made flesh.[33] Consider the following rites:

Baptism   Baptism is the public act of what God's grace is already doing: changing us and leading us to grow in Christ. Baptism is a public, tangible, concrete, watery mark of what God is doing in our lives and in the life of the body of Christ.

For the purposes of pilgrimage, I would add that baptism is a profound public declaration that the one baptized is understood as a member of the pilgrimage toward heaven's gates. I have proposed to several groups that walking sticks, scallop shells, and perhaps small backpacks or rucksacks may be located near the baptismal font or pool of water, signifying that the one who is being baptized is a member of this illustrative pilgrimage toward God's realm.

Holy Communion or Eucharist   These are but some of the names given to this sacramental meal that is another sacrament in the life of the church. Protestants, Catholics, and Orthodox can agree upon Eucharist as a major sacrament in the life of the church. Gerhard Lohfink writes that what makes the church the body of Christ is the very power of the Eucharist itself.[34]

What is most significant about Holy Communion is that the meal first was celebrated on Jesus' own pilgrimage of sorts. Jesus' last supper with his disciples was itself a celebration of the Passover meal, a meal whose origin is based upon the pilgrimage of the Israelites out of slavery in Egypt to the promised land. As Jesus is celebrating this pilgrimage meal with his disciples, Jesus himself is on a pilgrimage of sorts, having entered Jerusalem earlier in the week to the shout of loud hosannas. So this last meal with his disciples gathered together in a room takes on greater significance for Christians on pilgrimage as we remember the earthly pilgrimage Jesus was on, from birth in Bethlehem to his death in Jerusalem.

The Emmaus story in Luke 24 reminds us that Jesus is revealed as the Christ in the breaking of bread, a sign of hospitality and companionship, and then suddenly disappears. "According to Luke, when our risen Lord was at table with his disciples, he took the bread, and blessed and broke it, and gave it to them. Then their eyes were opened and they recognized him."[35] Martin

Robinson observes that the Eucharist is a key component in the devotional life of pilgrims for this reason: It is a reenactment of the "essential elements of the life, death, and resurrection of Jesus in the same way that the pilgrimage itself [is]."[36] As Jesus' earthly pilgrimage was a narrative of his life, death, and resurrection, the same holds true for those of us on pilgrimage: Ours is a story of life, death, and the resurrection we experience in Christ on this intentional, earthly pilgrimage.

Footwashing   Gerhard Lohfink writes that what is at stake in the rituals and sacraments we practice in the life of the church are the fundamental principles of Christian community. We esteem the other person above ourselves in the rituals, imitating what Christ himself lived: "Do nothing from selfish ambition or conceit, but in humility regard others as better than yourselves" (Phil. 2:3).[37] And as Paul notes a few verses later, Jesus "humbled himself and became obedient to the point of death—even death on a cross" (2:8).

A ritual that is full of powerful symbols but is not a sacrament is footwashing. As a ritual it is a humbling act and physically reminds us that, like Jesus, we are called to be humble. Daniel Armentrout writes that the glory of God is Jesus making himself humble enough to wash the feet of his disciples. On Maundy Thursday, through the washing of feet, those who wish to follow the broken, weeping Jesus—who became small, humbling himself to death on a cross—follow the same downward path in obeying the calling of Christ.[38]

This ritual has also been performed among pilgrims throughout time. The basis or scriptural model of footwashing is found in John 13. Jesus embodies the way we are to live in community with one another—not out of selfish ambition or conceit but in complete humility, regarding more highly the life of the other. The Lord of creation—on that night in which he enjoyed his last supper with his disciples and thus the night of his arrest—came to each disciple with a basin and towel and washed and then dried each one's feet. Simon Peter felt so awkward that he tried to get Jesus to stop doing it, but Jesus said that if he did not wash his feet, then Simon Peter would have no share in the life ministry of Jesus. Peter then asked that his whole body be washed.

The Lord and Teacher par excellence humbled himself to washing the feet of the lowly disciples. "If I, your Lord and Teacher, have washed your feet, you also ought to wash one another's feet. For I have set you an example, that you also should do as I have done to you. Very truly, I tell you, servants are not greater than their master, nor are messengers greater than the one who sent them. If you know these things, you are blessed if you do them" (John 13:14–17).

Armentrout and Lohfink rightly understand that we need these practices to remind us that the body of Christ on pilgrimage is a church in which we think of others more highly than we think of ourselves. After all, it is only out of the life, death, and resurrection event that the church came to be in the first place—and only on such a basis can the divisions that continually threaten our faith communities as a whole be overcome.[39]

Other Pilgrimage Rituals   There are three periods of time in each congregation's pilgrim life that rarely get our attention. The first is the beginning of a pilgrimage and the rituals of welcome that are often observed. For example, while on my first pilgrimage in New Mexico, each parish had representatives who would come out and greet us all, with their banner of the church's patron saint, and then march us into the church's sanctuary, singing us into their midst. Such welcome should occur in the church today.

The second period is when people are on the pilgrimage itself. On pilgrimages, we always sing songs, joke, pray, and encourage each other, in part reminding one another of our purpose. I was struck by the rituals of intensification at St. Patrick's Purgatory in which the most intense time of the pilgrimage was in the middle of the night and early morning as we kept moving onward and upward, not slowing down but speeding up in praying the prayers. The person who was responsible for leading us into this time of vigil prayers and movements kept on encouraging us throughout the night and cold morning hours.

The third period involves rituals of reaching destinations. On pilgrimage, there are not only the prayers and hymns sung when we depart for the pilgrimage, but there are also the rituals of returning or passing onward upon our return. When one is finished with a pilgrimage—a moment of gladness, tinged with sadness for the closing time of the pilgrimage together—there is a sense that we are now returning home. Martin Robinson notes that, upon the return of pilgrims to the place where they started, the "grateful pilgrims complete their journey with hymns and prayers in the place where they began. Worship helps to seal all that has taken place and points pilgrims to their ultimate destination."[40]

In the following chapter, I will explore the way that rituals of pilgrimage are a moral practice, where virtues shape character in the language, rituals, and the gestured performances in a growing, changing Christian life.

Chapter 9

The Character of the Pilgrim

By the tender mercy of our God,
  the dawn from on high will break upon us,
to give light to those who sit in darkness and in the shadow of death,
  to guide our feet into the way of peace.
                                        (Luke 1:78–79)

*I*n the Benedictine *Liturgy of the Hours*, one of the intercessory prayers begins, "God of mercy, you gave us new life through baptism, make us grow day by day in your likeness," and is followed by the refrain, "Lord, guide your people to walk in your ways." The prayer continues, "May our generosity today bring joy to those in need, in helping them may we find you. . . . Help us to do what is good, right and true in your sight, and to seek you always with undivided hearts."[1] I begin with this antiphonal prayer because it embodies one of the reasons for our growth: Our character, our very being, the core of who we are grows in the likeness of Christ on this pilgrimage. Through the performance of the gestured virtues of life—such as charity and generosity, self-control and humility, doing what is good, right, and true in Christ Jesus, and seeking unity with "undivided hearts"—the very core of our being is shaped and nurtured because of who we are as God's people.

On pilgrimage our character is shaped by the virtues we learn by living with one another along the pilgrim's way. The lessons that shape our character by highlighting which virtues we are to perform along the way involve more than giving the right answer on a final test in moral theology or Christian social ethics.

I am reminded on pilgrimage about the difference between *knowing* what is the good and right thing to do, *doing* the good and right thing, and *being* good. It is clearly important to know what is the right and good thing to do.

Without such knowledge, or without a community in which this knowledge is located and made accessible, we run the risk of not knowing the right and good thing to do in certain circumstances. However, the lessons that we know cognitively or intellectually may not be enough to actually lead us to practice or perform the gesture-laden virtue in a specific context, time, and group of people. Those who focus only on the abstract knowledge of virtue and character may not find an easily identifiable teacher to help guide them in an awkward situation that begs for a right and good act to be performed immediately. The one who thinks she or he is the teacher of virtues in the body of Christ needs always to be ready to be a student as well. Those who think they are the students in the life of the church might by God's prerogative be the teachers of virtue.

What makes teaching and learning the virtues of the Christian life an integral part of life's pilgrimage is simply this: One of the most powerful or dramatic ways of learning and teaching the virtues of life that shape our character as members of the body of Christ is right in the middle of life, sometimes in a crisis or conflict. Lessons of life are taught not only in a structured teacher-student classroom, where the teacher is the one with authority. On pilgrimage, it is amid the unplanned or unexpected experiences where pilgrims gain a deeper knowledge of who they are and where their abilities and inabilities may lie. On pilgrimage, one cannot help but learn about one's weaknesses and wounds, thereby gaining insight to where one's greatest fragility lies. One cannot help but learn the conflict between the virtues of hope, faith, love, forgiveness, joy, friendship, patience, self-control, and the vices paired with each virtue. These lessons about what matters in life may be learned on our pilgrimage and may last a lifetime. All the practices, gestures, rituals, and encounters with others on the pilgrimage serve as instructors, engaging our hearts, minds, and bodies, and may be more relevant than anything we have ever learned in a classroom.

The Shaping of Character and Learning of Virtues on Pilgrimage

One of the first graduate courses I taught on the subject of pilgrimage as education involved five white young men, all who were either in their third year in the master of divinity program or in the postgraduate master of theology program at Duke Divinity School. Throughout the semester we had read books on pilgrimage, and now, at the apex of the course, we were actually going to go on a pilgrimage. We would walk twenty-two miles over two days through bucolic fields and meadows. It is eternally green in this area of the country, the Piedmont area, even in the month of December.

On one early stretch of the road, the county sheriff pulled us over, inquiring as to what the cross and the six men carrying it were all about. In this part of the country, six white men and a cross did not mean the same thing as thirty pilgrims carrying a cross in northern New Mexico. Context matters in terms of interpreting gestures and symbols. In New Mexico, I was part of an activity sanctioned by the Catholic Church. It was part of the culture. In North Carolina, with so much Ku Klux Klan activity, we were a suspicious looking group, to say the least. I told the county sheriff that we were walking a pilgrimage as part of a course at Duke University, which seemed all right with him.

Having begun our trek at ten o'clock in the morning, it was late afternoon when we walked along Franklin Street in Chapel Hill, a main thoroughfare for the University of North Carolina's "flagship" campus. It is a street accustomed to seeing protesters for one cause or another, with a group of Goths usually huddled around the downtown post office and courthouse, or a card table set up for people who are protesting for peace in the Middle East. On Halloween and when a university sports team wins a national championship, the streets are packed with thousands of students, alumni, and friends. Nevertheless, some university students, faculty and staff, townspeople and tourists, adults and children pointed at us as we walked silently along on the sidewalk with our six-foot, roughly hewn cross. Now and then someone would wave at us; one person stopped and genuflected in front of the cross as we walked by; yet others gave us the "peace" sign or reached out to shake our hands warmly.

In one city block, the unexpected confronted us, and we had a momentary learning experience of the communal virtues of Christian community. Three men, all African American and older than any of us, confronted us with small white boxes on which a message was written that they were homeless and hungry and needed money for the upcoming evening. "Have any spare change, mister?" said one of the beggars to the pilgrim holding the cross in front of the line. The student holding the cross stopped in his tracks, and we stopped with him, almost running into him. "What do we do?" asked the befuddled student to the other pilgrims. "I don't know" was the reply after a pause that lasted a minute longer than it should have. The three men asking for money waited patiently, smiling at us, watching as we tried to figure out the moral issues before us. Then the student holding the cross looked at the cross itself, and it dawned on him that he needed to do what Jesus would do in this situation. He should engage the men in conversation, listen to what they wanted, and probably give them what they asked for and needed, rather than telling them what he thought they wanted and needed. At that moment, the men asked again for money. We each dug into our pockets, put some money in each person's box, and began a conversation.

The importance of this unexpected lesson was lost on no one. I was surprised that it took such a long time for these students—all in their last years of seminary studies and serious scholars—to figure out what they should do in this situation. Clearly, each student knew intellectually what it would look like to do an act of justice and to live a virtuous life. Yet it was a wholly other thing to act justly or to incarnate Christ's justice and charity in a specific situation. While I wanted to tell them what to do, I was held back by the competing desire to let them figure it out on their own, believing that they would learn the lesson better without my interruption. It was a godly "teaching moment" for all of us when the unplanned and the unpredictable provided an educational opportunity.

That evening, while we were preparing for dinner, it was clear to all that one theological virtue learned along this pilgrimage was performing the gestures of Matthew 25: "I was hungry and you gave me food. . . . Just as you did it to one of the least of these who are members of my family, you did it to me." This was an incredible lesson to learn as we exegeted the passage from real life rather than in a classroom with books and commentaries. We struggled with the meaningfulness of the passage of Scripture as we faced those who were hungry and homeless, and we responded to the request. We did so against the claims of some that this money might not be spent for food or housing. Our gestures were tied to Matthew's Gospel in the very context of Chapel Hill life. We were performing gestures of virtue, gestures of Christ narrated by Scriptures that bound the community of pilgrims and strangers closer together.

But the lessons did not stop there. The next morning, while carrying the cross on a busy thoroughfare, we were stopped again, this time by a car with two African American men who wanted to know what our business was with the cross. We told them this was a class experience on pilgrimage. Satisfied with our answer, they went their way.

Further on down the road, one of the pilgrims developed severe muscle pains in one of his legs. We counseled each other and agreed that some of us would go racing forward to get assistance in the way of a car to pick up the hurting pilgrim, while the rest of us waited with the hurt sojourner.

By the end of the pilgrimage, all the pilgrims were amazed with the powerful lessons we learned along the way. Not one of these lessons was planned. The lessons of life happened along the way. The unexpected made the lessons of charity and justice that much more impressionable as we were immersed in the very drama of life itself. Scripture came alive in ways it never could in the context of a classroom. And each one of our lives was changed for the better.[2]

Shaping Character in the Christian Community on Pilgrimage

A person's character is not genetically inherited. The moral character of a person is taught, learned, and later revealed in patterns of behaviors and gestures. Alasdair MacIntyre writes that we learn from others who already possess the moral education—the kinds of virtues and thus character—that we may lack.[3]

It has been my experience that our very character—and the host of virtues and vices that shape our lives as pilgrims—is put to the test and realized along the unpredictable moments in our lifelong pilgrimage. By embodying the language, rituals, and virtue-laden gestures of the church, we have an opportunity to intentionally perform the virtue that will fit any given moment.

Traditionally, one of the primary reasons that one went on pilgrimage in the first place was because one had erred or blundered in one's personal life. As was mentioned earlier in the book, Edith and Victor Turner note that medieval pilgrims went with the high hopes of stripping themselves of their social personae and whatever hurt and heartache they brought upon themselves or their family and community, thus restoring through the rituals and encounters with the unexpected their individuality and their relationship with God that had been grievously hurt.[4] The virtues or vices that shape our character arise and are made known as we endure suffering in the soul, as well as in the mind and body. One goes to a place to be cured of the moral flaws that may cause physical, emotional, or spiritual pain. Consider the reason many go to Lourdes, St. Patrick's Purgatory, or Santiago de Compostela: for the sake of penance, to seek forgiveness for one's sins against God and the church, or for healing of a physical malady.

In a sense, the pilgrimage is an exteriorized mysticism, in which the private or personal mystical journey is made public, a journey in which the thoughts of one's heart and mind may be made visible or concrete. The physical or exterior pilgrimage thus becomes an allegory, well represented in such a pilgrimage text as John Bunyan's *Pilgrim's Progress* as a means for the person's body, mind, and spirit to journey back to God. Therefore, the way to seek reparation, to be forgiven for one's sinful ways, acts, gestures, or habits, is to go on pilgrimage. Pilgrimage, sin, and penance are bound together.

But along the way, as we read in so many pilgrimage texts, there are more virtues and vices to be considered. Consider the twin stories in Bunyan's

Pilgrim's Progress of his primary pilgrim, Christian, and of Christiana, his wife, and their sons. Christian encounters a series of persons, each of whom bears the name of a Christian virtue or vice, such as Obstinate, Mr. Worldly Wiseman, Hopeful, Faithful, and Talkative, to name just a few. Christian comes face-to-face with these various virtues and vices along the way, all personified. At times along the journey, Christian is challenged to practice one virtue or another, and these experiences influence his own personality, his interaction with others, and his moral way of being in the world. Through the relationships at certain crossroads, Christian is further excited, scared, bewildered, filled with hope, or lost in the "Slough of Despond," waiting to be pulled out by Help, of all people!

I am proposing that the lifelong pilgrimage we are all on is a sustained setting for educating Christians in the practices of virtue-laden gestures that embody the moral wisdom of the Christian church. Such virtues flourish in face-to-face relationships, where God in Christ is present. Wisdom, writes Gordon Jackson, is the "art of making good whatever life throws at us."[5] And behind it all is the God of creation, who is radically intimate with us—"a mystery we never fathom," writes David Ford.[6]

And what are the virtues that matter along this pilgrimage? The virtues of the Christian life are otherwise known as the "fruit of the Spirit" and are as follows: love, joy, peace, patience, kindness, generosity, faithfulness, gentleness, and self-control (see Gal. 5:22–23).[7] Learning the virtues of the Christian life along the pilgrim's way is done as follows:

First, we identify, name, and refer to the virtues and vices on pilgrimage. Patricia Hampl writes that sin, taken in the context of something like a spring journey, "is an incident along the longer, larger Way." She writes that "penitence is a trip toward life":

> It even looks like fun—a bunch of people on vacation. Here, with the Renaissance winking on the horizon, the medieval penitent seems to have the best of both public and private penance: Sin needn't be a shaming public exposure, and expiation needn't be a private hair-shirt, a half-step short of neurosis. Certainly pilgrimage as a form of expiation underscores the liberation that is meant to be at the core of the sacrament, the radiant lightness of the shriven heart.[8]

It is on the pilgrimage that is our life that we come face-to-face with and name what sin is and what the way of penance is. We go on pilgrimage for multiple reasons, but many of us do so because of the hurt we carry with us. Nancy Louise Frey writes that the journals of pilgrims show a multitude of reasons people go on pilgrimage: inner worlds that are askew, feelings of loss, failure, fear, shame, and addiction, which, if not tended to, will fester. Many people go on pilgrimage because of the control they feel certain vices have over their lives. Feeling marginalized and despondent over current conditions, people leave their home environment in search of a new land, a new beginning, a fresh approach to living.[9]

Paul Wadell reminds us that it is never enough to be ourselves. We have to grow, we have to be transfigured, which is a common occurrence on pilgrimage as we move from being sinners into accepting being friends of God. This is why we need to keep companions with us who can provide good company along the pilgrim's way. With friends, we can pursue a way of life together, growing and being transfigured or changed from sinners into friends of God.[10] Without friendships, we cannot grow and change in the way of the Christian life, for we will not know or be about the business of the good news and being good that we discover only in Christ.[11]

Consider the act of penance in the history of the Roman Catholic Church, in which it was understood that pilgrimage was actually a form of penance, and it was often imposed as a punishment for some secular offenses in the Middle Ages. The hardship of pilgrimage was thought to win the penitent God's forgiveness and grace. By voluntarily willing to undergo the unknown in pilgrimage, the devotee hoped for material favor, granted by the Holy of Holies at the shrine located at the destination point. Shrines became transformation or transfiguration stations between earthly and heavenly realms, in which sins, vices, and the necessity of the virtuous life were made all that much more real.[12]

Or consider the virtue of humility that is learned along the pilgrim's way. Kathleen Norris, on her own pilgrimage of sorts in the Dakota Plains, quotes Terrence Kardong as saying that the Great Plains is a "school for humility," because it is such an eccentric environment, making pilgrims of the land remember that we are not entirely in control.[13] Humility begins with the fear of God, with acknowledging the omnipresence of God in Christ. Humility is the act of lessening the self in the hope of increasing our awareness of God, whom we seek through ordinary events and experiences, such as pilgrimage.[14] In understanding that we are sinners and have fallen short of the glory of God, we are increasingly aware that our own frailty always exceeds that which we know of others. Therefore, we have no choice but to believe and understand that we are inferior to others, despite our background, skills, and education. Yet even though we are frail and fall short of God's glory, we are called by God in Christ "friends." Similarly, we are able to call one another brothers and sisters because each of us bears Christ to and with those among whom we live.[15]

Second, pilgrimage allows us to live the virtuous life.   There are long stretches of life as pilgrimage in which we are focused on continual movement, which may be painful, boring, or exhilarating.[16] In Paulo Coelho's pilgrimage, he wrote that the true path of wisdom is identified by three things: first, wisdom involves love on the way of pilgrimage. Second, wisdom is practical enough to be applied to life. Third, wisdom is a path that can be followed by anyone.[17] Along the way of the pilgrim, we will come to trials that test us in regard not only to our dedication to Christ but also to our compassion for one another. Time and again, we will be tested to name the virtue, to practice the virtue, and to apply the virtue to the situation that we are in at any given time along the pilgrimage. Opportunities to learn and teach the virtues of the Christian life come before us twenty-four hours a day, with no vacation from these educational moments in our character formation in the body of Christ. To live in Christ is to live always in an "educational" or "teaching" moment, if we accept the premise that life in the body of Christ is an ongoing pilgrimage.

Third, we are bound to relearn the virtuous life on Christian pilgrimage. The issue is making the virtuous life habitual, part of who and whose we are, and is ideally learned by approaching the life we live as a Christian pilgrimage. Living the virtuous life over the long haul takes practice, for every incident of life will call forth a reacquaintance with one of the virtues. Living the virtuous life will call upon us to be creative as we learn to live in fellowship with God, whose presence is all around us.[18]

Since God is the initiator of such virtues as grace, faith, and hope, and since we learn such virtues as self-control, charity, and perseverance through interactions with others in our daily lives on pilgrimage, as we are told to do in Scripture and taught to do through the lessons of the church's history, it will become clear that God is with us on this journey. As Paul Wadell reminds us, there is no way to God except that way to God made possible through God's grace. God is the initiator of our lives, and God in Christ is the pilgrim exemplar who is also the way of divine forgiveness and divine love.[19]

Patricia Hampl learned that life is like a pilgrimage when she traveled to Assisi. On this pilgrimage she learned the radical Christian idea that a people could be forged, be brought together, through the miracle of the imagination, or what Keats calls the "holiness of the heart's affections." It is in the most basic acts, like "eat this in remembrance of me . . . do this in remembrance of me . . . drink this in remembrance of me," Jesus' own words, that we discover on this pilgrimage a way out of the darkness of our own life. It is the way toward union with God, through union with others, as we are part of a tribe "seeking the All," writes Hampl.[20] In such things as the reaffirmation of our baptismal covenants, the celebration of the Eucharist, or footwashing, the virtues and vices of the Christian life are dramatized and tangible, made comprehensible for all the people of God of all ages, abilities, and ethnicities.

Martin Palmer notes that we take a risk in going on pilgrimage or living life as a pilgrimage. This is deeper than a physical risk; it is "the risk you might not return the same person who set out."[21] The risk is ever before us as we constantly learn and relearn to live and practice the gestures of grace, the gestures of faith, and the gestures of love, as well as other virtues. We may think we know what the risks are, only for our lives to blow apart because we failed to live faithfully, truthfully, or lovingly. There is not only the risk of things falling apart, but of joy that in entering the physical and metaphysical world of pilgrimage we will be taken beyond anything we could imagine. As Palmer writes, "True pilgrimage changes lives."[22]

Finally, as Coelho reminds us, God is not vengeful but is love. God's only punishment is to make someone who interrupts a work of love in one place of life to continue it somewhere else in life.[23] The struggle is always there before us not to interrupt God's good work in and for us. Bunyan's Christian shows us that while we are constantly facing the depths of hypocrisy and self-deceit on this lifelong pilgrimage, we are God's creatures who are forever being given opportunities to move onward, regardless of our unpreparedness for what lies before us. As Bunyan's Christian always has more than a second or third chance to right the wrongs in his life and the choices he makes, so do we.[24] We leave our homes to go on pilgrimage in order to find ourselves as we search for God. The familiar obscures the eternal, writes Martin Robinson, and so we move onward in life.[25]

Learning Virtues and Living the Moral Life
as Christ's Body on Pilgrimage

The challenge before us in the church is learning the virtues that shape not only the character of individual Christians but the very character of their Christian communities. The importance of living and practicing the virtues of the Christian life is a constant thread in the life of the church, from the simple act of hiring a pastor, a church musician, or a youth leader, to the more difficult discussions surrounding the ordination of gays or lesbians, the work of the church in peace movements, or the disciplining of someone who has violated a part of a church's life.

The occasion of learning the virtues in the body of Christ on pilgrimage and the shaping of the moral life may follow a similar pattern of processing as outlined in my story of encountering the hungry and homeless on the streets of Chapel Hill. We were immersed in the chaos of injustice, trying to think clearly and rationally of what we *should* do.

Pilgrimage in this earthly life brings us face-to-face with the injustices of the world. Basil Hume writes that the pilgrimage "cannot pass by the hungry masses or those who clamor for justice and the recognition of their human dignity. The pilgrim's mind and heart are fixed on far horizons but must never ignore or make light of injustice, pain, and deprivation here in the passing world. Each day provides for the pilgrim the tasks that have to be undertaken."[26]

One of the places that can try and test the heart, mind, and body of a Christian is a long, boring stretch along the pilgrim path. In the western portion of the United States, there are certain stretches of roadway that are straight and narrow and seem to go on forever toward a mountain that never seems to get closer. Rugged or barren wilderness can have the same hypnotic power. Gary Snyder writes that the wilderness can be a ferocious teacher, rapidly stripping down the inexperienced or careless.[27] The rugged and barren landscape can wear us down, making us vulnerable, able to be more candid than we normally would be when we are better rested and able to pretend or cope with the strain and stress of life.

What does the wilderness, the land, teach us? What is its methodology? We will explore these questions in the next chapter.

Chapter 10

The Land of Pilgrimage

Midway through life's journey, I was made aware that I had strayed into
a dark forest, and the right path appeared not anywhere.

(Dante, The Inferno*)*

In [God's] hand are the depths of the earth;
  the heights of the mountains are his also.
The sea is his, for he made it,
  and the dry land, which his hands have formed.
      (Ps. 95:4–5)

Wordsworth urged us to travel through landscapes to feel emotions that
may benefit our souls.

(Alain de Boton, The Art of Travel*)*

The Plains illuminate the inner landscapes. Watching a storm pass . . .
fills our soul with reverence.

(Kathleen Norris, Dakota*)*

*G*enesis makes it clear that the earth and the cosmos we live in were created
by God. The light of the day, the darkness, the seas, the dry lands, the air, and
the creatures are a result of God's doing. Many psalms repeat the refrain several times that the earth is the Lord's, that God created the depths of the earth,
the mountains, and the waters. The creation of the earth is God's gesture, as
are the gift of Christ to the world, ourselves, and the imagination that saw fit
to make us the church with one another.

On my pilgrimage to Chimayo, I was told that the Roman Catholic Church
was celebrating its four hundred years in that area with banners all over the
various small Catholic churches where we stopped and ate throughout the

week. But some pilgrims reminded me that God had been in this land long before the Catholic Church and that it is because of God that the land we walk upon is considered holy ground.

Our connection to and dependence upon the land, water, and air was reinforced on a trip to a museum I took with my son's kindergarten class. The museum's science teacher told us that the water on this earth is all the water that we have ever had since the world was first created. There is no possible way to bring water in from any other locale outside of this planet. Or as the teacher reminded us, we drink the water that dinosaurs first drank. With the increase in population on this planet, this seemingly renewable resource we now know to be limited.

Historically, pilgrimages have had different themes, depending on the time and culture of the pilgrimage. For example, in medieval Europe people went in search of historic relics of the saints, or to see the sights of the Holy Land. The early colonists of the United States were engaged in a pilgrimage over the sea, exploring new destinations. The American frontier pilgrimage of the nineteenth and early twentieth centuries went over land from the east coast to the west coast, charting the land. In Australia the early white settlers, like their American counterparts, explored a nation that was already inhabited by a native people, but they nevertheless gave themselves the titles of "explorers" and "discoverers" of a land and people.

In this book, much has been made about the people on pilgrimage. In this chapter, the focus is on the land, sky, and water. Not only do we move over land or through the water or air, but on pilgrimage the land, the water, and the air move through us as well.

Pilgrimage Stories of the Land, Sky, and Water

For four years, since I first went on pilgrimage to Chimayo, New Mexico, I took my classes at Duke Divinity School on pilgrimage in the great outdoors. For an introductory class on educating Christians, we would walk a two-hour pilgrimage, and for a class on pilgrimage as education, we would take an entire day, walking up to or over fifteen miles. It is amazing to see what an indelible impression such a venture has upon the students and the teacher. For example, we began each pilgrimage by building a cross to carry. The students first gathered in a large circle for instructions and were then sent out into a forested area to look for twigs and branches. They returned to the circle in a few minutes with a branch or stem that was no thicker than a finger and no longer than my hip to my toe. With twine in hand, or a natural vine twine, we bound the twigs and branches together as I pointed out that fragments of the cross of Christ could be found within the local area that very day, for the earth is the Lord's, who is creating a new heaven and a new earth with us. Along the pilgrim way, we took flowers, scraps of paper with Bible verses, and leaves, sticking them to or into the cross so that at the end of the journey the cross was filled with bits and pieces of our experience as God's pilgrims.

I relearned the importance of teaching Christians about earth, sky, water, and fire while on the first early morning walk in northern New Mexico when we pilgrims were passed by a large, shaggy, smelly, chocolate brown elk that ignored us completely. Horses, on the other hand, were suspicious of our line of thirty pilgrims, which undulated snakelike on the road. The horses charged us in their protected pens, fearing the snake before them—us! Meanwhile, cows nearby chewed their cud and grass as we walked by. In the early morning hours as we left towns, dogs barked to protect their property. In my mind I thought they were wishing us well, perhaps telling us "Bon voyage" as we woke them from their sleep.

Those of us who walk the land on pilgrimage, or who ride over it in a wheelchair, are reminded that this experience is different from riding in a minivan over the interstate highway system or flying over the land in a plane. We pilgrims feel like the tortoise compared to the faster hares of modern travel. When walking on a pilgrimage, however, the crusty surface of the earth becomes far more fascinating. For example, when walking I am far more aware of the dips and bumps in the roadway, and the small creeks and rivulets that cross the soil. I smell the putrid aroma of a dead animal, once a deer, now torn apart by vultures and other birds. On one pilgrimage, I sat in a field full of ticks, then suddenly became aware of them as they crawled over my white socks and up my hairy legs. I appreciate anew the gift of a large shade tree on a hot, cloudless summer day.

In Rancho de Taos there was a team of young people from the church mending the walls of the adobe structure and the giant wall that made for an entrance space. I saw the wooden beams and layers of straw and mud being applied on the beamed framework, with the young people smoothing the rough texture with their bare hands. Inside, the white walls and the bare wooden beams of the ceiling were dramatic in their height. The uneven and rough wooden flooring of the sanctuary itself created the feeling of walking on waves. In Taos Pueblo itself, the church looked like it rose from the ground, with the reddish-brown mud of the adobe church the same as the ground color.

We were nearing the end of the pilgrimage to Chimayo. We left Rancho de Taos and walked steadily to Carson National Park, nine miles up a zigzagging road over a mountain pass toward the town of Penasco. The road is called "US" not out of patriotism, but because it first makes a big "U" shape and then is followed by an even longer "S" pattern. Suddenly, without warning, against the dark blue sky of early morning, there was a sudden rip of brilliant white light bursting from a nearby military base. A rocket shot forward into the stillness of white stars and crescent moon. After this initial burst, all that was left was a mist of gaseous substance that soon disappeared into nothingness. One of the pilgrims whispered in my ear, "Roswell is nearby—aliens, *X Files*, intrigue, mystery, wonder. . . ."

I turned around before we entered the heavily forested area and saw spread before me the city of Taos set against the mountainside, looking like a collection of sparkling diamonds placed upon a jeweler's black velvet cloth. The sounds of nature that early morning were everywhere, yet their sources were invisible to the naked eye: the chirping of crickets, the howling of a wild dog, the scurrying of chipmunks near roadways, the flapping of a bat's wings, or a falcon gliding on a gust of wind, whispering "whose" as she searched for a morning meal. The opening lines of a hymn, "This is my Father's world, and to my listening ear," sprang to mind.

Throughout the trek, the drama of this land fit my life, giving me daily sustenance while nurturing and refreshing my soul. Unlike North Carolina's dense corridors of pine and kudzu-laced poplar trees, the terrain of New Mexico fit my life of extreme moods. I marveled at the vast sweep of desert land interrupted by the verdant arroyos, these magnificent rock-striated chasms scarring the otherwise parched land, filling it with water and bounteous deciduous trees and teeming with life. That morning, jagged mountains topped with snow came into view through the outstretched arms of the crucified Christ in my hands as I carried the *guia* into the high country. As St. Paul wrote to the Colossians (1:15–18), this land is God's land, and Christ, the firstborn of this new heaven and new earth, has and is redeeming it, ruling over all that surrounds us. He rules over the scruffy pine trees and the other soaring evergreen trees with brown underbrush that hides the dawdling porcupine, the hungry eagle soaring on the air current through the mountain pass. The land throbs with life; it pulsates with the steady hum of creatures that are born, live, and die upon the earth and is shaped to rugged perfection by swiftly changing weather patterns, falling trees, rolling rocks, and four seasons of the year. The slightly nuanced texture of God's land breaks open into beautiful vistas that are more fantastic than the mind's eye can take in all at once. Who are we who strut through and over God's ever changing creation with the perverse assumption that our twisted powers even come close to rivaling the Creator's handiwork?

We prayed that morning, "With beauty before me, may I walk; with beauty behind me, may I walk. . . . Wandering on a trail of beauty, lively I walk," stressing "lively" with imaginative glee. A genuine sense of wonder and thanksgiving to God filled my entire being as I marveled at the creation surrounding me. Georgia O'Keeffe was astute in her observation that Christianity is like a veil over the land as Christ's spirit permeates all that was, is, and will be in this earth.

Finally arriving in Chimayo, we found in the middle of a small adobe chapel on the side of a larger sanctuary a hole in which the soil is said to be sacred. Touching, tasting, smearing one's brow with it, even smelling it, are said to have curative properties. This idea of tasting soil for curing what ails one is found also in Esquipulas, Guatemala, where I was given a small clay-like brick, *Pan del Señor*, with an impression of a cross, crucifix, or imprint of a Christian medallion on it. A friend tells me that in the past many of the people believed that when they ate the clay when they were ill, whether that illness was of mind, body, or spirit, they would be healed. The ingestion of such gritty earth is novel to this Protestant mouth.[1]

Reflections on Pilgrimage Stories of the Land

The lack of attention in the way we educate Christians today regarding our place upon this earth and our role as caretakers of this creation that God has given us has only recently become a cause of concern in the church universal. Writers such as Wes Jackson, Wendell Berry, Thomas Berry, Barry Lopez, David James Duncan, Edward Abbey, Annie Dillard, Terry Tempest Williams, and William Least Heat Moon—to name a few—have shown us that seeing, knowing, touching, and smelling the earth is not only good for the earth but good for us as well. Another way to sharpen our senses and awareness of the environment is by going on a pilgrimage.

Our awareness of the earth and our connection to it is a phenomenon of the last half of the twentieth century. As rainforests face the danger of extinction, we find more and more natural, homeopathic cures that are right under our feet, from St. John's Wort for depression to aloe leaves for burns. The rising use in Western medicine of herbal remedies long practiced among Eastern healers has been nothing short of dramatic. That the plants around us may actually provide ways to bolster our immune system against the common cold is an amazing discovery. What we take to be common weeds in our backyards may have curative power. Plenty of sun, water, simple exercise— all natural—can also help keep us healthy. Belden Lane holds that our place in the land reminds us of our humanity, our creaturehood, our limits, our brokenness and lack of certainty about life, and therefore our dependency upon the grace of God that bursts forth from absurd and unpredictable sources.[2]

A necessary part of pilgrimage, especially the pilgrimage that is the Christian life, is coming to know the earth, the land, the air, and the sky that we inherit, and understanding why we are drawn to them. To be caretakers of this earth we have been given is to move from a place of self- or human importance to a place of adventure in the world where, as Annie Dillard says, the holy is stuffed into it. Dillard continues:

> God is subtle, but not malicious. Again, Einstein said that "nature conceals her mystery by means of her essential grandeur, not by her cunning." It could be that God has not absconded but spread, as our vision and understanding of the universe has spread, to a fabric of spirit and sense so grand and subtle, so powerful in a new way that we can only feel blindly of its hem. It is making the thick darkness a swaddling band for the sea, that God sets "bars and doors" and said "Hitherto shalt thou come, but no further." But have we come even that far? Have we rowed out to the thick darkness, or are we all playing pinochle in the bottom of the boat?[3]

Dillard took the time to go on pilgrimage in her own backyard to investigate Tinker Creek in Virginia. She calls creation an "extravagant gesture":

> After the one extravagant gesture of creation in the first place, the universe has continued to deal exclusively in extravagances, flinging intricacies and colossi down aeons of emptiness, heaping profusions of profligacies with ever-fresh vigor. The whole show has been on fire from the word go. I come down to the water to cool my eyes. But everywhere I look I see fire; that which isn't flint is tinder, and the whole world sparks and flames.[4]

The Importance of Land, Sky, and Water
in the Church's Pilgrimage

How much does the land shape our pilgrimage in this Christian life? I was told often in Lindisfarne, England, that the northern part of the country has the footsteps of pilgrims all over it but that since they have not been used often in recent times, the trails of the pilgrims are now lost. Philip Cousineau writes that pilgrimage seems to come almost naturally to Tibetans with their ritualistic circling around mountains and sacred spaces. They are far more aware of the sacred awakened by mountains that reveals a reality that has a power for them to transform life.[5] Cousineau suggests that even we who are

Christians may make or transform the very ground beneath us into holy ground. Whether it is the Appian Way in Italy or the parking lot near where we work or go to school, if we walk the contemplative walk, a sacred walk in which we watch and listen more attentively to life around us despite our being bombarded by sights and sounds that try to distract us, we make the ground holy.[6] There are three important reasons why we need to consider carefully the place of land, sky, and water on our Christian pilgrimage.

First, pilgrimage is a way of rediscovering the earth.   Since Abraham and Sarah lived as nomads, and since Jesus spent forty days in the wilderness, the God of the desert has thrived on what Belden Lane calls "fierce landscapes," which force God's people into wild and wretched climes where trust (of and in God) must be absolute. God's people are deliberately forced into the desert, an exacting exercise of "radical faith."[7] God knows that the edges of the world, considered by some to be godforsaken, are where God in Christ's identity as Messiah has to be revealed. This was true in the case of Jesus, whose messiahship was tested and tried in the wilderness for forty days. During this time Jesus came to understand better the trials and tribulations that he would face as the world's messiah. Out in the wild, in the wilderness, anything can happen, for God is found often on the outer edges of human experiences.[8]

The land, sky, and water teach us about our relationship to God in a variety of ways. For example, stand at the ocean's edge in the middle of a storm. The power of the waves slapping upon the shoreline, rising higher than a two-story house and slapping the earth again, reminds us of our smallness and lack of power. We come to know God in a different way than if we are simply reading about the power and wondrous love of God in a classroom, tucked away from the drama and humor of creation.

Second, pilgrimage reveals God in earth's details.   We often miss the beauty before us because our eyes, ears, noses, and fingers fail to stop long enough to pay attention to our surroundings. It usually takes a friend's visit to remind us of the beauty of where we live. Though we are shaped by the spaces where we live, we fail to pay attention to them because we are focused on what is right before us. Throughout the ages pilgrims have sought wisdom about life at large through going on pilgrimages in perilous places. Yet there are lessons to learn of life in the God who is present in the wide-open lands and tree-heavy forests right around us. The sons and daughters of Israel traveled for over forty years in the wilderness. It was this sojourn to which the pilgrims who came to the American shores in the 1600s compared themselves.[9]

Lane writes that there are two ways of describing the mystery of God: the way of darkness and the way of light.[10] Junichiro Tanizaki says that Westerners wrote about the "mysterious Orient" because they could cut off the light from an empty space, "imparting a world of shadows that formed there a quality of mystery and depth superior to that of any wall painting or ornament." Those who are from a country in Asia tend to "seek our satisfactions in whatever surroundings we happen to find ourselves, to content ourselves with things as they are; and so darkness causes us no discontent, we resign ourselves to it as inevitable. If light is scarce, then light is scarce; we will immerse ourselves in the darkness and there discover its own particular beauty."[11] Meanwhile, Westerners try to brighten up their lots with many lights. There is something about the darkness of shadows that provides a mystery representing age, depth, perhaps wisdom, and a beauty that is lost when light comes upon it. God is in the shadows. And God is also light.

In lightness and darkness we go on pilgrimage to discover God in the world. On the one hand, we walk with Bunyan's pilgrim through the wilderness of this world that God created.[12] We go on this pilgrimage believing that we will find something—God, friendship, ourselves, and others. In part, pilgrimage stories are about moving through the landscape, learning from the odd encounters, refuges, refugees, and people. The journey brings a powerful feeling of being guided toward a goal that may or may not be in view.

On the other hand, the places where we walk move through us as well. There is an imprinting of some kind that goes on, by which we remember vividly images of the desert, sounds along the way, the feeling of the sun's heat on our shoulders, the pain of a pebble in our shoes. These all make a distinct impression that we cannot shake off. The landscape marks the body. There is a growing awareness of how our bodies act and react upon different terrains or upon the sea, depending on where the pilgrimage takes us.

Alain de Boton believes that sublime places repeat in grander terms lessons that ordinary life typically introduces. The universe is mightier than we are, and we are frail and temporary with no alternative but to accept limitations on our will. We are the playthings of forces beyond our control. The vast spaces of nature provide us with the finest, most respectful reminder of all that exceeds us and goes beyond us.[13]

Third, there is solace in the high country, the deserts, and the shorelines of life.   Lane writes that there is an "unaccountable solace that fierce landscapes offer to the soul," the benefits of which provide for us a period of silence in the high-volume chatter of this world, the possibility of the comfort of prayer, and a sense of divine presence not to be sought as an end in itself but as a place in which we may reconnect with the God of creation who is still creating.[14] There are long stretches of silence along the pilgrim way during which we keep moving—whether we are in pain, bored, or exhilarated. With our fellow pilgrims we pray, think, meditate, or sing.[15] We tend to overlook these terrains until we are given pause to reflect upon them. Prompted by God, we may find in the solitude a sense of awe and wonder as we graciously accept the great, unfathomable events that disturb our lives and inevitably turn us back to dust.[16] "Dust to dust, ashes to ashes" are the words we say at the time of burial and on Ash Wednesday.

On pilgrimage we find places of wide diversity, in which one person's oasis is another person's desert, and vice versa. What matters to the individual is the land on which we grow up, or the geography that best fits our mind, body, and spirit and that seems to dictate where a person's place of solace or oasis is amid life's rough times. I have friends who love the wide-open plains of western Kansas, while others thrive in mountainous western Colorado. There are those who need to live in a place that is tropical, while others love winter.

Of Chapels, Shrines, and Churches: Sculpting Sacred Space

An important part of pilgrimage, tied to destination (see chapter 12) as well as to the focus of this chapter, has to do with the churches, chapels, and shrines that one comes upon during a pilgrimage. Both the outside and the inside of a chapel, shrine, or church is a living testimony of God's people in a certain place. Mircea Eliade believed that every shrine is an archetype of a sacred center, marked off from the profane space around it, where heaven and earth intersect and there exists the possibility of the holy breaking through. That is why pilgrimage sites are closely associated with manifestations of the Divine. It explains the human propensity to approach the Divine in such places.[17]

Within these chapels, shrines, and churches, there is an attempt to sculpt the sacred space. Architects are designers not only of the materials they use but of the sense of space they try to achieve within a building or structure. There are those spaces that draw a person's vision upward—a Gothic cathedral, for example. Without such a soaring ceiling our eyes may be brought to look right and left toward the walls with their sculpture or furniture arrangement; when there is a large mosaic pattern on the floor, we may look downward.

Within the walls of a place of worship, the process of interior design is evident, including the placement of furniture, art, lamps, tables, and pictures or a cross on the walls, and perhaps mobiles, along with lights, hanging from the ceiling. All of these human-made objects, structures, and designs are attempts to craft or shape holy space. Created in the image of God, we depend upon material objects, textures, forms, and colors to envision the world God has given us, and to envision the holy as well. Thus, we have the sacred rituals and sacraments of water, bread, and wine to remind us of God's presence in our lives in the past, present, and future. W. Paul Jones writes that the earth is a Eucharist in which the wheat to make the bread and the grapes for the wine are of this earth, and his hermit life is the chalice.[18] There is something incarnational about the land, the sky, and the water where we live and in which we therefore may find the holy as pilgrims.[19] Indeed, as Walter Brueggemann notes, the world itself is remade each time the liturgy of the church is reenacted, as God is doing a new thing each time Christ's people gather in prayer, sing the hymns, pour the water, break the bread, drink the wine, and walk the earth.[20]

On the other hand, the words of the people of Esquipulas resonate within me: "The Christ you seek you will not find unless you bring him with you." What makes the chapel, shrine, or church a sacred space is the people within whom the sacred resides. The pilgrim body is a conduit of knowledge, a medium of communication, and the means of connecting. We are, as pilgrims of Christ, agents of social change.[21]

Perhaps the challenge for us this day is to remember that the holy resides within each one of us, rather than in inanimate objects. However, one cannot dispute the power of a place that feeds our imagination and sense of holiness, whether that place holds a relic of St. Benedict or the pulpit where the Reformer John Knox preached in Edinburgh. After all, we look at the books of Jane Austen and plays by William Shakespeare in the libraries of England, and we are in awe.

Land, Sky, and Water on the Body of Christ's Pilgrimage

One way to remember the place of land, sky, and water is by being sure these three elements, along with fire, are represented in our worship spaces. For earth we may have plants in the places where we worship, bouquets of flowers, or a single rose in a large sanctuary. One of the most dramatic presentations of earth I have seen was the bare limb of a tree shooting out of a big clay pot and rising over seven feet into the air in the middle of the white-washed Sacred Heart Chapel in St. Benedict's Monastery during Lent. I have taken to having pots of dead tree branches decorating the chapel space at other churches where I am pastor. These branches are exchanged for lilies at

Easter, a pattern that keeps changing throughout the church year. For sky, I hang ribbons and banners from the ceiling. For water, I touch and stir the water in the large stone baptismal font in Sacred Heart Chapel, with its small invisible pump pumping in and disturbing the water throughout worship.

Another practice that I have taken up with groups of pilgrims during the summer months is going in the evening to a large meadow or area that is free from both trees overhead and lights from a city at night. We take blankets and pillows outside, or perhaps sleeping bags, and lie down. Our task is to focus on the moon and a star. By staying focused, with our heads held perfectly in place, we see that we are actually moving. This gives us a sense of place in our universe.

A similar experience during the day when on pilgrimage is watching the movement, placement, and length of shadows along our way. Both of these exercises, along with the changes in our spaces of worship, remind us of our movement upon this earth. The moon and the sun are moving, as we are, by being on this orbiting planet.

On our pilgrimage journey we are bound to experience many different kinds of landscapes, places on the water, and perhaps spaces in the air as well. The next chapter focuses on an aspect of pilgrimage that the land may call us to, namely, solitude and prayer. John Main says that faith is tied not necessarily into words but into silence. The test and sign of faith is silence that is neither sullen nor timid. It is a silence that speaks for itself.[22]

Chapter 11

Contemplation on Pilgrimage:
Solitude and Prayer

> *Contemplation is not a vacation from life. Contemplation is the pursuit of meaning. Those who find the will of God everywhere are the real contemplatives.*
>
> *(Joan Chittister,* Wisdom Distilled from the Daily*)*

Somewhere along a pilgrimage there is, to paraphrase Qoheleth, a time to talk and a time to be silent, a time for community that is united in its speaking and a time to be community known for its faithful silence and hopeful solitude. There is a time for great action and a time for contemplative living. It is a balancing act of sorts, though it leads neither to a place of rest nor to true equilibrium. It is a never-ending balancing act of the life of doing, producing, and performing—and also being contemplative.[1] Solitude and the contemplative life are not taught in Sunday schools, let alone in youth groups or many adult Bible studies. For years, it seems that many Protestants kept solitude and contemplation in the realm of "things Catholic" and not often to be discussed. But today, more seminaries, institutions of higher education, and retreat centers are investing time and talent in creating programs and continuing education courses on the themes of solitude and contemplation.

At the core of the contemplative life is the deeper longing to take off the masks and costumes we wear to satisfy other people. With this longing we strive by God's grace to be loved for who and whose we are, rather than always seeking favor through what we do, say, look like, perform, or produce. Parker Palmer writes that contemplation is any way "that we can unveil the illusions that masquerade as reality and reveal the reality behind the masks. . . . Contemplation happens any time that we catch the magician deceiving us and we get a glimpse of the truth behind the trick."[2] Writing as one whose life is based upon performing well before oneself and others for praise, I must conclude that this is easier said than done. Freedom from feeling the need to perform and from seeking acceptance through a "job well done"—that is, being courageous enough to just be in God, to receive God's abundant and salvific grace—is an extraordinary gift. It is also a gift that seems elusive at best. The contemplative life undermines the driven, consumer culture of modern society, where our value is based upon what we do rather than whose we are.

The contemplative aspect of pilgrimage is not all sunshine and roses. I have found that it is in walking in different landscapes, with a new group of people, that I may best see the reality behind my veils of illusions. This is the true gift of contemplation. Learning to contemplate and growing in the contemplative life is another aspect of how we are growing and changing in the pilgrimage of our lives.[3] The life of prayer and solitude may also cause great strife. I have felt like Job on occasion in this pilgrimage of life, praying as I sat and pondered my out-of-control life. I have come to appreciate that the prayer of *this* pilgrim—to be more aware of the illusions I live with in my life—is an attempt to be in a more authentic, more transparent relationship to God and others. But as one friend wisely reminded me, "Be careful what you pray for, because you might get it!" That is what has happened. While the prayer sounded good and sincere at first, I did not think God would take me up on the request. In order to live a more honest and thus more faithful life, there were certain parts of my life that had to be addressed in order for me to be the person God wants me to be. Where was God amid the questions I was raising? In the fierceness of God's grace I discovered God anew. There were no comforting words, just the fury and fantastic brightness of the light of Christ. I read the Psalms and confessed the sins (Ps. 51 leading my lips), seeking comfort, but I found the fierceness of grace throwing me into a place of desolation and want. The trick for me is living in the questions of this life as I search for and struggle in my relationship with the holy. This earthly pilgrimage is not a form of escapism; rather, it thrusts us deeper into the muck and mire of a faith that defies words or images. It demands we listen to the hushed voice of God. What follows is a compilation of moments on various pilgrimages where I discovered the necessity of prayer and came to savor the solitude of the active yet contemplative life, which I found on many pilgrimages.

Pilgrimage Stories of Solitude and Prayer

On the pilgrimage to Chimayo, there were thirty-minute periods sprinkled throughout each day when we would walk but not talk among ourselves. The span of thirty minutes was for prayer, for silence, for just being. For someone who was working in a theological seminary during this time, whose "worth" was dependent upon what I produced and said, from articles and books to sermons and lectures, this time of silence, of just walking, swinging my arms, and focusing on the land, was novel if not plain weird at first.

The first few times I walked in silence I was still bound to and hounded by *chronos* time. I tried to gauge how many minutes I was in silence, waiting to see when I could talk again. I counted how many steps I would have to walk before we could begin to talk again. Needless to say, the desire to talk, to do, to be active, to be productive, was the first thing on my agenda.

But on the second day I began to let go of *chronos* time and enter *kairos* time, what W. Paul Jones calls those "special moments when God is particularly present for God's own particular reason." Jones calls Jesus the *Kairos* of all *kairoi*, "that special Incarnation that appeared in the 'fullness of time.'"[4] What I especially feared during these times of silence was that most of my life was caught in the doing, the producing, the performing cycle of activities. Silence was not only audible but deafening to me and eerily haunting. I remembered being on a "silent retreat" in my young twenties, sitting on the deck of a home overlooking the Atlantic Ocean near Cape Henlopen, Delaware, led by one who was masterful in leading such retreats. During that time I felt the mask that I presented to the world slipping slowly from my face. Every time I tried to push the mask back on, it would slip even quicker.

On this first pilgrimage, as with the experience at Cape Henlopen, I found myself talking to myself, the pace hastening onward as I grew more uncomfortable with the silence. Everyone else around me had their eyes on the ground, perhaps counting steps as well but not acknowledging it. Out of desperation I wanted to shout. The quiet of other people's lives scares us. We talk to those who are in crises, hoping that our talk will calm our nerves, rarely thinking of the other person's nerves. We become like Job's friends, not wanting at all to switch places with Job but visiting upon him our wise counsel. We may come to a place of silence not because we are comfortable with it but, having thrown all the words we can at Job, we know of nothing better to do.

I am a Presbyterian minister of the *Word* (and Sacrament). Presbyterians are well known for our ability to use words adroitly and with theological exactness. Presbyterians like words and the sound of our words in describing in great detail God and the nature of all that is holy. I was not taught prayer and solitude when I was a student at Princeton Theological Seminary. Writing out of that strange world between Catholicism and Presbyterianism, Belden Lane states that kataphatic, or affirmative, theology makes "generous usage of metaphor and analogy in describing the mystery of God. It is concrete and incarnational, speaking of the divine by way of vivid imagery and storytelling." It operates on the "metaphorical character of all thought. God is father and lover, judge and friend, raging fire and still small voice."[5] God is mindful of our discomfort. God is wise to our neurotic willfulness, to our stubborn streak, to our stiff-necked quality, and knows full well that the silence of God does not rest well within us. We clamor, as children seeking a parent's attention, to get God's attention, clawing our way, banging doors, taking a passive-aggressive approach to the Holy of Holies, as if such human tantrums will change God's mind.

On the pilgrimage to Chimayo, I remember when my sense of frustration with silence began to subside and I became more welcoming of the growing mindfulness in my life. The steps of my walk became a rhythm for my thinking, which was lyrical and beheld its own quiet tune. I experienced an increasing consciousness of God, of what was going on within me, and of my relationships with others and the world around me. Others around me also grew quieter, or so it seemed. Soon, I came to crave the times of silence on pilgrimage. I yearned for the solace, inviting the quiet moments when I did not have to think of any witty remarks or engage in any discussions with anyone else. Keeping an eye on the roadside to my left, the person in front of me, and the road debris on the right, I found myself welcoming silence and solitude, listening to the shuffle of our feet on the loose gravel on the side of the road. We were pilgrims of God. Soon the time that seemed to stretch toward eternity was flying by me. Before I knew it, the time of silence was over and we were talking. On the third day of the pilgrimage, I discovered that we walked quicker when we were silent than when we talked. Talking tends to slow us down, but walking in rhythm, in the silence, in the solitude, frees us up to concentrate on the things that matter in life and quickens our pace.

In the Christian community of L'Arche, Jean Vanier insisted that people become comfortable with being—just being in God and with one another—without the worry, the hassle, the cover of doing for, to, and by others. The question was this: Can we just be the persons God created us to be? Or is such a thought so frightening that we cover it over with activity after activity, doing, hiding, masquerading as someone we are not, and following someone else's agenda for us with little regard about ourselves? Real contemplation, real solitude, does not take us out of reality. On the contrary, writes Joan Chittister, it puts us in touch with the world around us by giving us the distance we need to see where we are more clearly headed. Contemplation or solitude is the ability to see the world and ourselves through God's eyes. Contemplation reminds me of our holy obligation to care for the world we live in and are members of. It is a pursuit of meaning as we discover, in the deep quiet, a fuller sense of who we are in God and feel the presence of God everywhere.[6]

The Place of Solitude and Prayer in a Prayerful Life on Pilgrimage

Solitude and prayer are part and parcel of any pilgrimage. While they are usually inextricably bound together, solitude is more a way of being in the world and may or may not involve action on our part, while prayer is not only an act but a way of being in the world.

Solitude on Pilgrimage   Important for all pilgrimages is the state of being solitary, without others, in a time of aloneness or remoteness. This is not to be confused with radical or hyperindividualism. Rather, solitude may be achieved and maintained in a crowded room. It is not that we are now disconnected from life but that we are more connected to the life in Christ and the communion of saints when we are in solitude and prayer. To be in solitude means that one's intercourse with the world is at a minimum. It is not the same as being alone, nor is being in a state of solitude the same as loneliness. One can be alone and not in solitude if one is filled with fear and foreboding, anxious to quell the uncertainties of life with being busy. One may be in a state of solitude yet be around a large gathering of people, be lonely yet not be in solitude. One may be in prayer while in a state of solitude, or just simply be.

Those who have shown me the art and the act of solitude in an exemplary fashion are my sisters and brothers who practice the life of the hermit. I have been in monasteries and abbeys that include a certain number of hermits, who are on a kind of spiritual pilgrimage, learning to live in the space of "As if . . ." or the subjunctive, writes W. Paul Jones. To be in solitude is to find that place that is like our personal sanctuary, to which we can escape from the clamor and distractions of daily living—where, in the healing touch of quiet, we can reduce life to its basics. Jones adds that living in solitude is to not miss the important in the unimportant, such as sunrise and sunset, winter and summer.[7]

Jones went on his own pilgrimage from being an ordained minister in the United Methodist Church to becoming a Roman Catholic monk. He found that being on a pilgrimage as a hermit was hard at first, that in losing everything he experienced a sort of emptiness. This was followed by a sense of oneness, of acceptance of his place in God's cosmos. Finally, he experienced a sense of illumination, in which he felt himself totally dependent upon God.[8] To be in this space of illumination, in the embrace of such a life, is to live fully in the words of the Westminster Shorter Catechism: to glorify God and enjoy God forever.[9]

What this meant for Jones was the withdrawal from all protections and the busyness and noise of life that kept him from encountering the solitude of his existence. This is to live an authentic life, rather than a life that is false and full of pomposity or pretentiousness. When we withdraw, we discover that the "enemy" of our happiness and joy in Christ is not the "other," whoever the other may be, but we ourselves: "I become the serious problem for me," writes Jones.[10]

For Belden Lane, the pilgrimage in the desert—whether it is the geographical desert, the desert of a "waiting room of radiation oncology, the nursing home . . . or the AIDS hospice nearby"—is a place of learning the life of solitude and the life of prayer.[11] After all, says Flannery O'Connor, sickness may be more instructive in some respects than a long trip to Europe if you want to learn something about life.[12] As Jones discovered, so has Lane: In the hermitages and the deserts of life, we will find the benefits of silence, of solitude, as well as the comfort of prayer and a sense of the divine presence, but these are not to be sought as ends in themselves.[13] Rather, it is because of God, who is always here, though we may not be aware in what ways God is manifest in the world today, that we are brought to a place, to people, to a span of time in which we may focus on the solitude of life amid the crowded roadways of pilgrimage.

Discovering solitude on pilgrimage came to me as a complete surprise. When I was told that we would have thirty minutes for prayer and solitude on the initial pilgrimage to Chimayo, I was scared of having so much time. There were no books for me to hide behind or read, there was no music to listen to, no play or movie to watch, no artwork to focus on, no opportunity to "people watch" like at an airport. Instead, there was just the trudging of footsteps, one after another, in a barren desert landscape.

Begrudgingly I began this span of time focusing on the footsteps before me, with a strong desire to talk to someone, anyone, though that was forbidden. So I wallowed in silence, not knowing what to do next. Then I remembered a time in North Carolina when I suddenly escaped from the routine of my life and ran to the North Carolina Zoo in Asheboro in the middle of the week and spent an entire afternoon there without telling a soul. I smiled broadly as I remembered that time of clearing out my head of ideas and thoughts that were troubling me so much. For over an hour, I watched polar bears swim in their tank. I was satisfied with life. I did not feel it was a waste of time. I came back home refreshed that evening.

Suddenly, those thirty minutes of silence became a greater joy. The solitude's gift was discovery of the things in this world that God has made possible, that make me not only happy, but fulfilled and pleased and settled and less anxious. I began to crave the thirty minutes of silence. The solitude was not aloneness but a sense of satisfaction with the self in God and God in me, in us.

Prayer on Pilgrimage   The connection between solitude and prayer on pilgrimage may be this: We worship a God who is a "door-kicking God," who breaks through our self-protective barricade, and who may scare us into prayer.[14] Another way of connecting solitude and prayer is this: Prayer is a pilgrimage, a journey unlike all others. John Main writes that if we make the pilgrimage of prayer we do so by becoming still, which is what we attempt to be in times of solitude and contemplation. He says that progress is in the stillness and that accepting the stillness of the now, of God, leads us into the eternal.[15] Of course, this runs counter to how we currently understand education, growth, and change in the life of the world, as well as in many churches. But does not God often speak in the still, small voice?

Jones writes that without prayer as a powerful viability, "God is a less honest word than Nothingness." Why do we say "in the name of Christ" at the end of our prayers? "Life is a procession marching to a death chamber unless the crucified one leads the way," writes Jones.[16] The centrality of prayer and solitude is well told in the story of the anonymous nineteenth-century Russian peasant in *The Way of a Pilgrim*. This pilgrim wants to find the way of prayer, because he has found that true knowledge and wisdom are practiced by those who know the ceaseless prayer, otherwise known as the Jesus Prayer. This short prayer is simply "Lord Jesus Christ, have mercy on me," repeated time and again, until it becomes the ostinato pattern of one's existence.[17] Why this short prayer? Because it contains the summary of the gospel, and the hope of the pilgrim is that by ceaselessly reciting it, there following the injunction of Scripture to pray always, God may respond.[18] The pilgrim is open and receptive, earnestly hoping and searching for a method of prayer to satisfy his longing for uninterrupted communion with God. "By the grace of God, I am a Christian, and by my deeds a great sinner, and by my calling a homeless wanderer of humblest origin," he says.[19] This is an alien way of living the Christian life to my Protestant sensibilities.

The power of this simple prayer is that it is believed to reach beyond the intellect and human knowledge, beyond all human efforts to find meaning in life. The peasant pilgrim had heard the homilies and the lectures on prayer, but they were all instructions *about* prayer in general, covering such topics as what prayer is, the necessity of prayer, the fruits of prayer, but no one spoke of the way to succeed in prayer.[20] This power *through* prayer and *by* prayer is the source of all good actions and virtue.[21]

The pilgrim reminds us that prayer is not to be confused with a means or method toward achieving the fruits of the Spirit (virtues), for to understand prayer as a work, a technique, is to depreciate the power of prayer. More powerfully put: without prayer it is impossible not only to do but also to know what is the good. Only fidelity to prayer will lead a person to enlightenment and union with Christ.[22]

Prayer makes possible our tasting the divine love of God. Emotionally we experience warmth in our relationship with God through prayer. How many times have we been emotionally troubled when entering prayer, only to come out of the time of prayer more at peace with ourselves and the world around us? Revelation, the enlightenment of the mind, is also possible through prayer. On the pilgrimage, prayer becomes a way of kindling the imagination, the creativity that is part of the inner life of the pilgrim.[23]

The promise of prayer is this: All people who believe in God can pray, and this prayer can change our weakness, limitation, and suffering, thus bringing God glory.[24] As Paul Jones reminds us, the Reformers of the church believed that prayer affects outcomes that would not otherwise occur, for God responds when asked. This makes prayer truly a courageous effort of human will, more exhausting than all other kinds of works in the life of the church on pilgrimage.[25] Change and growth will occur in the life of all pilgrims through and with the assistance of prayer. Our Russian peasant pilgrim is deeply in love with God not because he always gets his way but because God never tires of him, and the pilgrim is overwhelmed. The pilgrim reminds us that the message is this: Prayer is both the first step on the pilgrimage and the crown of a devout life, and the gospel directs us to pray constantly.[26] For this peasant pilgrim, the pilgrimage is more than walking: it is all prayer.

Solitude and Prayer in the Life of the Church on Pilgrimage

Jesus Christ, as the incarnation of the living God, is God's promise to us to be in a committed, covenantal relationship and to participate in our living, dreaming, and yearning. The God of salvation is present not only in our sanctuaries when we worship but in the fellowship halls as we greet good friends and visitors, in church offices when we write funeral homilies, and in the playgrounds and classrooms where our children learn and build relationships.

Because Christ's Spirit is present in all these places, we may take advantage of the Spirit's presence by declaring in our gestures of prayers our need and thankfulness for grace. Jones says that our healing depends upon our ability to stand naked before God, opening our hands as gestures of faith or dropping to our knees while letting go of all the fragments of self-acclaim, so that we may humbly receive what we really need and what we really want: God's love to fill our very thirsty and love-hungry lives.[27] All this is made possible through faith by grace. It is through prayer that we come to see, hear, and take part in this divine pilgrimage, in which we encounter the incarnate God in history, who moves us forward to a new consciousness.[28]

There is a great need in both Catholic and Protestant churches to teach the pilgrimage practices of solitude and prayer. These spiritual disciplines are not usually figured into the current matrix of educational activities in the life of the church. To practice such disciplines is to experience a kind of wakefulness to God in the world and the world in God.[29]

A practice that I recommend is sitting in a room in a comfortable position—with the lights turned down low and perhaps soft music in the background—closing your eyes for five or ten minutes, then praying the Jesus Prayer. To be still and calm for a few moments like this, not worrying about much of anything, slows one down.

The next task is to look at the space immediately around you—at your hands and clothes, at the rug and the light up above. Take note of one thing in the room and focus on that for three or four minutes. Perhaps thank God for that object. Then every few moments, expand your viewpoint by looking at objects and people farther away, taking in each new sight, color, form, texture, and remembering it. Then close your eyes again. Focus on one item that stands out. Why does it stand out? How is God present in this object?

This can also be done outside—in a backyard, a city park, or any place of natural beauty. Sit in silence for a few minutes, meditating on what you see around you. Then explore what strikes each one of your senses, and thank God for each of these things.[30]

I learned another act of solitude, prayer, and wakefulness in an art gallery full of people. It was the closing day of the show. Lost amid the clutter of people, I was instructed by a friend to walk into a room, take a cursory glance at the artwork, and choose one work of art that I would like to take home with me. Suddenly I was no longer aware of the people, but only of the artwork. I chose my piece of art and went right to it. With the objective of taking a "mental photo," I stared into the work, seeking God's presence, God's movement in the hands of the artist, becoming "one with the art" as it were.

But learning these practices and trying these activities does not come easily without someone to accompany us on our first attempts. As was true on pilgrimage we need someone to guide us in the disciplines of solitude and prayer along the path way of our collective pilgrimage. Having centered on the importance of being aware of those we are journeying with on this pilgrimage—our companions and the communion of saints—it is also important to remember that we are to balance such time on this earthly pilgrimage with periods of solitude and prayer.

In the next chapter we draw closer to the end of the journey. But the surprise is that the journey goes on, even after we think we have to come to an end.

Chapter 12

The Destination of Pilgrimage

At last the march shall end; The wearied ones shall rest;
The pilgrims find their home at last, Jerusalem the blest.
Rejoice! Rejoice! Rejoice, give thanks, and sing!
                    (Edward Hayes Plumptre, "Rejoice, Ye Pure in Heart")

Christians now wander as on pilgrimage through time, looking for the
kingdom of eternity.
                                        (St. Augustine, City of God)

What we find exotic abroad may be what we hunger for in vain at home.
                                        (Alain de Boton, The Art of Travel)

At the beginning of *Pilgrim's Progress,* Christian leaves his home, wife, and
children because he sees that "our city will be burned with fire from Heaven,
in which fearful overthrow, myself, with thee, my wife, and you my sweet
babes shall miserably come to ruin."[1] This is the genesis, the beginning point,
of his departure: this scene of total annihilation of the City of Destruction.
And where is he to go? The Evangelist gives him a vision of a "Wicket Gate"
that becomes his destination; through that gate Christian will come upon the
Celestial City![2] And so, with Obstinate and Pliable by his side, Christian flees
the city and follows the light that leads him to the Wicket Gate. This is his
goal, his destination, a most powerfully motivating force in his life, for which
he is willing to go on a difficult journey through a land not his own.

Destination is the last characteristic of pilgrimage. The first question on
pilgrimage is: Why are we leaving? The second question is equally important: Where are we going? The genesis and destination of our pilgrimage
matter. The treasure we seek at the end of our pilgrimage brings the challenges we face in living life to an end. Though the answer to the first question
is within us, for Christ is within us, we seem to need to venture to a faraway

138

land to tap our memory.[3] Thus, we need to go on the pilgrimage to get away from the normal and mundane in order to see anew the question and to find the answers we search for in this life. Ultimately, our life is that much more meaningful because of our pilgrimage.

Chaucer's pilgrims are on a trek to visit the relics of St. Thomas à Becket; they seek healing or a break from the life of the villages from where they came. In *The Way of a Pilgrim*, the pilgrim leaves his home in search of a way of praying that will be more fulfilling. Egeria goes in search of liturgical practices. She confirms and vivifies her faith in the truths of Scripture through personal visits to places marked by the action of God and humankind, and she prays with those who exemplify the Christian life, be they in the Sinai, Palestine, Mesopotamia, or Iran.

It is a great moment when we see, however distant, the goal of our wandering. What was once a part of our imagination—something other pilgrims showed us in pictures, sang about in songs, or told us in stories—suddenly becomes a part of our experience.[4] But there is always the lingering question: Is the journey the important thing for the pilgrim, is it the destination, or is it both? This question lingers in the journals of many pilgrims.

Pilgrimage: Points of Origin

In *Dakota*, Kathleen Norris writes that "fear is not a bad place to start a spiritual journey." If we know what makes us afraid, we can see more clearly that the way out is through the fear.[5] A friend of mine put it this way: That which is *in* the way, *is* the way.[6] Where we come from on the pilgrimage is not always a place of rest or repose. It can be a place of agitation and fear.

Earlier in this book I pointed out the importance of knowing where one has come from, for the past is as important a teacher in our lives on pilgrimage as is our present and future. Children and adults who are adopted crave to know where they came from, what the circumstances of their birth were, and what led to their birth parents' decision to place them up for adoption. Consider how many times in your life you are asked the question: Where is home? Where do you come from?

Likewise, on an actual pilgrimage, people will want to know where we come from and why we are on the pilgrimage. When I showed up in Costilla, New Mexico, for the beginning of the pilgrimage to Chimayo, people wanted to know why I was on *this* pilgrimage. I was white and Protestant, and English was my primary language. Why did I come to New Mexico, where I was a minority on several counts? I told them that I was throwing a challenge to my everyday life in North Carolina. Yet since being on this first pilgrimage I have never been able to find my way back to what used to be home. Everything has changed: my job, my family configuration, and how I understand education in the life of the church. Such change is not necessarily in the people and places; it was I who changed in significant ways.

On each subsequent pilgrimage I have undertaken, whether it was to the Basilica of Christ Crucified in Esquipulas, or to Canterbury, Lindisfarne, or St. Patrick's Purgatory, I have always approached these pilgrim times with feelings that can best be expressed as a mixture of excitement and anxiety. I am excited because I know that I will discover something about myself in God that I had not known or considered before, but I feel anxious as I wonder what kind of change it will make upon me and my relationship to God and others. My family and friends tell me that I come back from these pilgrimage experiences more at peace with myself and the world around me, and I know each time it has been good to get away and set my life to the rhythm of the pilgrimage. I reenter into home life and live differently for awhile, but I feel that I must be on an actual pilgrimage again soon in order to keep the experience alive. By going on a pilgrimage on a yearly basis, the characteristics of pilgrimage in my daily life are freshened.

Pilgrimage's Destination: A Divine Extravagance

Knowing the destination, we can discern best what progress we are making toward that goal. However, pilgrimage-as-education differs greatly from other types of education. The goal of pilgrimage may be as simple as facing the right direction, which is not necessarily of our doing but is made possible through God's grace. That is why, in hindsight, I have come to see that pilgrimage is a divine extravagance. Pilgrimage is divinely inspired, and it is an extravagance because when people go on pilgrimage, they are not making money, and they are spending time and energy. The call to be a follower of Christ is considered by many a divine extravagance.

The divine extravagance is embodied in this closing pilgrimage story of visiting the statue of *El Cristo Negro*, the Black Christ, of Esquipulas, Guatemala. It is the destination place for generations of pilgrims. Even before the image of the Black Christ came to the town of Esquipulas, generations of pilgrims of the indigenous culture visited this spot. The Black Christ is a beautiful image of the dying Christ on the cross. It was carved in Antigua over four hundred years ago out of an orange tree. It was then covered with cloth and painted black, which has worn to a rich brown color. When the statue was first brought to Esquipulas, it was carried in procession like a traveling shrine, and people confessed that they experienced miracles throughout its journey to this southeastern border town. Almost two hundred years later the archbishop of Guatemala, who himself declared that he experienced a miracle in connection with the statue, built a basilica in Esquipulas to thank the Christ for the miracle that saved his life. In 1959 Benedictine monks were invited to come to minister to the pilgrims and maintain the basilica.

Around the basilica is evidence of the crass commercialism often found in areas of pilgrimage. For example, there is the Hotel El Peregrino, or "Pilgrim Hotel," with "TV, cable, and hot water," next door to the basilica—in clear view of the humblest and poorest of pilgrims who save all year to come back to Esquipulas to give thanks to the Christ for miracles or blessings in their lives. I watch, listen, touch, smell, and walk with this living procession and open market of people who gather together around the basilica. I am only too aware that I am but the latest pilgrim to come upon this spot of holiness, to the basilica that houses *El Cristo Negro*. The knowledge of this pilgrimage site is not communicated through books, photographs, essays, travel videos, Web sites, or television specials, though most of these now exist. The knowledge of the Black Christ comes primarily through the personal testimonies of Christ's pilgrims who are of this land, and through the architecture and souvenirs, or *recuerdos*, of pilgrims' past visits.

Whether sitting in the choir stall of the basilica, walking in the park in front of the basilica, running along the streets of the town, or stopping by a booth selling *recuerdos*, I am in awe of the gestures of faith and grace performed effortlessly or with great élan by these pilgrims. For example, one morning during mass, I hear a shuffling of fabric against the hard, geometrically designed flagstone and tile floor of the basilica. Coming through a corridor of candles secured with wax to the floor, in native dress, three women shuffle forward on their knees. They have been shuffling from the tall, wooden doors of the basilica all the way to the front of the altar, past confessionals that look like squat wooden phone booths and side altars with life-size statues of Mary, Joseph, Santiago, Veronica, and Anthony hovering over them. One of the women has a child on her back in a woven papooselike sack, and the child is lulled to sleep by the swaying motion of the mother crawling upright on her knees. The women softly murmur prayers on their way to the black, wrought iron altar rail, carrying candles forward to offer to the Christ. Then, without turning around—for one never turns one's back on the Black Christ—they shuffle backward on their knees in a single file out to the light of day.

Why have they come? To give thanks to Christ. To many, the statue of the Black Christ is not Christ, but is just a statue. But the statue is attractive to the native people of this land. The darkness of the Christ is the familiar complexion of the native people of Guatemala. The five-foot Christ, surrounded by Mary his mother, Mary Magdalene, and John the Evangelist, is on a silver cross richly decorated with sculptured vines and grape leaves.

For over a week I watch the faithful stream in and walk purposefully toward the Black Christ. The way close to the figure of the Black Christ is through a serpentine back entrance and through a chapel that contains a figure of Christ on his knees, half-naked, with his back flayed open and bleeding, his face caught in utter pain. The pilgrims of Central America and Mexico can identify with this kind of suffering. When I approach the image of the Black Christ, I come from behind the shrine and circle around it. Fresh flowers have been placed around the glass shield that protects the figures from human touch, humidity, or harm. The smell is often pungent with such freshly cut foliage. The glass is smeared with oil from human hands, and attendants wipe it down frequently. In front of the Christ, I can kneel or touch the glass, as have at least a million others throughout the year. The face of the dying Christ is sweet and kind. The artistry is breathtaking. I am told that it is proper never to turn one's back on the Christ and so, like the others, I walk backward away from the figure, keeping my eyes on the Christ.

"The Christ you seek you will not find unless you bring him with you." The verse I hear repeated often throughout Esquipulas makes a foothold on my Anglo-Protestant sensibilities. We pilgrims come with Christ within us already. It is Christ within us who makes this place, this procession, this gathering around the Black Christ, holy. The statue is not holy without the people who surround it—the people who travel with Christ, who is in us as we are in Christ. It is Christ within us who gives each pilgrim the impetus—the unspeakable, unnameable urge or nudge, sometimes the burning desire or unquenchable need within—to venerate the Christ of Esquipulas.

Outside I watch the groups of pilgrims that hover around the basilica. I especially note a group of pilgrims from Livingston, Belize; they are Catholic and of African descent. From afar, I am struck by the large-boned women and the slender men. The women wear bright clothes with yellows, whites, pinks, reds, and green plaids or floral patterns. Each woman also wears a bandana or straw hat. Some women are easily balancing straw baskets, or black luggage, or large plastic tote bags on the tops of their heads, while others carry large cloth handbags full of *recuerdos* such as candies, cookies, and small figurines of the Black Christ. They stand in two lines at the bottom of the stairs leading up to the sanctuary, praying out loud and singing songs of praise. An older, larger woman, gripped by extreme passion, throws herself prostrate onto the pavement, beating her fists against the hard stone. The voice of the people around her, a Greek chorus of sorts, swells in volume as the people join the chant and pray and sing hymns of praise in Creole around this woman who is obviously gripped by a fervent appeal to the Almighty God.

There is an illogical necessity of the divine extravagance being played out and performed among the pilgrims who gather here before the Black Christ. It is an extravagance, perhaps even madness, to leave one's home in order to take one's immediate and extended family on a trip over some distance that takes maybe an entire day if not two. Many leave jobs that already pay too little. Many of these families live day to day, meal by meal.

Many families and single people cannot normally afford to make this trip, but the divine drive that pilgrims feel within them pushes them in this direction. It is the belief bred within them, generation after generation, that all of life is a gift from God, and that any healing of body, mind, and spirit comes from God alone who, in the person of Jesus Christ and the tangible presence of the Holy Spirit, sides with and advocates for the oppressed, the poor, the homeless, the widow, the orphan, the sick, and the political outsider.[7]

Reflections on the Genesis and Destination of Pilgrimages

All pilgrimages have a genesis or beginning point that we can turn to and name, perhaps by date or by place, or because of the people we were with at the point of our departure. Likewise, all pilgrimages have destinations, ending points, whether they conclude in a specific place of worship such as a chapel or shrine, in meeting a group of people, or in meeting on a certain anniversary date.

Focusing primarily on destination can debase the present moment on pilgrimage, playing down the significance of what occurs along the pilgrim's way.[8] Zygmunt Bauman writes that we are all pilgrims in this life and that there is little we can do about it even if we wished, as the "earthly life is a brief overture to the eternality of the soul."[9] Nevertheless, there is a desire within us, a need to know where we are going and toward what end, purpose, or goal, regardless of how long or short, crowded or lonely, the pilgrimage is. People need to know when they are going to graduate from school, when they are going to be confirmed in the church, what the opportunities are for raises in the places where they work. And people want to know where they are going after they die and what happens when they die. Sometimes we are consumed by learning where we are headed and moving our lives toward that destination point, with God's help and grace. At other times we need to know where we are walking or moving to by looking at the footprints before us, reflecting on the roads of life that we have thus far traveled, speaking to others of the progress we have made, and searching for a sense of what is coming closer as we move forward.[10] Bauman writes that the destination gives form to the formless, making a "whole" out of the fragments of life and lending continuity in the episodes or chapters in our narrativelike lives. There is something within us that wants to know the distance between the goal we are headed toward and where we are at this present moment, as we want to conserve our energy, our time, our lives, and our finances for the future.[11] Knowing that there is a destination, a reason we are on the pilgrimage, gives us a sense of solidity in a world that feels unpredictable and indeterminate. We depend upon the footprints of others, while hoping that we are leaving our own footprints, conscious that each move has a consequence that cannot be reversed.[12]

Three characteristics of reaching the destination of the pilgrimage may be helpful in understanding pilgrimage as growth and change in the Christian life.

First, we assess all that has gone on during the pilgrimage.   As Martin Robinson observes, on pilgrimage we have an increased awareness of the holy that we do not want to dissipate. Place and land have an increased importance in our lives. So also we have an increased desire to worship God as we encounter ancient rituals, sites, and sounds. We value being in fellowship with those who are with us on the journey. We find ourselves trying to remember all the unexpected points and highlights from the pilgrimage itself, including the strangest moments, the strangest people, and the sudden realization that the journey has come to an end.[13]

When on the pilgrimage to Chimayo, the final evening before we actually reached El Santuario de Chimayo, we spent the evening singing songs that we had learned throughout the week and sharing with one another our impressions of the journey. We also shared the pocket-full of prayers written by others on slips of paper that we had picked up along the way, leaving them at the foot of the cross we had brought with us thus far. The next day, at the sanctuary itself, we had time to listen to the stories of the other pilgrimage routes. We celebrated the youngest pilgrim and the oldest. The oldest was Sarah, a woman in her eighties, who had walked with her group over one hundred miles from Wagon Wheel, New Mexico. As a part of worship among the pilgrims and our respective family and friends, a person from each of the five bands of pilgrims shared a highlight from the pilgrimage.

Second, this is only one more step along the way.   Though it is a momentous last step among the many steps we have made on pilgrimage, it is but one among many. Whether it is the destination or the journey itself that matters, it is important to remember that the destination is part of the journey and that the two are inseparable. The journey of pilgrimage would be meaningless without knowledge of what awaited the pilgrim at the journey's end.

While arriving at the destination is one more step on the pilgrimage, it is as momentous as the first step we took. Each experience of a story, ritual, conflict, and relationship with a friend or stranger shapes and nurtures us as we grow and change throughout the period of pilgrimage. We are surely not the same people who left some time earlier, for we have all had deeply meaningful experiences.

Third, we are celebrating a milestone in reaching the destination. In reaching the destination there is a sense of accomplishment, of a journey well-completed. In the daylong pilgrimages I took with students in Chatham County, North Carolina, there was no denying that on reaching the end of our journey the students felt a certain sense of accomplishment and satisfaction. After a prayer for pilgrims upon their return, the students would collapse where they were and take a nap.

Victor and Edith Turner describe how toward the end of a pilgrimage the pilgrim discovers some newfound freedom from mundane or profane structures. The churches, the rituals, the icons, the banners, and the stories told along the pilgrimage remind us of who the God is whom we worship and follow.[14]

In Chimayo, we were drummed into the gathering of other pilgrims and friends by the same drummers who welcomed us to Taos Pueblo. Each band of pilgrims carried its cross, its flag, its heart of Jesus and gathered them in a central location. First, the groups brought the satchels of earth that they had gathered along the route and poured them out in a central place among all the pilgrims in rivers of brown and tan. Second, they brought together the processional crosses of Jesus. The same pattern was repeated with the flags of Our Lady of Guadalupe and the puzzle pieces of the heart of Jesus, which were put together. All at once, the various parts of the pilgrimage were together for all to behold. Our journey had come to an end.

Pilgrimage Genesis and Destinations in the Church on Pilgrimage

The genesis of the pilgrimage in the life of the church is made public and most manifest in the sacrament of baptism. Our time of growth and change in the presence of others as Christians may begin as early as our very conception and birth, but baptism is the ritual of entrance or initiation into the life of the body of Christ on pilgrimage. Tom Wright says that our passport for pilgrimage is the Easter story, and the Easter story is why we are baptized in the first place. Theologically, we can say we were saved not in our baptism, but when the crucified Christ rose from the dead. The resurrection spreads out before us the map of God's new world, made possible through the Easter story. And what was begun with Christ's resurrection will be continued, as a pilgrimage, until it is thoroughly finished—every act of faith and love, justice and mercy. Beauty and truth will be revealed in that final destination when Christ comes again in glory.[15]

The destination that is set before us has been mentioned throughout this book: being and becoming more like Christ, aspiring toward living most fully in God's realm or kingdom. Through a life of pilgrimage as members of Christ's body, perhaps taking some side roads that others are not acquainted with, while at other moments being fully a part of the throng of pilgrims, we move inexorably toward the reign of God, experiencing growth and change that only Christ could imagine possible.

The purpose of our journey is a growing reliance upon God. This pilgrimage is neither merely personal nor communal but, as W. Paul Jones states, is cosmic. To name the Spirit "Holy" is to believe that the whole cosmic procession is a divine pilgrimage. God as our redeemer is disclosed as the incarnate God of history, as pilgrimage moves only forward toward a kind of raised consciousness of who and whose we are in God.[16] The God of Israel who pitched his tent with his people, the God who led a wandering pilgrim life among his people in the person of Jesus Christ, and the Holy Spirit who accompanies us in our time of this cosmic pilgrimage is drawing us ever closer to the love of the Creator. If the church is a path, a place to walk and to practice the faith, says Craig Dykstra, we may be surprised along the way by the living God and recognize and know that Christ is present to us.[17]

Herein lies a secret truth: Because Christ is always present to and with us, the destination of our pilgrimage as the body of Christ, which is being and becoming more like Christ, is already within us and among us. Because pilgrimage is always in search of the holy, we have a tendency to believe that the holy is outside of us, and thus we go on pilgrimage in search of God, who is constantly searching for us.[18] But like the pilgrims throughout the ages, we go on pilgrimage to comprehend this God-framed reality.

I want to propose ways of assessing and affirming the lives of each pilgrim within a congregation or parish. This means that a congregation, parish, or denomination would have to consider the pilgrimage of each person's life, discerning in what ways each person is progressing on the personal pilgrimage within the body of Christ. Currently there is no way to assess this. What needs to be developed is a way for people to share their experiences on the pilgrimage of their daily lives.

Imagine a congregation keeping a timeline on each person's life. Along this timeline each person's gifts, talents, and services to the community would be discerned, and every effort would be taken by the community to ensure that each person be given possibilities for nurturing these gifts, talents, and services. In discerning where we are in relationship to the destination of our pilgrimage, we must ask the following questions:

> What Scripture passages do we believe people should be aware of in the church's pilgrimage?
> What level of participation in the sacramental and ritual life of the church enhances the Christian's pilgrimage?
> Are people involved in weekly fellowship or worship?
> Are people engaged in daily spiritual devotions and prayer?
> Are people aware of their gifts, talents, and services for the greater good of the body of Christ?
> In what ways are people engaged in service to others in the body of Christ? How do we make a social witness to the world around us?
> Do we have weekly, monthly, or yearly occasions to share our stories with others about the pilgrimage that we are all on as the body of Christ?

Finally, regarding death, we must ask: Is death our final destination? Paulo Coelho reminds us that only we human beings are aware that we are going to die. Death is our constant companion, and it is death that gives each person's life its true meaning. To see the face of death, we have to know a person's anxieties and terrors.[19] But death is not the final word. And as the Scriptures remind us, death has lost its sting in the face of resurrection. Even in our death, the pilgrimage continues as we are welcomed into and among the communion of saints, as we are welcomed into the realm of God's eternal love.

The Pilgrimage Goes On

Martin Robinson writes that the end of a pilgrimage implies a new beginning: "The pilgrim enters on a pilgrimage not as an end in itself, but in the hope of gaining clarity of the continuation of the journey of faith. . . . Just as the pilgrimage itself needs to be prepared for, so pilgrimage itself is merely preparation for that greater journey which has as its end the imitation of Christ."[20] In the final chapter, we will look at how the journey continues as a church.

Chapter 13

The Church: The School of the Pilgrim

There is meaning in our journey. We in search of God, and God in search of us. . . . I saw clearly that the Stranger who had become my friend was himself God who had become [human].

(*Basil Hume*)

Stay with us, Lord Jesus, for evening draws near, and be the companion on our way, to set our hearts on fire with new hope.

(The Liturgy of the Hours)

*T*he morning after I finish the pilgrimage to El Santuario de Chimayo, I awake singing the song I learned in Spanish over the past six days. After going to Esquipulas and worshiping in the presence of the Black Christ, I open the *New York Times* and find a picture of a man carrying a cross that is over six feet tall, on which is the figure of the Black Christ—but this time it is in Panama. I still carry the rosary I was given by Brother Robert in Esquipulas, which was carved in Bosnia. After I come back from Lindisfarne and teach my classes about the pilgrimages of St. Aidan and St. Cuthbert from the book written by the Venerable Bede, I bring out photographs of the Holy Isle, and I am flooded with emotions and memories. A few months after returning to the United States from Ireland, I attend a conference of religious educators. I share with my friend Tom Groome and his friend Kieran Scott, both from Ireland, my trek to St. Patrick's Purgatory. Both of them are amazed and tell me that they rarely meet Americans who have actually walked, barefoot and all, on Station Island in Ireland.

The lesson learned is an easy one: When one gets to the destination of pilgrimage, it isn't necessarily the end of the journey. The journey continues onward, and never leaves the pilgrim's memory-filled life. As going on a pilgrimage is often a "baptism by fire," a process of immersion that envelops one's entire life, so the task afterward is no less consuming. It involves finding, creating, adapting practices, and performing gestures, that keep us open to the art, the act, or the gestures of pilgrimage in our daily life. *The Christian life is a pilgrim life, and the Christian pilgrim life is the Christian life.* It usually takes people a few weeks after going on an actual pilgrimage for the initial impact of being on pilgrimage to wear off. But the effect can never completely wear off. One's very life is marked, and all other experiences of the Christian life will be prefigured by the experiences of the pilgrimage. That is why the School of the Pilgrim is not only meant to keep the door open for other pilgrimages in the future but to welcome and initiate others into the art, the act, and the gestures of pilgrimage. As well, it is meant to keep alive the lessons learned from an actual pilgrimage so that we may continue to deepen our experiences of living in the body of Christ on pilgrimage.

In a sense I began pilgrimage as a test of God. I wanted God to prove to me that pilgrimage was everything that all these other pilgrims found to be true throughout time and in various locales. I was not sure of the veracity of pilgrimage. I was a doubter, a skeptic, whose rational Protestant sensibilities were already in play in my life. No one in the United Methodist Church of my earlier childhood in Maplewood, New Jersey, ever taught me about pilgrimage. Likewise, neither the youth group of my Presbyterian church (United Presbyterian in those days) nor the Young Life chapter in Beaverton, Oregon, to which I belonged ever broached the word. I was raised to think that a pilgrim was one of the early founders of the Massachusetts colony of Plymouth. A pilgrim wore black and gray clothes with unfashionably big white collars and stiff cuffs, large black hats, and silver belt buckles on shiny black shoes.

In many of the congregations I have pastored, the people feel they have "arrived" at the gates of heaven. They have found their chair or their pew, and every Sunday they sit in that space for an hour or so with no one else venturing into that space. Their "heaven" is a wooden pew by a certain stained glass window. In colonial American churches the same phenomenon occurred, except that a church usually marked off a boxed-in pew with the name of the people who gave money for it. There is no sense of movement, of pilgrimage, within these places.

I get excited when I visit Roman Catholic churches and hear the priest or liturgist state that the church is a "pilgrim church," and I wonder if anyone else understands what that means. Several hymns sung in the Episcopal Church fit under the rubric or title of "pilgrimage," but I am not sure if anyone else notices. On the other hand, after I taught the practices of pilgrimage to the Duke Youth Academy of Duke Divinity School, the academy began borrowing more of the language of pilgrimage for its sales brochure.

There is always the danger that a pilgrimage or pilgrimage theme may become a passing fad, though the practice and naming of pilgrimage seems to be rather resilient, having been part of the universal church's history for almost two thousand years. One priest told me the story of the donkey that became a pilgrimage site. The donkey, which was carrying all kinds of wares, died along the road. The owner, not wanting to dig a deep hole, made a stone pyramid over the donkey. Soon passersby were fascinated by the structure and the story of the donkey and began to spread the story that something important or powerful or holy happened on the site. Over time the place became a pilgrimage shrine for the donkey that carried the holy family on its pilgrimage to Egypt. Meanwhile, people stream to New Jersey to venerate the Virgin Mary's image on a window, or to Florida to seek out the larger-than-life image of Mary on a black-paned office building. Strange apparitions, fads, and gimmicks happen.

But pilgrimage endures. Thousands of people join pilgrimages to St. Patrick's Purgatory, Chimayo, Esquipulas, Canterbury, Mexico City, and other places throughout the world. In Dorchester, England, there is a groundswell of people visiting the church where St. Birinus's relic was once housed. From the large and well-known, to the small and personal places, pilgrimage appears to be an art that has never been lost, a movement that needs little in the way of publicizing.

Pilgrimage is more than a period or time in a person's life. As I have proposed throughout this book, pilgrimage is a way of comprehending and living life today as Christians, and the School of the Pilgrim is one possible way of teaching Christians to live life today as pilgrims.

Consider in what ways the language of journey is already a part of congregational life, beginning with Advent, which is understood as the coming of the Light of Christ. During the season of Advent we focus on peace in the wilderness of God's world, in which wolf and lamb shall lie down together. We hear of the pilgrimage of Joseph, Mary, and Jesus to Jerusalem and then to Egypt. We hear of the pilgrimage of the Wise Men. Ash Wednesday is a beginning of the next stretch of road in the Christian calendar as we follow Christ.

Lent reinforces our pilgrimage, as each Sunday we remember in vivid detail the trek that Jesus took upon this earth and the imprint of his ministry upon our lives. This time culminates with Palm Sunday and Jesus' pilgrimage into Jerusalem to meet his accusers and death on Good Friday. The language of pilgrimage runs throughout Holy Week as we remember Jesus' triumphal entry into Jerusalem. This segment of the journey ends at the foot of the cross.

Easter heralds a new beginning of our pilgrimage with Christ. This is a significant marker in the life of pilgrims as we join our lives today with the pilgrims of Christ from all those years in the past, moving forward to the "city not made by human hands, the new Jerusalem, where with God and the Holy Spirit, Christ lives in glory forever."[1]

As I have suggested since the beginning of this book, there is a sense that the church, the body of Christ, does not often have the sensation of being on the move. Our churches feel like they are stuck in a rut on the roadside, unable—or so it seems—to move forward. With the language of pilgrimage as part of our biblical mandate and our historical tradition, the question is obvious: Why don't we live as if we are on a pilgrimage?

What follows are ways we may create areas in the life of the church with the goal of teaching people to live as God's pilgrim people.

Leave

Jesus knew what it was like to leave something in order to move on with his mission. Having left the side of the Father, Christ the Son was sent to earth in the form of a helpless baby. Upon his arrival, he is already concerned about his leaving. In the Gospel of John, with his troop of disciples still at the apprentice stage, Jesus tells them that he is about to go: "Little children, I am with you only a little longer" (13:33). Upset by this news, Simon Peter asks him where he is going, to which Jesus answers, "Where I am going, you cannot follow me now; but you will follow afterward" (13:36). Further on, Jesus tells them, "I go and prepare a place for you, [and] I will come again and will take you to myself, so that where I am there you may be also." Thomas asks how they will know the way. "I am the way, and the truth, and the life," replies Jesus (14:3, 6).

Jesus calls us today to leave those things that try best to take our attention away from the grace-inspired works of God. At times, like Jesus' followers, I sense the presence of Christ behind me, urging me to get on with life's pilgrimage. As Jesus called his disciples to leave families, to leave jobs, to leave friends, to leave environs that were familiar and safe, Jesus asks us to live life to the fullest in Christ.

I have learned that this does not mean that the pilgrim life will be easier. In truth, the sense of risk, of worry, and anxious moments are still present. More times than I can think of I have asked Christ in the last few years, "Where are you taking me, and why?" But I have found that with friends, in reading the

Psalms daily, in the preaching moments throughout the church season, I have come upon necessary reminders of what I left behind and of who has called me to leave and follow him.

Come

Jesus offers this invitation: "Come to me, all you that are weary and are carrying heavy burdens, and I will give you rest. Take my yoke upon you, and learn from me; for I am gentle and humble in heart, and you will find rest for your souls. For my yoke is easy, and my burden is light" (Matt. 11:28–30). This invitation of Jesus to trade our burdens for his yoke is an invitation almost too good to believe.

Along life's pilgrimage we will find among us those who pick up everything they see in the roadway, as well as those who fail to carry their share of the load. We will be forever called to share the material we are carrying in life, for that is what we do as Christian pilgrims. We have Jesus the Pilgrim walking side by side with us.

Follow

Mark tells of the calling of Jesus' first disciples: "As Jesus passed along the Sea of Galilee, he saw Simon and his brother Andrew casting a net into the sea—for they were fishermen. And Jesus said to them, 'Follow me and I will make you fish for people.' And immediately they left their nets and followed him" (Mark 1:16–18).

To follow Christ always creates tension in our lives. We follow Christ because without him we would be lost. In following Christ we envision him before us on this pilgrimage, beckoning us on. Michael Casey writes that in following Christ, we will rightly attempt to imitate Christ, consciously and unconsciously. Of course, there is more to following Christ than simply conforming to a series of instructions or playing a game of "Simon Says." It is a matter of living as Christ lived, acting as Christ acted, aspiring to be like Christ.[2] Slowly, in the process of conversion we progress to a point of subjective participation in the reality of Christ.

Casey notes that there is a price to be paid for this transfiguration, this transparency: Our egotism needs to be diminished, since Christ's involvement in our action is inhibited by our self-centered concerns. By giving ourselves over to Christ, being opened by grace to the God who changes history, we offer to

God the opportunity to revolutionize the whole tenor of this segment of earth's history that is our little life—all this from leaving, coming, and following the Christ on our earthly pilgrimage.[3]

Walking Together with the Pilgrim Jesus

In his book *Caminemos con Jesus*, Roberto Goizueta writes that throughout life's pilgrimage, God is changing us all, causing us to grow into the freedom that is found within the body of Christ. In the cry *"Caminemos con Jesus"* we are "proclaiming Jesus as the source of our community, our solidarity, and therefore our liberation."[4] In our every gesture on this pilgrimage we proclaim Jesus crucified and resurrected. We walk, we move with Jesus hand in hand with other pilgrims, throughout time yet in this time, in this place, constantly being reminded that the journey continues toward the New Jerusalem. It is a journey in which we will know love, experience hope, and travel places in faith, inspired always by the gift of God's grace.

Journey on!

Notes

INTRODUCTION: BEING A PILGRIM

1. This study was the core of my senior paper at Princeton Theological Seminary, which I wrote for the late Dr. James Loder in 1983.

2. See Brett Webb-Mitchell, *God Plays Piano Too* (New York: Crossroad, 1993).

3. See Brett Webb-Mitchell, *Follow Me* (New York: Seabury Press, 2006), 36–37.

4. John Calvin, *Institutes of the Christian Religion* 3.7.3; ed. John T. McNeill, trans. Ford Lewis Battles, LCC (Philadelphia: Westminster Press, 1960), 1:693.

5. Webb-Mitchell, *Follow Me*, 47.

6. Throughout this book I will continue to have this conversation between three kinds of pilgrimage experiences. The first are actual pilgrimages that I have gone on in the past few years that were usually a weeklong journey with others to a place or shrine. The second are the result of reading several pilgrimage narratives in which I have found myself on another kind of pilgrimage experience as I have come to see where the writer or storyteller is taking me in his or her life. The third come from these first two experiences of pilgrimage. I have come to see the same characteristics or variables of pilgrimage as central in my approach and understanding of life outside the intentional pilgrimage or pilgrimage narrative. While the first two kinds of pilgrimage are important, they set the framework by which all of life may be understood as a pilgrimage.

CHAPTER 1: THE STORY OF CHRISTIAN PILGRIMAGE

1. Philip Cousineau, *The Art of Pilgrimage* (Berkeley, CA: Conari Press, 1998), 173, 177.

2. Diana Webb, *Pilgrims and Pilgrimage* (New York: I. B. Tauris & Co., 1999), 2.

3. See Bruce Chatwin, *The Songlines* (New York: Penguin Books, 1987).

4. Michael Sallnow, "Pilgrimage and Cultural Fracture in the Andes," in John Eade and Michael Sallnow, *Contesting the Sacred* (Chicago: University of Illinois Press, 2000), 148.

5. Smith cited in Cousineau, *Art of Pilgrimage*, 107, 108.

6. "Pilgrimage" in *The Oxford Dictionary of the Christian Church*, ed. F. L. Cross and E. A. Livingstone (New York: Oxford University Press, 1978), 1091.

7. Cousineau, *Art of Pilgrimage*, 13.

8. Ibid., 14.

9. Quoted in ibid.

10. See Eade and Sallnow, *Contesting the Sacred*.

11. Cousineau, *Art of Pilgrimage*, 9.

12. Ibid., 153.

13. Ibid., 9.

14. Ibid., xxvii.

15. Ibid., 119.

16. Ibid., xxiii.

17. Quoted in ibid., xii.

18. Ibid., xxx.

19. Martin Robinson, *Sacred Places, Pilgrim Paths* (San Francisco: HarperCollins, 1997), 1.

20. Ibid.

21. John Eade, "Introduction to the Illinois Paperback," in Eade and Sallnow, *Contesting the Sacred*, xvii.

22. John Eade, "Introduction," in Eade and Sallnow, *Contesting the Sacred*, 4.

23. Quoted in ibid., 6.

24. Ibid., 9.

25. Christopher McKevitt, "San Giovanni Rotondo and the Shrine of Padre Pio," in Eade and Sallnow, *Contesting the Sacred*, 78.

26. Michael Sallnow, "Pilgrimage and Cultural Fractures in the Andes," in Eade and Sallnow, *Contesting the Sacred*, 148.

27. McKevitt, "San Giovanni Rotondo," 79.

28. W. Paul Jones, *A Table in the Desert* (Brewster, MA: Paraclete Press, 2001), 49.

29. Cousineau, *Art of Pilgrimage*, xxiv.

30. Robinson, *Sacred Places, Pilgrim Paths*, 13.

31. Ibid., 3.

32. Ibid., 3–4.

33. Zygmunt Bauman, *Life in Fragments* (Cambridge: Blackwell, 1995), 84.

34. Belden Lane, *Solace of Fierce Landscapes* (New York: Oxford University Press, 1998), 18.

35. *Egeria, Diary of a Pilgrimage*, trans. George Gingras (New York: Newman Press, 1970), 7.

36. Robinson, *Sacred Places, Pilgrim Paths*, 5.

37. Ibid.

38. Ibid., 6.

39. Ibid., 7.

40. *The Way of a Pilgrim*, trans. Helen Bacovcin (New York: Vintage, 1978), 194.

41. Victor and Edith Turner, *Image and Pilgrim in Christian Culture* (New York: Columbia University Press, 1978).

42. Geoffrey Chaucer, *Canterbury Tales* (New York: Bantam, 1982), 3.

43. John Bunyan, *Pilgrim's Progress* (New York: Penguin Books, 1987), 12.

44. Robinson, *Sacred Places, Pilgrim Paths*, 7.

45. Annie Dillard, *Pilgrim at Tinker Creek* (New York: Harper & Row, 1974), 269.

46. Rosemary Mahoney, *The Singular Pilgrim* (Boston: Houghton Mifflin, 2003), 17–18.

47. Ibid., 19.

48. Quoted in Jean Clift and Wallace Clift, *The Archetype of Pilgrimage* (Mahwah, NJ: Paulist Press, 1996), 29.

49. Webb, *Pilgrims and Pilgrimage*, 1.

50. Mahoney, *Singular Pilgrim*, 5.

51. Robinson, *Sacred Places, Pilgrim Paths*, 10.

CHAPTER 2: GROWTH AND CHANGE ALONG THE PILGRIM'S WAY

1. James Fowler, *Stages of Faith* (San Francisco: Harper & Row, 1981), 182.

2. Roberto Unger, *Knowledge and Politics* (New York: Free Press, 1975), 55.

3. Ibid., 199–220.

4. Doris Pilkington-Nugi-Garimara, *Rabbit Proof Fence* (New York: Hyperion, 2002).

5. John Main, "The Witness of Monastic Prayer," *Monastic Studies* 18 (Christmas 1988): 39.

6. See ibid., 46.

7. Quoted in Joan Chittister, *The Rule of St. Benedict* (New York: Crossroad, 1995), 21.

8. Quoted in Joan Chittister, *Scarred by Struggle, Transformed by Hope* (Grand Rapids: Wm. B. Eerdmans, 2005), 27.

9. Joan Chittister, *Wisdom Distilled from the Daily* (San Francisco: Harper & Row, 1990), 5, 6.

10. Main, "Witness of Monastic Prayer," 30.

11. Columba Stewart, *Prayer and Community: The Benedictine Tradition* (Maryknoll, NY: Orbis Books, 1998), 28.

12. I am aware that other religions practice pilgrimage. However, I am not writing from that perspective, nor in this small book do I have room to cover the various ideas and practices of pilgrimage found in each religion.

13. John Seabrook, "Child's Play," *New Yorker*, December 15, 2003, 69.

14. Craig Dykstra, *Growing in the Life of Faith* (Louisville, KY: Geneva Press, 1999), 39.

15. Main, "Witness of Monastic Prayer," 32.

16. Paul puts no chronological age on this sense of being an "infant in Christ."

17. Chittister, *Scarred*, 34.

18. See Dorothy Day, *A Long Loneliness* (San Francisco: HarperSanFrancisco, 1997); Jean Vanier, *Community and Growth* (Mahwah, NJ: Paulist Press, 1989).

19. William Poteat, *A Philosophical Daybook* (Columbia: University of Missouri Press, 1990), 2–3.

20. Bruce Morrill, "Initial Consideration: Theory and Practice of the Body in Liturgy Today," in *Bodies of Worship*, ed. Bruce T. Morrill (Collegeville, MN: Liturgical Press, 1999), 12–13.

21. There is a diference between being *authoritative*, which is based upon one's competence, expertise, or qualifications, and being *authoritarian*, which demands unquestioning obedience, thereby curtailing freedom of judgment and action.

22. Chittister, *Wisdom Distilled*, 46.

CHAPTER 3: GESTURES OF CHRISTIAN PILGRIMAGE

1. Henri Nouwen, *Bread for the Journey* (San Francisco: HarperCollins, 1997), 1.

2. John Spalding, *A Pilgrim's Digress* (New York: Harmony Books, 2003), 73.

3. Joan Chittister, *The Rule of St. Benedict* (New York: Crossroad, 1995), 123.

4. Dame Maria Boulding, "Prayer and the Paschal Mystery," *Downside Review* 94, no. 317 (1976): 277.

5. Brett Webb-Mitchell, *Follow Me* (New York: Seabury Press, 2006), 42–43.

6. Cintra Pemberton, *Soulfaring* (Harrisburg, PA: Morehouse Publishing Co., 1999), 10.

7. Tom Wright, *The Way of the Lord* (Grand Rapids: Wm. B. Eerdmans, 1999), 65.

8. Pemberton, *Soulfaring*, 10, 12.

9. Fenton Johnson, *Keeping the Faith* (Boston: Houghton Mifflin, 2003), 295.

10. Marilynne Robinson, *Housekeeping* (New York: McGraw-Hill, 1980), 182.

11. Johnson, *Keeping the Faith*, 295.

12. Ibid., 297.

13. See Brett Webb-Mitchell, *Christly Gestures* (Grand Rapids: Wm. B. Eerdmans, 2003).

14. Paulo Coelho, *Pilgrimage* (San Francisco: HarperCollins, 1998), 40, 41.

15. Ibid., 41.

16. Ibid., 61.

17. Ibid., 62.

18. Helen Bacovcin, "Introduction," in *The Way of a Pilgrim and the Pilgrim Continues His Way*, trans. Helen Bacovcin (New York: Doubleday, 1992), 7.

19. Ibid.

20. Ibid., 8–10.

21. Ibid., 13.

22. Ibid., 17.

23. Ibid., 41.

24. Ibid., 51.

25. Ibid., 157.

26. Coelho, *Pilgrimage*, 48.

27. Ibid., 54.

28. See Patricia Hampl, *Virgin Time* (New York: Random House, 1992), 121.

29. Augustine, *City of God* (New York: Penguin Books, 2003), 18.54; 14.13, 28.

30. Ibid., 15.14, 17.

31. Gerhard Lohfink, *Jesus and Community* (Minneapolis: Fortress Press, 1989), 181, 183.

32. Augustine, *City of God*, 15.1.

33. Wright, *Way of the Lord*, 53.

34. Ibid., 42.

35. Flannery O'Connor, *Mystery and Manners* (New York: Farrar, Straus & Giroux, 1991), 111.

36. Ibid., 118.

37. Gerhard Lohfink writes of the following biblical admonitions as keys to living the Christian life, which are "far from exhaustive": outdo one another in showing honor (Rom. 12:10), live in harmony with one another (Rom. 12:16), welcome one another (Rom. 15:7), admonish one another (Rom. 15:14), greet one another with a holy kiss (Rom. 16:16), wait for one another (1 Cor. 11:33), have the same care for one another (1 Cor. 12:25), be servants of one another (Gal. 5:13), bear one another's burdens (Gal. 6:2), comfort one another and build one another up (1 Thess. 5:11), be at peace with one another (1 Thess. 5:13), do good to one another (1 Thess. 5:15), bear with one another lovingly (Eph. 4:2), be kind and compassionate to one another (Eph. 4:32), be subject to one another (Eph. 5:21), forgive one another (Col. 3:13), confess your sins to one another and pray for one another (Jas. 5:16), love one another from the heart (1 Pet. 1:22), be hospitable to one another (1 Pet. 4:9), meet one another with humility (1 Pet. 5:5), have fellowship with one another (1 John 1:7; Lohfink, *Jesus and Community*, 145). Lohfink goes on to explain how these gestures are a form of edification, which

he understands as a pair of concepts to "build up and tear down" so that God can build up a nation and uproot it, thus planting the church in the ways of God (ibid., 146).

38. Lohfink, *Jesus and Community*, 145, 146.

CHAPTER 4: DISCOVERING THE WHOLE PERSON ON CHRISTIAN PILGRIMAGE

1. Pete McCarthy, *McCarthy's Bar* (New York: St. Martin's Press, 2001), 285–86.

2. Brett Webb-Mitchell, *Follow Me* (New York: Seabury Press, 2006), 139–52.

3. In the next chapter I will discuss the importance of the community for stimulation itself.

4. Quoted in Philip Cousineau, *The Art of Pilgrimage* (Berkeley, CA: Conari Press, 1998), xxvix.

5. Ibid., 23.

6. Christopher McKevitt, "San Giovanni Rotondo and the Shrine of Padre Pio," in *Contesting the Sacred*, ed. John Eade and Michael Sallnow (Chicago: University of Illinois Press, 2000), 78.

7. Quoted in John Eade, "Introduction," in Eade and Sallnow, *Contesting the Sacred*, 6.

8. Lonni Pratt and Daniel Homan, *Benedict's Way* (Chicago: Loyola Press, 2000), 229.

9. John Eade, "Introduction to the Illinois Paperback," in Eade and Sallnow, *Contesting the Sacred*, xvii.

10. Nancy Louise Frey, *Pilgrim Stories* (Berkeley: University of California Press, 1998), 109–13, 118.

11. Alain de Boton, *Art of Travel* (New York: Pantheon, 2002), 248; Eade and Sallnow, *Contesting the Sacred*, 5.

12. Roberto Unger, *Knowledge and Politics* (New York: Free Press, 1975), 36.

13. Ibid., 40, 42.

14. Zygmunt Bauman, *Life in Fragments* (Cambridge: Blackwell, 1995), 85.

15. Bruce Morrill, "Initial Consideration," in *Bodies of Worship* (Collegeville, MN: Liturgical Press, 1999), 2.

16. Joan Chittister, *Wisdom Distilled from the Daily* (San Francisco: Harper & Row, 1990), 5.

17. Ibid., 5.

18. Joan Chittister, *Scarred by Struggle, Transformed by Hope* (Grand Rapids: Wm. B. Eerdmans, 2003), 19.

19. Jean Vanier, *Community and Growth*, 2nd ed. (Mahwah, NJ: Paulist Press, 1989), 104.

20. See Craig Dykstra, *Growing in the Life of Faith* (Louisville, KY: Geneva Press, 1999), 20.

21. W. Paul Jones, *Teaching the Dead Bird to Sing* (Brewster, MA: Paraclete Press, 2002), 77.

22. Michael Casey, *Sacred Reading* (Ligouri, MO: Ligouri Press, 1996), 38.

23. Cousineau, *Art of Pilgrimage*, 88, 92.

24. Cintra Pemberton, *Soulfaring* (Harrisburg, PA: Morehouse Publishing Co., 1999), 9.

25. De Boton, *Art of Travel*, 32.

26. Ibid., 145, 157, 167.

27. Ibid., 58.

CHAPTER 5: COMPANIONS AND COMMUNITY ON PILGRIMAGE

1. Quoted in Martin Robinson, *Sacred Places, Pilgrim Paths* (San Francisco: Harper-Collins, 1997), 82–83.

2. Brett Webb-Mitchell, *Follow Me* (New York: Seabury Press, 2006), 61–63.

3. Anthony C. Meisel and M. L. del Mastro, *The Rule of Saint Benedict* (New York: Image, 1975), 53.

4. John Spalding, *A Pilgrim's Digress* (New York: Harmony Books, 2003), 220.

5. Quoted in Amy Mandelker and Elizabeth Powers, *Pilgrim Souls* (New York: Simon & Schuster, 1999), 103.

6. Meisel and del Mastro, *Rule of Saint Benedict*, 63.

7. Ibid., 67.

8. Quoted in Robinson, *Sacred Places, Pilgrim Paths*, 71.

9. Joan Chittister, *Wisdom Distilled from the Daily* (San Francisco: Harper & Row, 1990), 46.

10. Quoted in Robinson, *Sacred Places, Pilgrim Paths*, 71.

11. Jean Vanier, *Community and Growth*, 2nd ed. (Mahwah, NJ: Paulist Press, 1989), 265.

12. Ibid., 266.

13. Quoted in Robinson, *Sacred Places, Pilgrim Paths*, 82–83.

14. Paul Wadell, *Friendship and the Moral Life* (Notre Dame, IN: University of Notre Dame Press, 1989), 51.

15. Ibid., 98.

16. Sidney and Mary Lee Noland as quoted in Robinson, *Sacred Places, Pilgrim Paths*, 81.

17. Ibid., 11.

18. Cintra Pemberton, *Soulfaring* (Harrisburg, PA: Morehouse Publishing Co., 1999), 25.

19. J. F. Webb and D. H. Farmer, *The Age of Bede* (New York: Penguin Books, 1998), 9, 15.

20. Vanier, *Community and Growth*, 267.

21. Ibid., 266.

22. Ibid., 267.

CHAPTER 6: THE SAINTS AND MEMORY ON PILGRIMAGE

1. In the Presbyterian Church (U.S.A.)'s *Book of Confessions*, Presbyterians also acknowledge the importance or centrality of the communion of saints in the Scots Confession ("This Kirk is invisible, known only to God, who alone knows whom he has chosen, and include both the chosen who are departed, the Kirk triumphant, those who yet live and fight against sin and Satan, and those who shall live hereafter"; 3.16), the Heidelberg Confession ("that believers one and all, as partakers of the Lord Jesus Christ and all his treasures and gifts, shall share in one fellowship"; 4.055), the Second Helvetic Confession, and the Westminster Confession of Faith ("All saints being united to Jesus Christ, their head"; 6.146–6.148).

2. Martin Robinson, *Sacred Places, Pilgrim Paths* (San Francisco: HarperCollins, 1997), 116.

3. Geoffrey Chaucer, *Canterbury Tales*, trans. David Wright (New York: Oxford University Press, 1985), 1.

4. Robinson, *Sacred Places, Pilgrim Paths*, 116.

5. Quoted in Zygmunt Bauman, *Life in Fragments* (Cambridge: Blackwell, 1995), 83.

6. *Book of Confessions*, 5.026.

7. Venerable Bede, *The Age of Bede* (New York: Penguin Books, 1998), 49.

8. Brett Webb-Mitchell, *Follow Me* (New York: Seabury Press, 2006), 124–36.

9. Bauman, *Life in Fragments*, 86.

10. Robinson, *Sacred Places, Pilgrim Paths*, 126.

11. Shirley du Boulay, *The Road to Canterbury* (London: HarperCollins, 1994), 109.

12. Marilynne Robinson, *Housekeeping* (New York: McGraw-Hill, 1980), 194.

13. Quoted in Robinson, *Sacred Places, Pilgrim Paths*, 118.

14. Bauman, *Life in Fragments*, 83.

15. Hannah Green, *Little Saint* (New York: Modern Library, 2001), 9.

16. John Eade, "Introduction," in *Contesting the Sacred*, ed. John Eade and Michael Sallnow (Chicago: University of Illinois Press, 2000), 16, 24.

17. Green, *Little Saint*, 29.

18. Cintra Pemberton, *Soulfaring* (Harrisburg, PA: Morehouse Publishing Co., 1999), 4.

19. Bruce Morrill, *Bodies of Worship* (Collegeville, MN: Liturgical Press, 1999), 15.

20. John Main, "The Witness of Monastic Prayer," *Monastic Studies* 18 (Christmas 1988): 30.

21. Thomas Gillespie, "Making Other Plans," *Princeton Theological Seminary Bulletin* 24, no. 3 (2003): 305.

22. Nancy Louise Frey, *Pilgrim Stories* (Berkeley, CA: University of California Press, 1998), 38.

23. Quoted in Philip Cousineau, *The Art of Pilgrimage* (Berkeley, CA: Conari Press, 1998), xxvix.

24. Ibid., 8.

CHAPTER 7: TEACHING AND LEARNING TO BE A PILGRIM

1. Brett Webb-Mitchell, *Follow Me* (New York: Seabury Press, 2006), 63–64.

2. Ibid., 141.

3. Tom Wright, *The Way of the Lord* (Grand Rapids: Wm. B. Eerdmans, 1999), 53.

4. Zygmunt Bauman, *Life in Fragments* (Cambridge: Blackwell, 1995), 85.

5. Paulo Coelho, *The Pilgrimage* (San Francisco: HarperCollins, 1998), 22.

6. Ibid., 34.

7. Ibid., 27–28.

8. Ibid., 35.

9. Joan Chittister, *Wisdom Distilled from the Daily* (San Francisco: Harper & Row, 1990), 19.

10. Bauman, *Life in Fragments*, 86.

11. Nancy Louise Frey, *Pilgrim Stories* (Berkeley: University of California Press, 1998), 87.

12. Mark Edmundson, *Teacher* (New York: Vintage Press, 2003), 239.

13. Chittister, *Wisdom Distilled*, 156.

14. Belden Lane, *Solace of Fierce Landscapes* (New York: Oxford University Press, 1998), 15.

15. Gerhard Lohfink, *Jesus and Community* (Minneapolis: Fortress Press, 1989), 262.

16. John Eade, "Introduction to the Illinois Paperback," in *Contesting the Sacred*, ed. John Eade and Michael Sallnow (Chicago: University of Illinois Press, 2000), xvii.

17. Frey, *Pilgrim Stories*, 56.

18. Ibid., 58.

19. Ibid., 61.

20. See Lonni Pratt and Daniel Homan, *Benedict's Way* (Chicago: Loyola Press, 2000), 120–21.

21. Paul Wilkes, *Beyond the Walls* (New York: Doubleday, 1999), 44–50.

22. Paul Trachtman, "Too Hot to Handle," *Smithsonian* 34, no. 9 (December 2003): 28.

23. Ibid.

24. Jerome Bruner, *Theory of Instruction* (Cambridge, MA: Harvard University Press, 1966), 151.

25. Chittister, *Wisdom Distilled*, 144.

26. John Main, "The Witness of Monastic Prayer," *Monastic Studies* 18 (Christmas 1988): 33.

27. Chittister, *Wisdom Distilled*, 144.

28. Joan Chittister, *Scarred by Struggle, Transformed by Hope* (Grand Rapids: Wm. B. Eerdmans, 2005), 40–41.

29. Joan Chittister, *The Rule of St. Benedict* (New York: Crossroad, 1995), 68–69.

30. Lane, *Solace of Fierce Landscapes*, 167.

31. Ibid., 171.

32. Chittister, *Wisdom Distilled*, 72.

33. Ibid., 144.

34. *The Liturgy of the Hours*, 426.

35. Chittister, *Rule of St. Benedict*, 27.

36. Chittister, *Scarred*, 16.

37. Chittister, *Wisdom Distilled*, 167.

38. W. Paul Jones, *Teaching the Dead Bird to Sing* (Brewster, MA: Paraclete Press, 2002), 77.

39. Main, "Witness of Monastic Prayer," 39.

40. Ibid., 36.

41. Jones, *Teaching the Dead Bird*, 169.

CHAPTER 8: RITUALS OF CHRISTIAN PILGRIMAGE

1. Patricia Hampl, "Penance," in *Signatures of Grace: Catholic Writers on the Sacraments*, ed. T. Grady and P. Huston (New York: Dutton, 2000), 57.

2. Quoted in Rosemary Mahoney, *The Singular Pilgrim* (Boston: Houghton Mifflin, 2003), 5.

3. Brett Webb-Mitchell, *Follow Me* (New York: Seabury Press, 2006), 53–59.

4. Catherine Bell, *Ritual Theory, Ritual Practice* (New York: Oxford University Press, 1992), 13, 54.

5. George Gringas, *Egeria: Diary of a Pilgrimage* (New York: Newman Press, 1970), 18.

6. Ibid., 7, 11.

7. Ibid., 19.

8. Ibid., 66.

9. Ibid., 19.

10. Ibid., 123.

11. Tom Wright, *The Way of the Lord* (Grand Rapids: Wm. B. Eerdmans, 1999), 9.

12. Ibid., 10.

13. Ibid., 8–9.

14. John Westerhoff, *A Pilgrim People* (Minneapolis: Seabury Press, 1984), 7, 9.

15. Ibid., 3.

16. John Eade, "Introduction," in *Contesting the Sacred*, ed. John Eade and Michael Sallnow (Chicago: University of Illinois Press, 2000), 6.

17. Philip Cousineau, *The Art of Pilgrimage* (Berkeley, CA: Conari Press, 1998), 62, 65.

18. Ibid., 67.

19. Freud called dreams the "royal road of consciousness."

20. Michael Sallnow, "Pilgrimage and Cultural Fracture in the Andes," in Eade and Sallnow, *Contesting the Sacred*, 149.

21. Jean Corbon, *The Wellspring of Worship* (Mahwah, NJ: Paulist Press, 1988), 38–39.

22. Cousineau, *Art of Pilgrimage*, xxiii.

23. Corbon, *Wellspring of Worship*, 47.

24. Wright, *Way of the Lord*, 130.

25. Corbon, *Wellspring of Worship*, 47.

26. Ibid., 47, 64.

27. Noted in Jennifer Westwood, *Sacred Journey* (New York: Henry Holt, 1997), 8.

28. See Don Saliers, *Worship as Theology* (Nashville: Abingdon Press, 1994), 27.

29. Cousineau, *Art of Pilgrimage*, 23.

30. Dame Maria Boulding, "Prayer and the Paschal Mystery," *Downside Review* 94, no. 317 (1976): 282–83.

31. Corbon, *Wellspring of Worship*, 154.

32. Wright, *Way of the Lord*, 33.

33. Ibid., 54.

34. Gerhard Lohfink, *Does God Need the Church?* (Collegeville, MN: Liturgical Press, 1999), 259.

35. Presbyterian Church (U.S.A.), *Book of Common Worship* (Louisville, KY: Westminster/John Knox Press, 1993), 68.

36. Martin Robinson, *Sacred Places, Pilgrim Paths* (San Francisco: HarperCollins, 1997), 141.

37. Lohfink, *Does God Need the Church?* 259.

38. Daniel Armentrout, "Kissing Feet," *Sewanee Theological Review* 44, no. 4 (2001): 409–11.

39. Lohfink, *Does God Need the Church?* 260.

40. Robinson, *Sacred Places, Pilgrim Paths*, 141.

CHAPTER 9: THE CHARACTER OF THE PILGRIM

1. *The Liturgy of the Hours* (Collegeville, MN: Liturgical Press, 1987), 420.

2. Brett Webb-Mitchell, *Follow Me* (New York: Seabury Press, 2006), 80–84.

3. Alasdair MacIntyre, *Whose Justice? Which Rationality?* (Notre Dame, IN: University of Notre Dame Press, 1988), 113.

4. Cited in John Eade, "Introduction to the Illinois Paperback," in *Contesting the Sacred*, ed. John Eade and Michael Sallnow (Chicago: University of Illinois Press, 2000), xvii, 4, 78.

5. Quoted in David Ford, *Shape of Living* (Grand Rapids: Baker House, 1997), 96–97.

6. Ibid., 111.

7. Ibid., 92. Ford also includes a list of virtues, such as faith, hope, love, prudence, justice, courage, and self-control, and a list of vices, which includes pride, anger, envy/jealousy, greed, sloth, lust, and gluttony.

8. Patricia Hampl, "Penance," in *Signatures of Grace*, ed. Thomas Grady and Paula Huston (New York: Dutton, 2000), 57.

9. Nancy Louise Frey, *Pilgrim Stories* (Berkeley: University of California Press, 1998), 44, 46.

10. Paul Wadell, *Friendship and the Moral Life* (Notre Dame, IN: University of Notre Dame Press, 1989), 1.

11. Ibid., 6.

12. John Eade, "Introduction," in Eade and Sallnow, *Contesting the Sacred,* 22, 24.

13. Kathleen Norris, *Dakota* (New York: Ticknor & Fields, 1993), 9.

14. Columba Stewart, *Prayer and Community* (Maryknoll, NY: Orbis Books, 1998), 28, 88, 118.

15. Ibid., 68.

16. Frey, *Pilgrim Stories*, 118.

17. Paulo Coelho, *The Pilgrimage* (San Francisco: HarperCollins, 1998), 27.

18. Wadell, *Friendship and the Moral Life*, 91.

19. Ibid., 92.

20. Patricia Hampl, *Virgin Time* (New York: Random House, 1992), 121.

21. Quoted in Jennifer Westwood, *Sacred Journeys* (New York: Henry Holt, 1997), 8.

22. Quoted in ibid.

23. Coelho, *Pilgrimage*, 54.

24. Roger Sharrock, "Preface," in *The Pilgrim's Progress,* by John Bunyan (New York: Penguin Classic, 1965), xix.

25. Martin Robinson, *Sacred Places, Pilgrim Paths* (San Francisco: HarperCollins, 1997), 11.

26. Quoted in ibid., 97.

27. Quoted in Belden Lane, *The Solace of Fierce Landscapes* (New York: Oxford University Press, 1998), 117.

CHAPTER 10: THE LAND OF PILGRIMAGE

1. Brett Webb-Mitchell, *Follow Me* (New York: Seabury Press, 2006), 69–72.

2. Belden Lane, *The Solace of Fierce Landscapes* (New York: Oxford University Press, 1998), 33.

3. Annie Dillard, *Pilgrim at Tinker Creek* (New York: Harper & Row, 1985), 7.

4. Ibid., 9.

5. Philip Cousineau, *The Art of Pilgrimage* (Berkeley, CA: Conari Press, 1998), 94.

6. Ibid., 105.

7. Lane, *Solace of Fierce Landscapes*, 43.

8. Ibid., 46, 49.

9. Amy Mandelker and Elizabeth Powers, *Pilgrim Souls* (New York: Simon & Schuster, 1999), 149.

10. Lane, *Solace of Fierce Landscapes*, 217.

11. Junichiro Tanizaki, *In Praise of Shadows* (Stony Creek, CT: Leete's Island Books, 1977), 21, 31.

12. See Nancy Lousie Frey, *Pilgrim Stories* (Berkeley: University of California Press, 1998), 71.

13. Alain de Boton, *The Art of Travel* (New York: Pantheon Press, 2002), 157, 167, 171, 176.

14. Lane, *Solace of Fierce Landscapes*, 216, 219.

15. Frey, *Pilgrim Stories*, 113, 117–18.

16. De Boton, *Art of Travel*, 176, 182.

17. John Eade, "Introduction," in *Contesting the Sacred*, ed. John Eade and Michael Sallnow (Chicago: University of Illinois Press, 2000), 6.

18. W. Paul Jones, *Teaching the Dead Bird to Sing* (Brewster, MA: Paraclete Press, 2002), 104.

19. Cintra Pemberton, *Soulfaring* (Harrisburg, PA: Morehouse Publishing Co., 1999), 5.

20. Quoted in Lane, *Solace of Fierce Landscapes*, 225.

21. John Eade, "Introduction to the Illinois Paperback," in Eade and Sallnow, *Contesting the Sacred,* xvii.

22. John Main, "The Witness of Monastic Prayer," *Monastic Studies* 18 (Christmas 1988): 40.

CHAPTER 11: CONTEMPLATION ON PILGRIMAGE: SOLITUDE AND PRAYER

1. Parker Palmer, *The Active Life* (San Francisco: Harper & Row, 1990), talks about being active and contemplative at the same time. This is echoed in the writings of W. Paul Jones, a former United Methodist minister, now Catholic, who discovered the contemplative life in Kentucky.

2. Ibid., 17.

3. Ibid., 18.

4. W. Paul Jones, *A Table in the Desert* (Brewster, MA: Paraclete Press, 2001), 50.

5. Belden Lane, *The Solace of Fierce Landscapes* (New York: Oxford University Press, 1999), 64. The opposite of kataphatic theology is apophatic theology, born in the fourth century, which is the way of negation. Lane calls this the "less is more" tradition (62).

6. Joan Chittister, *Wisdom Distilled from the Daily* (San Francisco: Harper & Row, 1990), 103–4.

7. W. Paul Jones, *Teaching the Dead Bird to Sing* (Brewster, MA: Paraclete Press, 2002), 21.

8. Ibid., 40.

9. The Westminster Shorter Catechism, in the *Book of Confessions* (Louisville, KY: Office of the General Assembly, 1991), 7.001.

10. Jones, *Teaching the Dead Bird*, 58.

11. Lane, *Solace of Fierce Landscapes*, 232.

12. Cited in ibid., 29.

13. Ibid., 219.

14. Jones, *Teaching the Dead Bird*, 73.

15. John Main, "The Witness of Monastic Prayer," *Monastic Studies* 18 (Christmas 1988): 39.

16. Jones, *Teaching the Dead Bird*, 79.

17. An ostinato is a short melodic and rhythmic phrase that is persistently repeated by the same musical instrument or human voice.

18. Helen Bacovcin, "Introduction," in *The Way of a Pilgrim*, trans. Helen Bacovcin (New York: Doubleday, 1992), 8.

19. Ibid., 13.

20. Ibid.

21. Ibid., 17.

22. Ibid.

23. Ibid., 41, 74.

24. Ibid., 8.

25. Jones, *Teaching the Dead Bird*, 71.

26. *The Way of a Pilgrim*, 131.

27. Jones, *Teaching the Dead Bird*, 123.

28. Ibid., 169.

29. Lane, *Solace of Fierce Landscapes*, 188.

30. Claudia Horwitz, *The Spiritual Activist* (New York: Penguin Press, 2002), 30.

CHAPTER 12: THE DESTINATION OF PILGRIMAGE

1. John Bunyan, *Pilgrim's Progress*, ed. Roger Sharrock (New York: Penguin Books, 1987), 11.

2. Ibid., 12.

3. Philip Cousineau, *The Art of Pilgrimage* (Berkeley, CA: Canori Press, 1998), 34.

4. Ibid., 159.

5. Kathleen Norris, *Dakota* (New York: Ticknor & Fields, 1993), 130.

6. Charlie Layman told me of this saying, which he learned at a Quaker gathering.

7. Brett Webb-Mitchell, *Follow Me* (New York: Seabury Press, 2006), 99–105.

8. Zygmunt Bauman, *Life in Fragments* (Cambridge: Blackwell, 1995), 83.

9. Ibid.

10. Ibid., 86.

11. Ibid.

12. Ibid., 268.

13. Martin Robinson, *Sacred Places, Pilgrim Paths* (San Francisco: HarperCollins, 1997), 156.

14. Cited in ibid., 171.

15. Tom Wright, *The Way of the Lord* (Grand Rapids: Wm. B. Eerdmans, 1999), 109–11.

16. W. Paul Jones, *Teaching the Dead Bird to Sing* (Brewster, MA: Paraclete Press, 2002), 169.

17. Craig Dykstra, *Growing in the Life of Faith* (Louisville, KY: Geneva Press, 1999), 10.

18. Cintra Pemberton, *Soulfaring* (Harrisburg, PA: Morehouse Publishing Co., 1999), 7.

19. Paulo Coelho, *Pilgrimage* (San Francisco: HarperCollins, 1998), 139.

20. Robinson, *Sacred Places, Pilgrim Paths*, 174.

CHAPTER 13: THE CHURCH: THE SCHOOL OF THE PILGRIM

1. *Book of Common Worship* (Louisville, KY: Westminster/John Knox Press, 1993), 253.

2. Michael Casey, *Sacred Reading* (Ligouri, MO: Ligouri Press, 1996), 37–39.

3. Ibid., 41, 47.

4. Roberto Goizueta, *Caminemos con Jesus: Toward a Hispanic/Latino Theology of Accompaniment* (Maryknoll, NY: Orbis Books, 1999), 211.